# THE ARABS
# A SHORT HISTORY

# Expanded Edition
# with Documents

## selected and edited by
# Luke Yarbrough
## and
# Oded Zinger

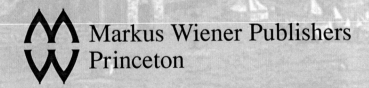

Markus Wiener Publishers
Princeton

# THE
# ARABS
## A Short History

## HEINZ HALM

Translated by
Allison Brown and Tom Lampert

For information write to:
Markus Wiener Publishers
231 Nassau Street, Princeton, NJ 08542
www.markuswiener.com


**Library of Congress Cataloging-in-Publication Data**

Halm, Heinz, 1942-
[Araber. English]
The Arabs : a short history / Heinz Halm ; translated by Allison Brown and
Tom Lampert ; with documents selected and edited by Luke Yarbrough and
Oded Zinger. — Expanded ed.
     p. cm.
Includes bibliographical references and index.
Translated from the German.
ISBN 978-1-55876-545-0 (hardcover : alk. paper)
ISBN 978-1-55876-546-7 (pbk. : alk. paper)
1. Arabs--History.  2. Arab countries—History.  I. Title.
DS37.7.H3513 2012
909'.04927—dc23
                          2011039254

# Table of Contents

# APPENDIX

## Primary Source Readings from the
## History of the Arabs ................................. 179

# Notes on Pronunciation

Arabic names and terms have been transliterated in a form facilitating pronunciation for English-speaking readers. The macron always denotes a long vowel. If a word has only one long vowel, this is generally also the accented syllable. The *r* indicates an *r* rolled at the tip of the tongue, and the *gh* is a glottal *g*; *k* corresponds to the English *k*, while a *q* is a throaty, dark (velar) *k* (not *qu*); *kh* is pronounced like a hard *ch* as in the German *Bach*; *th* corresponds to the voiceless English *th* in *thing*, whereas *dh* is pronounced as a voiced *th*, as in English *the*; *s* is always voiceless, and *z* is always voiced. The *h* is always an audible consonant and not used to make a long vowel (e.g., *Mahdi*).

The right half ring, ' (hamza), indicates a glottal stop, whereas a left half ring, ' ('ayn), is a voiced pharyngeal fricative that is difficult for non-Arabs to pronounce. Since it is a consonant, words such as *Ka'ba or San'ā'* have two syllables.

# 1

# Pre-Islamic Arabia

*Ruins of the Mārib dam*

From Klaus Shippman, *Ancient South Arabia* (Princeton: Markus Wiener, 2001)

# Name and Origin

Arabs call themselves *al-'Arab*, a collective term used to designate the Arab people as a whole. *Al-'Arabī* is the term for an individual member of that people. This affiliation is based first of all on the use of the Arabic language: An Arab is someone who speaks Arabic. There are approximately 280 million Arabic-speaking people in North Africa and the Middle East today, from the Atlantic Ocean to the western edge of the Iranian plateau, that is, from Morocco and Mauritania in the west to Iraq in the east, and from Syria in the north to Oman, Yemen, and Sudan in the south. This expansion of the Arab people and the Arabic language is a relatively recent historical phenomenon related to the spread of Islam beginning in the seventh century CE.

The first known use of the term Arab is found in an inscription of the Assyrian king Shalmaneser III from 853 BCE celebrating a victory of the Assyrians over the coalition of Syrian kings (including the King of Israel) at the Battle of Qarqar in Syria. According to the inscription, the Syrian coalition was supported by a contingent of a thousand camel riders of Gindibu, King of the Arabs (*Aribi*). Inscriptions of Assyrian kings from the eighth and seventh centuries BCE repeatedly mention kings and queens of the Arabs, for the most part as tributaries and auxiliary forces of the Assyrians.

The *Aribi* mentioned in Assyrian inscriptions appear to

have been nomadic groups living in the Syrian Desert, in other words, on the inner margins of the Fertile Crescent (Palestine/Jordan, Syria, and Iraq). As Shalmaneser III's inscription indicates, the name *Aribi* was from the beginning tied to the use of dromedaries. As pack and riding animals but also as sources of meat and wool, these animals enabled human life in the desert steppe (*bādiya*). It is from the latter term that Arab nomads or Bedouins derive their name (*al-badawī*). Numerous Assyrian reliefs from the era of King Sennacherib (705–681 BCE) depict Arabic camel riders in battle. For the Assyrians, whose imperial claims included all of Syria, controlling the Arabs of the Syrian Desert was of great strategic importance.

There were no significant changes in the Neo-Babylonian Empire after the fall of Nineveh in 612 BCE. Nabonidus, the final king of Babylon (556–539 BCE), even continued to live for ten years in the palace he had built in the northwestern Arabian oasis of Taimā, leaving Babylon to his son Belshazzar, the crown prince. His sphere of control extended to Yathrib, which later became known as Medina. After 549 BCE, Persian kings do not appear to have ruled the Arabs directly, but rather to have sought them as allies. Herodotus reported (III, 88) that before the Persian king Cambyses conquered Egypt in 525 BCE, he obtained consent from the Arabs. Xerxes also used Arabs as archers on camelback during his campaign against Greece (480 BCE) (VII, 69; 86).

Almost all of these reports portray the *Aribi* as inhabitants of the inner periphery of the Fertile Crescent in the Syrian-Mesopotamian desert and in northern Arabia, where they initially appeared as nomadic camel herders, but also as farmers in the oases of northwestern Arabia. It is here that the name "Arab" appears for the first time (we do not know the origin of the term), and it is here as well that the (North) Arabic language – the bond that continues to unite the Arab people – has its roots.

Arabic is one of the Semitic languages, a language family named after Shem, the son of Noah, according to the Table of Nations in the Old Testament (Genesis 10) the progenitor of both the people of Israel and the Arabs. Arabic is thus closely related to the languages spoken in the Fertile Crescent during antiquity (Akkadian = Babylonian/Assyrian, Phoenician, Canaanite, Hebrew, and Aramaic), as well as to Old South Arabian and the languages of Abyssinia (Ethiopian, Tigre, Tigrinya, and Amharic). The oldest evidence of the (North) Arabic language are brief inscriptions found at the oases extending like a chain of pearls from the south of present-day Jordan through the Ḥijāz and down to ʿAsīr. Such graffiti has been documented since the era of Assyrian rule. It was initially written in alphabets that were closely related to Old South Arabiia and that developed – like Greek and Latin – from a Phoenician prototype. The Arabic alphabet used today thus has the same roots as our Latin alphabet, even if its appearance would hardly suggest it. As this alphabet had less than thirty letters to denote spoken phonemes, it spread across the entire Middle East, replacing the much more complicated writing forms of the ancient Orient, cuneiform scripts and hieroglyphics.

# Ancient South Arabia

The territory that constitutes present-day Yemen lay outside the Assyrian Empire's sphere of influence, although the kings of Sheba are occasionally mentioned in Assyrian inscriptions. With 10,000-foot mountain peaks and heavy monsoon rains, the southwest of the Arabian Peninsula is a world unto itself. The ancient landscapes here of terraced fields and stonewalled cities present a marked contrast to the rest of the peninsula. Since time immemorial, people in this area had mediated trade between the Indian Ocean and the Mediterranean. In particular, frankincense (a tree resin) extracted around Dhofār in present-day Oman was traded through the kingdoms of South Arabia to the north, where large amounts were used in temples and later in churches of the Middle East and Greece. The Incense Road led from Dhofār through several dominions that, while not producing any incense themselves, controlled and thereby profited from the trade in it: Ḥaḍramawt, and west of this Qatabān with its capital of Timnaʿ; Sheba with its capital Mārib; and Maʿīn with its cities in al-Jawf (northeast of Ṣanʿāʾ). The Old Testament tells of the Queen of Sheba (almost certainly a legendary figure) who is said to have visited King Solomon in Jerusalem. Sheba and Ḥaḍramawt (*Hasarmaweth*) also appear in the Table of Nations in the Old Testament (Genesis 10).

The Kingdom of Maʿīn, which can be documented from approximately 550 to 125 BCE, extended at times into

6

northwestern Arabia. It established a trade colony in Dedan (present-day al-'Ulā) in the fourth century BCE, and its merchants reached Egypt and Syria. At times Ma'īn fell under the rule of neighboring Sheba. Karib'il Watar, the king of Sheba from approximately 510 to 490 BCE, had his conquests immortalized in victory inscriptions. The Old South Arabic language, like modern Arabic a Semitic language, had its own written alphabet. Several thousand inscriptions provide us with insight into the culture of Sheba. Numerous large buildings such as temples have survived in the capital Mārib. However, the most important construction here was the Great Dam of Mārib, approximately 2000 feet long, which was used to dam the waters of the Wādī Adhana between two mountain ridges. A complicated system of locks and canals was used to irrigate the entire region around the capital city.

# Arabia in the Hellenistic Period

Alexander the Great did not touch Arabia during his military campaign. However, Alexander's admiral Nearchus, on his return from India through Cape Musandam, did reach the northern point of what is today Oman, before leading his fleet back to Mesopotamia through the gulf. Alexander's own plans for oceanic exploration were interrupted by his early death in 323 BCE. Of Alexander's wealthy successors or Diadochi – the Seleucids in Syria/Mesopotamia and the Ptolemaeans in Egypt – especially the latter had close ties to Arabia, as they exercised maritime control over the Red Sea. The Greeks were familiar with the southern Arabian kingdoms of Ḥaḍramawt, Qatabān, Sheba, and Ma'īn. Greek geographers mentioned their capital cities and the Chatramotitai, Kattabaneis, Sabaioi, and Minaioi peoples – the last named were the Minaeans from Ma'īn.

Most of the surviving inscriptions written in the precursors of present-day (North) Arabic were created during the Hellenistic period. This includes several thousand inscriptions, most of which are brief graffiti etched in rocks, in which travelers immortalized their presence or called for assistance from certain gods. While these inscriptions are written in alphabets derived from Old South Arabian (Sabaean), the language is clearly North Arabic and thus has been designated as proto-Arabic. The two most signifi-

cant of these written forms are Lihyanic and Thamudic.
Both written forms have been dated from at least the fifth
century BCE up into the Common Era. Thamudic graffiti
has been found throughout the entire Ḥijāz and 'Asīr, the
Sinai, southern Palestine, and Transjordan.

The Nabataeans were also Arabs. Their capital city
Petra was located in a rocky basin east of the Dead Sea. The
first historical reports of the Nabataeans appear directly
after the death of Alexander the Great. In 312 BCE, Antigonus, one of Alexander's generals, attempted to take Petra.
The Nabataeans controlled the Incense Road to the east of
their city. Antigonus had taken spoils of frankincense and
spices in Petra, and the Roman historian Diodorus express-
ly noted that the Nabataeans transported frankincense and
myrrh to the Mediterranean Sea. However, they also
engaged in piracy on the Red Sea, which led to conflicts
with the Ptolemaeans in Egypt. The Nabataeans gradually
brought the entire Transjordan and southern Palestine
including Gaza under their control. The Nabataean King
Aretas III (in Arabic *al-Ḥāritha*, 87–62 BCE) was even able
to take control of Damascus in 85 BCE. Although the
Nabataeans spoke Arabic, as indicated by the names of their
kings, they employed a script developed from the Aramaic
alphabet for their correspondence and inscriptions. The
Nabataeans' material culture was also influenced by the
north, as is evident even today in the impressive Hellenistic
façades of the rock tombs of Petra. The epithet of Aretas III
was *Philhellenos,* or friend of Greece.

The Greeks' familiarity with Arabia during the
Hellenistic period is also evident in the work of the geographer Ptolemy of Alexandria (second century BCE), which
maps the entire Arabian Peninsula including the interior.

# Arabs and Romans

The Roman proconsul Pompey traveled to Syria in 64 BCE in order to reorganize political relations in the Levant along Roman lines. In the preceding year, Roman troops had driven the Nabataean king Aretas III out of Damascus and occupied the city. Pompey now transformed Syria into a Roman province. In 63 BCE, Pompey himself advanced from Antioch through Damascus to Jericho and Jerusalem. He permitted the small Jewish kingdom of the Hasmoneans and the Nabataean kingdom to exist as Roman client states, content to have subjugated the Middle East to the *Pax Romana*. The subsequent Roman civil wars were often fought in Asia Minor. After Octavian (Augustus) annexed Ptolemaic Egypt in 30 BCE, Roman influence extended also to the Red Sea.

Like the Greeks before them, the Romans distinguished between *Arabia Deserta* or "Desert Arabia" and the "happy" *Arabia Felix*, Yemen. This epithet is the result of a misunderstanding of an Arabic term. For Arabs, who were "oriented" to the east, the south lay to the "right" (*al-Yaman*) and the north lay to the "left" (*al-Shām*). In contemporary Arabic these two words are still used to designate Yemen and Syria. Yemen, in other words, is actually the land "on the right side." However, "right" also means "propitious," and in this way the "land to the right" became "happy Arabia" (*Arabia eudaimon* in Greek). The name, however, could also be understood in a different sense: The luxury goods that Romans so desired came from here. According to the geographers Strabo and Pliny the Elder, *Arabia Felix* or Yemen was the Roman source for incense and myrrh, cassia and nard, silk, jewels, and pearls – that is, products not produced in Yemen itself but in southeastern Arabia or beyond the Indian Ocean and the Persian Gulf in India and China. Augustus' decision to send a military expedition into "happy Arabia" in 24–25 BCE was probably motivated above all by his desire to control trade in these goods. A Roman official, Aelius Gallus, commanded the Roman troops, ostensibly ten thousand in number. Syllaios, the minister of the Nabataean king, assumed leadership of the expedition, and the Nabataean king and the Jewish king Herod provided auxiliary forces. The troops were transported on 130 cargo ships from the Gulf of Suez to Leuke Kome (Yanbu') and from there they made the grueling march through 'Asīr. They conquered Najrān and the cities of Ma'īn, but had to abandon the siege of Mārib after six days due to lack of water. The Roman army was forced to withdrawal with significant losses. The geographer Strabo, who was acquainted with Aelius Gallus, recorded the various stages of the march.

The enterprise was a complete disaster both militarily and politically, although there was no significant political force in Yemen at the time and city princes ruled the country. However, a new force was rising in the south of Yemen: the tribe of the Himyarites, whose capital city Ẓafār with the citadel Dhū Raydān (75 miles south of Ṣan'ā) now became the main city of *Arabia Felix*. Immediately after Aelius Gallus' failed campaign, old Sheba and the new Himyarites joined to form the "Kingdom of Sheba and Dhū

Raydān." This new kingdom successively subsumed the smaller kingdoms of Maʻīn, Qatabān, and Ḥaḍramawt. The *Homeritae*, as the Romans called the Himyarites, ruled southern Arabia during the entire Roman imperial era. Trade relations between the two empires seem to have remained close, and the Romans never again attempted to take direct control of *Arabia Felix*.

The situation was different in northern Arabia. Here Arabs were not only the immediate neighbors of the Roman province of Syria, but they also lived in increasing numbers within the Roman Empire itself. Nomads moved between the villages on the edge of the Syrian Desert, occasionally settling permanently there or in one of the cities. Arabs trickled into the settled areas of the Fertile Crescent in the same way that Semitic-speaking peoples – the Akkadians, Aramaeans, Canaanites, and the Israelites – had done for thousands of years. Under the Seleucids, the Itureans (*Itouraioi*), who were almost certainly South Arabian, had pushed into Galilee in the second century BCE and taken control of the Beqāʻ plain between Lebanon and Antilebanon. Safā inscriptions, Arabic graffiti in the Safā Hills southeast of Damascus, from the first century BCE to the fourth century CE testify to the presence of Arabs there. In 70 CE, after the destruction of Jerusalem by Titus, Judea became a Roman province, and in 106 CE, Emperor Trajan also annexed the Nabataean kingdom, turning it into the Roman province Arabia. In this way, the entire western horn of the Fertile Crescent was incorporated into the Roman Empire. In the autumn of 129 CE, Emperor Hadrian visited Palmyra, Damascus, Beirut, and Petra, before spending the winter in Gerasa (Jerash in northern Jordan).

Emperor Philip the Arab (244–249) was born in the Jabal al-Druze in a hamlet that he renamed Philippopolis (present-day Shahba, fifty miles southeast of Damascus), in which he built a theater and other magnificent structures.

Further northeast, the oasis city of Palmyra (*Tadmur* in Arabic), which owed its ascent as a trade city to the decline of Petra, gradually became Arabized. The rulers, who attempted to establish a vast Middle-Eastern empire between the Roman and the Parthian empires in the third century, had Arabic names: Odaenathus (*'Udhayna*), his bride Zenobia (*Zaynab*), and their son "Augustus" Vaballathus (*Wahb Allāt* = "Gift of the Goddess Allāt"). Emperor Aurelius ended the Palmyrians' imperial dreams in 272, bringing Zenobia and her son to Rome as captives.

Like Palmyra, Hatra in northern Mesopotamia also flourished in the second and third centuries as a result of its location at the border between the Roman and the Parthian empires and its function as a trade emporium. The city had a predominantly Arab population. It was not far from the Tigris (60 miles southwest of Mosul) but had never belonged to the Parthian Empire and had successfully resisted Roman legions, both those of Emperor Trajan (117 CE) and those of Septimius Severus (197 CE). Not until 240 CE were the Persians able to take the city.

# Arabia between Byzantines and Persians

Two events outside of Arabia marked epochal changes for Arabs as well. In 226 CE, the Persian king Ardashir ended Parthian rule of Iran and Mesopotamia. The new ruler assumed the old title of *King of Kings*, establishing a Sassanid Neo-Persian Empire. The Parthian royal city of Ctesiphon on the Tigris (25 miles southeast of present-day Baghdad) became the residence of the new great kings. In 330 CE, the Roman Emperor Constantine established his capital city of Constantinople on the site of the old Greek city Byzantium, which became the new metropolis of the Eastern Roman Empire. As a result, the Syrian Desert and the Arabian Peninsula became an area of conflict for these two neighboring major powers of late antiquity, which clashed here in the north as well as in the south.

The Arabic Lakhmid tribe established their rule west of the lower Euphrates around 300 CE. The Lakhmid kingdom served the Persian Empire as a buffer state against the Eastern Roman Empire. The royal residence of the Lakhmids was al-Ḥīra (from the Aramaic *Herta* or "camp"; cf. Hatra), which was located south of what later became Kūfa (present-day Najaf). We know of more than twenty Lakhmid kings up to the beginning of the seventh century. The grave stelae for Imru al-Qays (died in 328), designating him as the "King of all Arabs," have been uncovered in Ḥawrān in Syria. Al-Nuʿmān I (ca. 400–418) built magnificent castles, including the fabulous al-Khawarnaq Palace near al-Ḥīra, which has survived in the legends and poems of later eras. As a vassal of the Sassanids, al-Mundhir III (ca. 505–554), a contemporary of Justinian, engaged in raids against Byzantine Syria, which brought him into the vicinity of Antioch. His son 'Amr (554–569) is renowned as the patron of poets. At least three of the seven most important pre-Islamic Arab poets are reputed to have lived at his court. His mother was Christian and founded a monastery in al-Ḥīra. Starting in the early fifth century, there was a bishop in the city, although in all probability only the final Lakhmid king, al-Nu'mān III (ca. 580–602), was himself a Nestorian Christian.

The Arab buffer state on the Byzantine side, in which the Banū Ghassān clan shielded the Syrian provinces from the desert, is much younger. The center of the Ghassānid kingdom was Jābiya in Jawlān (Golan), a cross between a nomadic camp and a settled city. There were also palatial buildings along the edge of the desert steppe, where the Ghassānids could receive the leaders of allied tribes. As vassals of Byzantium, they were Christians, although they belonged to the Monophysite (Jacobite) Church predominant in Syria. The Ghassānids reached the apex of their power in the sixth century. In 529, Emperor Justinian named al-Ḥārith II (ca. 529–569) *phylarchos* and gave him the title *patricius*, making him one of the highest dignitaries in the Roman Empire. Justinian prepared a magnificent reception for him in Constantinople in 563. His son al-Mundhir (*Alamundaros*) was also received at the court in 580, but the relationship subsequently deteriorated, not least because the Ghassānids refused to abandon their "heretical" Monophysite beliefs. Al-Mundhir was finally deported to Sicily and his son al-Nuʿmān was imprisoned in Constantinople. Ghassānid rule was brought to an end in 613–614, after the Sassanid king Khosrow II Parvez captured Damascus and Jerusalem. The last Ghassānid Jabala VI fought on the side of the Byzantines against the Arab Muslims in 636, but later converted to Islam.

Another battleground for the rivalry between the Byzantine and Persian Empires was Yemen. The Himyarites (*Homeritae*) had ruled over the former empire of Sheba since the third century. There was a coup around 500 CE, in which the ruling dynasty was deposed and a usurper with the epithet *Dhū Nuwās* ("he with the curl") assumed power. Dhū Nuwās was Jewish and called himself Yūsuf after the Biblical Joseph. Following the Roman destruction of Jerusalem in 70 CE, Judaism appears to have been spread by refugees and exiles along the Incense Road to the south and there also seem to have been some conversions among Arab tribes and clans. At the time of Muḥammad, three of the five Arabic tribes living in Yathrib (Medina) were Jewish. The Yemenite king Yūsuf /Dhū Nuwās is said to have to have persecuted the apparently large Christian population in his empire as retribution for Roman-Byzantine oppression of the Jews. In response, Christian Ethiopians, backed by Christian Byzantium, intervened. The negus or sovereign of Ethiopia conquered Yemen between 523 and 525, dethroned the persecutor of Christians, and established Christian Ethiopian viceroys as rulers, thus bringing an end to the Kingdom of Sheba and Himyar.

Abraha, one of these Ethiopian viceroys, is said to have built a magnificent church in Ṣanʿāʾ, almost certainly on the site of today's great mosque, the famous al-Qalīs (*ekklesia* in Greek). Another epochal date in South Arabian history occurred during his reign: the final destruction of the Great Dam of Mārib. Several dam catastrophes were reported in the fifth and sixth centuries. According to one inscription, Abraha was still able to make repairs in 542. A short time later, however, the dam appears to have burst a final time, turning the lowlands of Mārib, the heartland of Sheba, into desert. The memory of this has been preserved in sura 34 of the Qur'ān, "The Sabaean" (verses 15–17). Abraha is also mentioned in sura 105, "The Elephant": He is said to have taken part in a military campaign against Mecca, in which he served as an elephant leader. According to several accounts, the "Year of the Elephant," in which God miraculously allowed the Christian assault to fail, is also the year in which the Prophet Muḥammad was born (ca. 570).

Soon after this – the entire chronology of ancient South Arabia remains sketchy – the Yemenites rose up against Ethiopian foreign rule, calling for assistance from the Persian king. The Sassanids had already established themselves on the western side of the Persian-Arabian Gulf – numerous castles in Oman can be traced back to this time – and they did not hesitate to intervene in South Arabia, thereby bringing the entire trade along the Incense Road under their control as well. King Khosrow I Anushirvan sent an army, which drove the Ethiopians out of Yemen. The Persians installed local viceroys, who administered the southern Arabian satrapy for them. Yemen remained a Persian province for almost sixty years until the Islamic conquest.

# Old Arabic Language, Poetry, and Script

Three developments in the north of the Arabian Peninsula on the inner perimeter of the Fertile Crescent during the sixth century proved constitutive for the development of the Arab world: the (North) Arabic language, the Arabic script (which emerged as part of a continuing development of the Nabataean alphabet and which appears to have been used throughout northern Arabia on the eve of Islam), and ancient Arabic poetry.

The Arabic language (*al-'Arabiyya*) appears to have emerged quite suddenly in the sixth century with an already highly developed form of poetry. We have no record of the formative phases that must have preceded this. Its central form was the *qaṣīda* (a longer ode) and it possessed over a dozen complicated quantitative meters. This rich prosody was without parallel or precursor among the Semitic languages of the Fertile Crescent. The poetry had its origins in the tribal milieu. The poet (*shā'ir*), who was believed to be inspired by spirits (*jinn*), initially functioned as a representative of his tribe and his clan, celebrating his own tribe and reviling others. Praise and censure, panegyric and satire were often the subject of the qaṣīda as well, even after its content had become more diverse. In the sixth century, the poets already appeared as self-assured individuals leading an autonomous poetic existence. The influence of poets was evident not only at the great annual markets on the Arabian

Peninsula (such as in ʿUkāẓ near Mecca), where poets competed with their rivals, but also at the Lakhmid court in al-Ḥīra and the Ghassānid court in Transjordan, where the figure of the court poet and the panegyrist appeared. The poet Nābigha, for example, can be regarded as a court poet of the king of al-Ḥīra.

Poems were presented orally. The great poets of the sixth century were often surrounded by a group of reciters or *rāwī*, who ensured the dissemination of their qaṣīdas and thus of the authors' fame. Many poems of the pre-Islamic era were collected in the eighth century – several hundred complete qaṣīdas and countless fragments are extant – and were recorded in *dīwān*s (the word, taken from Persian, means "index" or "list"). Two of these collections are particularly noteworthy: the *Muʿallaqāt* (literally, "the suspended" or "hung," although the precise meaning of the title has never been clarified); and the *Ḥamāsa* ("zeal," "enthusiasm," or "courage") by Abū Tammām. The *Muʿallaqāt* is comprised of ten qaṣīdas (originally seven with three added), each from a different poet. Even today, this collection is regarded as the classic model of Arabic poetry. A rāwī from the eighth century compiled the initial seven poems that constitute the basis of the collection. Three of the odes are directed at a Lakhmid king from al-Ḥīra. The *Ḥamāsa* is an anthology of pre-Islamic poetry compiled by poet Abū Tammām in the ninth century.

Arabic is an enormously rich language. With its guttural (velar) and emphatic sounds, it possesses greater phonetic diversity than English. It also has a highly differentiated system of verb forms and an enormous vocabulary with numerous synonyms and a variety of nuanced expressions,

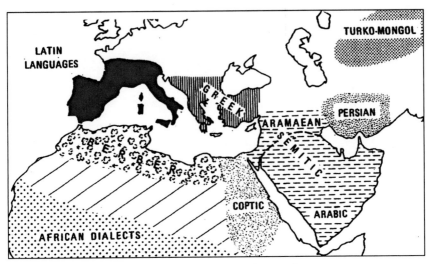

*Distribution of languages before the Muslim conquests*

From Maurice Lombard, *The Golden Age of Islam* (Princeton: Markus Wiener, 2003)

such as for different types of deserts, physical peculiarities, age levels, and characteristics of cattle. One reason for this enormous variety might be the tendency and ability often attributed to Arabs (not without some justification) of becoming intoxicated with the melodiousness of their own language.

The Arabic script consists of twenty-eight letters, all of which are consonants. (Short vowels are not written, and long ones are only implied.) Most of these letters, however, have a different form depending on whether they appear at the beginning, middle, or end of a word, or whether they appear alone. This rich variety of letters also lends itself to ornamental decoration, which has contributed to an astonishing development of calligraphy in books as well as in epigraphy. Arabic is written in a cursive script running from right to left, although not all letters can be connected to the left. Naskh, the Arabic script primarily in use today, has rounded forms and emerged in Baghdad during the tenth century. It developed from Kufic script, an older calligraphic form with its straight lines and angles, which was named after the city of Kūfa on the Euphrates. However, in addition to a special Maghrebi script and the Nastaʻlīq calligraphy style in Iran with its slanted script (from the top right to the bottom left), there is also a variety of decorative forms of epigraphy, for example, "flowering Kūfī," whose extended letters can assume leaf and blossom-like forms. These developments, however, all occurred during the Islamic era.

# 2

# Arabia and Islam

*Hunting castle Qasr al-Hayr al-Gharbi near Damascus*

From Bertold Spuler, *Age of the Caliphs* (Princeton: Markus Wiener, 1996)

# Arabia on the Eve of Islam

There was no comprehensive political order on the Arabian Peninsula prior to the emergence of Islam. The kingdoms of ancient South Arabia were limited to the southwestern corner of the peninsula. The entire region was characterized by a tribal social order; not only the Bedouin herders were organized in tribes, subtribes, and clans, but also the sedentary urban dwellers and farmers. The population of the city of Mecca was comprised of members of the Quraysh tribe, which was in turn divided into a dozen clans, including the powerful Makhzūm and 'Abd Shams, as well as the less influential Hāshim. The neighboring city of Ṭā'if belonged to the Thaqīf tribe, and five Arab tribes inhabited the Yathrib oasis (later Medina). In pre-Islamic times, the tribes of the Arabian Peninsula were already organized on a genealogical basis predicated on the assumption that all tribes had descended from common ancestors. Qahṭān was regarded as the progenitor of the South Arabian tribes, whereas the North Arabian tribes were said to have descended from 'Adnān. This distinction was evident in a profound antagonism between the two groups that continued to exist far into the Islamic period. Later – we do not know the precise date – the two lines were brought together in a genealogy based on the Old Testament: Qahṭān was equated with the Biblical Joktan, a grandson of Noah's son Shem (Genesis 10:25), whereas 'Adnān was considered a descendant of Ishmael, the outcast son of Abraham and Hagar

(Genesis 16:15). Arabs from South Arabia were regarded (or regarded themselves) as "true, pure Arabs," the *'āriba,* while Arabs from North Arabia were considered *musta'riba,* "arabized Arabs."

Although the various tribes spoke their own dialects, poets had already created a uniform high language that was evidently understood everywhere. The annual fairs served as a means of exchange and also led to a leveling of differences. The locations of the fairs rotated throughout the entire Arabian Peninsula, and periods of a general, binding ceasefire guaranteed that they could be carried out in peace. Important meeting places were also the shrines to different gods and goddesses, such as the Ka'ba, a cube-shaped temple in Mecca dedicated to the god Hubal, and many other places of worship northeast of Mecca, which even today are sites of Islamic pilgrimages (*hajj*), of course devoid of such pagan idols.

We know of the world of the Arab gods, at least in broad outlines, through allusions in the Qur'ān and especially through *Kitāb al-Aṣnām (The Book of Idols)* by the Iraqi author Ibn al-Kalbī (737–821). According to the latter, certain tribes controlled the shrines dedicated to particular gods or goddesses, although members of other tribes were also permitted to worship them. The deities appeared as stones or as trees, whose rustling was interpreted as an oracle, and sometimes also as primitive statues of wood or stone. Certain clans were entrusted with caring for the shrines. Hubal, the main god of the Quraysh of Mecca, also appears to have been worshipped under the name *Allāh* (contracted from *al-ilāh,* "deity"). His oracle in the Ka'ba functioned through casting lots with arrows. At his side stood a "goddess," *Allāt,* whose holy district was near the city of Ṭā'if. Manāt, the goddess of fate, was embodied in a black stone on the road from Mecca to Medina, whereas al-'Uzza, the planet Venus, was worshipped in three trees in Nakhla, east of Mecca. The rituals connected with the worship of the god of the Ka'ba and the other shrines in and around Mecca also predate Islam. Stripped of their pagan contexts they were later retained by Muḥammad out of reverence to the Prophet Abraham, Hagar, and their son Ishmael, who were regarded as the shrines' monotheistic founders even in pre-Islamic times.

Pilgrimages and markets, as well as traveling minstrels, provided the first interregional connections among the tribes scattered throughout the Arabian Peninsula. Trade, which was largely concentrated along the incense road from Yemen to Syria, that is, from the Indian Ocean to the Mediterranean Sea, also connected the peninsula to the rest of the world. Although Mecca did not lie directly along this route, it was a very active trading city. The Quraysh themselves lived from trade. The annual winter and summer caravans they outfitted (sura 106:2) are mentioned in the Qur'ān and according to Islamic tradition, Muḥammad himself traveled to Syria as a young man.

Judaism and Christianity reached western Arabia in pre-Islamic times both from the north and the south. Roman-Byzantine Syria, whose eastern regions had already been Arabized in antiquity, was Christian. Yemen had been ruled by a Jewish dynasty until a Christian Abyssinian governor took over. In Najrān, there was a strong Christian community led by a bishop; in Yathrib (Medina), three of the five Arab tribes that inhabited the oasis were Jewish.

Virtually nothing is known about how Judaism and Christianity spread in these regions. Contact with these two monotheistic religions, however, left very unambiguous traces in Islam. The Qur'ān is full of stories about Noah and Moses, the ancient patriarchs Abraham, Isaac, Jacob, and Joseph, King David and King Solomon, and the Prophet Jonah, although there are very few direct references to Christianity. While there does not appear to have been either a Jewish or a Christian community in Mecca, Islamic sources do tell of the ḥanīfs, a kind of monotheistic God-seekers without ties to either of the older religions, but no longer satisfied with the faded world of the ancient Arab gods. The Prophet Muḥammad, in other words, emerged in an environment that was by no means unprepared for his message.

# The Prophet Muḥammad

Islam is without a doubt a constituting element of the Arab world, at least in the early Islamic period, when the notions of Arab and Muslim largely coincided. According to the Qur'ān, God often says: "These (*letters*) are proofs of this profound scripture. We have revealed it, an Arabic Qur'ān" (sura 12:1–2; see also 41:1 and 43:1). Only the Arab-speaking segment of humanity is addressed in this particular divine revelation, which in another form, by other prophets, and in other languages had already been re-vealed to other peoples. The Qur'ān "is a scripture that con-firms, in Arabic," the mission of other prophets, such as Moses (sura 46:12). The notion that Qur'ānic revelation possessed a universal mission and validity appears to have developed only later.

Born around 570 as a member of the Hāshim clan in the Quraysh tribe in Mecca, Muḥammad was orphaned at an early age and like many Meccans first earned his livelihood as a trader. As an associate and trustee of the wealthy widow Khadīja, he is said to have accompanied a caravan to Syria. There he carried on business, whereupon Khadīja – about fifteen years his senior – married him. After receiv-ing his divine revelation around 610, when he was about 40 years old, he appeared as a prophet (in Arabic *nabī*, similar to the Hebrew *navi*) of a monotheistic faith that forebode a Judgment Day, thereby vehemently rejecting the ancient polytheistic religions of Arabia. In Mecca, the Prophet was able to gather only a small band of followers. The leading clans in the Quraysh tribe, which feared for their influential position and their income from the pilgrimages to the Ka'ba and other holy shrines in the environs of Mecca, were hostile to Muḥammad and his mission. They harassed his companions and even threatened him. Consequently, in 622 the Prophet and his companions made an emigration (*hijra*) to Yathrib (later al-Madīna), about 250 miles northwest of Mecca, referring to themselves as "ones who submit (to God)" (*muslimūn*) and to their faith as "submission" (*islām*) to God's will. The two non-Jewish tribes there had made an agreement with Muḥammad prior to this.

In Yathrib/Medina, the Prophet went from being a persecuted outsider to the powerful leader of an ever-growing community, whose cohesion was guaranteed by the profession of faith in the one God and loyalty to their prophet, rather than by kinship relations and occasional confederacies that existed up to then among Arab tribes. This new community (*umma*) competed with the traditional tribal order of society, although it was not yet in a position to replace it. It was open to all tribes and clans and was also considered indissoluble, as it was traced back to God himself.

During the tens years he was in Medina (622–632), Muḥammad managed to expand the Islamic *umma* virtually throughout the entire Arabian Peninsula. Numerous tribes – both sedentary and nomadic – voluntarily joined the community, which became increasingly powerful. Jews and Arab converts to Judaism living in the oasis of Khaybar in the Ḥijāz mountains agreed contractually to subordinate themselves to the *umma*, as did the Christian community in the bishopric seat of Najrān in northern Yemen. Yemen, which was ruled by the Persians, was won over, as was Muḥammad's hometown Mecca. There, the pagan aristocracy initially fought against the Prophet, with varying results, until the opposing pagan clans of the Quraysh finally decided their future was more secure in the *umma* than in opposition to it. They opened up to the Prophet and converted to Islam in 630. When Muḥammad died two years later, the entire Arabian peninsula was associated with the *umma,* that is, almost all Arabs were united in Islam. This loyalty, however, was tied to Muḥammad personally and was rescinded after his death by some tribes, where their own prophets now appeared. Muḥammad's successor Abu Bakr (632–634) was able again to subjugate the renegades through military force and end the "apostasy" (*ridda*).

# The Arab-Islamic Conquests

Only two major kingdoms existed in antiquity and usually opposed each other as rivals: In the west there was the Hellenistic world with the later Roman-Byzantine empire, and in the east, the great Persian empire under the Achaemenids, Parthians, and Sassanids. The Islamic *umma* added a third actor to the political stage for the first time. A state emerged where there had previously been none. It quickly began to expand and – similar to the other two – developed into an imperial power.

During the decade in which Muḥammad led the *umma* in Medina, preliminary structures for a state had already been created: the basic features of a system of law that bound the tribes together, a class of administrators sent from Medina, and the rudiments of a system of tributes and taxes. The tribal order of society was not simply abolished as a result, but new "state" structures were superimposed on it.

The political and military elite in the new polity were exclusively Arabs. For this reason, the historian Julius Wellhausen titled his classic description of early Islamic history *The Arab Kingdom and Its Fall* (1927, German 1902). The core of the new elite were Muḥammad's original fellow sufferers and comrades in arms, the first Muslims. The first four caliphs, or "successors" (*khalīfa*), also came from their ranks: Abū Bakr (632–634), 'Umar (634–644), 'Uthmān (644–656), and 'Alī (656–661), Muḥammad's cousin and son-in-law. All four were members of the Meccan tribe of

32

the Quraysh, who had been distinguished by their religious merit, in particular by their early profession of faith in the new religion (*sābiqa*). All four had also participated in Prophet's hijra, that is, they were "emigrants" (*muhājirūn*). In comparison, the Muslims of Medina, the "helpers" (*anṣār*), receded into the background very early on. None of them became a caliph, although they did at times raise such claims. Rather quickly, however, Mecca's old pagan elite of money and power reasserted its authority even within the Islamic *umma*, pushing out the class of religious meritocrats. The Umayya family, belonging to the Quraysh clan of the 'Abd Shams, assumed the leading role in this. Once a bitter enemy of the Prophet and his mission, they now joined the vanguard in the military expansion of the new state. The Quraysh aristocracy can be seen as one of the driving forces behind the ensuing conquests (*futūḥ*, literally "openings"). Their trade interests had already led them to Syria during the pre-Islamic era. It has been documented that a number of Meccans owned manors in eastern Syria even prior to the conquest. The Umayyad Mu'āwiya, a son of Muḥammad's former adversary Abū Sufyān, played a significant role in conquering Palestine and Syria. As a reward he was appointed governor of Damascus, a position he held for twenty years. His power base was in Syria, and from there he opposed the selection of the fourth caliph 'Alī. After 'Alī was murdered in 661, he was able to claim the title of caliph for himself and establish Damascus as the new capital.

The military expansion of the caliphate began under the second caliph, 'Umar, and quickly led to the conquest of Roman-Byzantine Palestine/Syria and Persian-Sassanid

Mesopotamia (al-'Irāq). In 636, a Byzantine army was defeated at Yarmūk, a left-bank tributary of the Jordan, after which the Byzantine army abandoned Syria. Almost all of the cities of Palestine and Syria surrendered in exchange for more favorable conditions: protection of life and limb, guaranteed property, the continued existence of churches and protection of their property, and the free exercise of religion. In return, the cities paid a tribute, usually in the form of a lump sum. This was later converted into a poll tax (*jizya*) on non-Muslims. According to these treaties, non-Muslims were given the status of "wards" (*dhimmī*). Under these conditions, Damascus surrendered in 635, Jerusalem in 638, Caesarea in Palestine in 640, and Alexandria in 642, bringing all of Egypt under Arab-Islamic rule. The contractual partners of the caliph were the Christian patriarchs and bishops, who were the only remaining public authority once the Byzantine military withdrew.

The decisive battle in Mesopotamia took place against the Persian imperial army around 636 near al-Qādisiyya, west of the lower Euphrates. Directly following this, the Arabs occupied Ctesiphon, residential city of the Great King on the left (eastern) bank of the Tigris (today Salmān Pāk, southeast of Baghdad). Arab Muslims also defeated the Persians in another battle at Nihavend in western Iran in 641 or 642, paving the way for the conquest of the Iranian highlands.

The rapid expansion of the caliphate is an astounding phenomenon that has been explained in various and at times contradictory ways. The most stubborn cliché, although long challenged by historians, is that of zealous masses setting off to conquer the world in order to spread Islam through fire and sword. However, it is difficult if not impossible to reconstruct the motives of actors at the time, as Arabic sources available to us were all compiled from oral tradition long after the events took place. The Qur'ān itself does not express any explicit missionary aims, nor do we have any evidence of a political program of conquest.

Reports about the initial conquests – which are chronologically confusing and uncertain – tell of individual bands of Bedouins who were and had always been active on the borders of the Fertile Crescent and who were encouraged to further endeavors by their momentary successes. The Arab conquests thus appear initially to have remained within the framework of a continuous process in the Fertile Crescent beginning in the third century BCE: the steady and at times wavelike expansion of Semitic-speaking Bedouins from the Syrian Desert – the Akkadians, Canaanites, and Aramaeans. Soon, however, these Arab incursions assumed a completely new dimension and quality, which is apparent in the fact that they expanded far beyond the Fertile Crescent – into Iran, Armenia, and Asia Minor, as well as into Egypt and North Africa. This development can be traced to the imperial desires of the new power center in Medina, although it appeared to have sought only gradually to coordinate the actions of independent armies at the peripheries of the Fertile Crescent. Most of the military leaders came from the Meccan Quraysh and the Medinan helpers *(anṣār)*, whereas the rank and file soldiers were predominantly from Bedouin tribes associated with the *umma* who were interested above all in booty. One-fifth of the spoils were traditionally reserved for the caliph, who assumed the role of the

pagan tribal sheikh. Later, after state structures had been
established, the central government became the recipient
and distributor of the regular tax revenues.

The conquests in Palestine and Syria were secured by
quartering the individual troop divisions in the larger cities;
in Mesopotamia, Egypt, and North Africa, on the other
hand, military encampments were set up, which gradually
developed into permanent cities: al-Basra in 635, al-Kūfa
on the Euphrates in 638, al-Fusṭāṭ (Old Cairo) on the Nile
in 641, and al-Qayrawān (Kairouan) in present-day Tunisia
in 670. The soldiers (*muqātila*) stationed there were organized according to tribal groups, camping and fighting under
their own leaders. They received payment (*'atā*) from their
regional commander (*amīr*), drawn from spoils and tribute
and later from the regular taxes and duties. Like the old religious meritocrats and their descendants, the warriors of the
individual tribes also received fixed shares of the endowments entered in an army list or *dīwān* ("list, register" in
Persian). The "warriors" – initially only Arabs and Muslims
– were thus the beneficiaries of this fiscal system based on
taxation of the non-Muslims. The need to subjugate an
increasing number of taxpayers to finance a steadily growing Muslim army was certainly one significant motive for
the expanding conquests. The capture of the Iranian highlands and central Asia was initiated from the military en-
campment cities of Basra and Kūfa and continued inde-
pendently from there. The Maghreb and the Iberian peninsula were taken by armies from Kairouan.

The system described above emerged during the conquests and lasted as long as the conquests continued, into
the seventh and eighth centuries, then becoming obsolete.

This was the basis of what Julius Wellhausen referred to as the "Arab Kingdom": the imperial rule of Muslim Arabs over non-Muslim non-Arabs. Nowhere were non-Muslims compelled to convert to Islam; the guarantee of protection (*dhimma*) for non-Muslim subjects became an established part of Islamic divine law (*sharī'a*). Mass conversions, after all, would have undermined the financial basis of the dīwān system. It was only gradual change that led to the fall of the "Arab kingdom." Although the religious motive for expanding the Arab empire might be merely one of many, we should not underestimate the role that religion played as the link between the rulers and as the legitimation for their rule. It was not the conversion of the non-believers, but the rule of Muslims over them that was regarded as God's will.

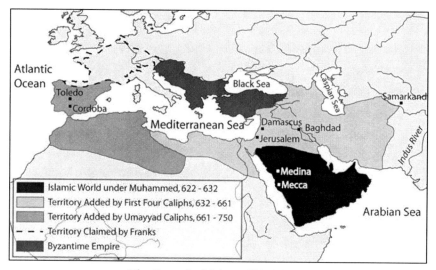

*The Spread of Islam, 622–750* CE

From Don and Jean Johnson, *The Human Drama, Vol. II* (Princeton: Markus Wiener, 2006)

# The Caliphate of the
# Umayyads (661–750)

Caliph Mu'āwiya (661–680) was able to ensure the succession of his son Yazīd (680–683) and thus start a dynasty that would rule the Arab empire for ninety years. This marked the definitive establishment of the old aristocracy of the Quraysh in Mecca over the religious meritocracy of young Islam. This rule, however, did not remain unchallenged. In the next generation, descendants of the companions of the Prophet asserted their claims against Yazīd, which led to a bloody intra-Muslim conflict (*fitna,* "strife, trial"). Al-Ḥusayn, son of 'Alī and grandson of the Prophet, was killed in 681 at Kerbela (Karbalā') while trying to incite a rebellion in Iraq. He became the first martyr of the oppositional party of the Shi'ites. The sons of al-Zubayr, a companion of the Prophet, were able to set up a counter-caliphate in Mecca that survived until 691. There continued to be uprisings after this, especially by 'Alid pretenders against the established caliphate.

In the meantime, the Umayyad 'Abd al-Malik (685–705) was able to bring down the Meccan counter-caliphate and reestablish the unity of the empire. He was the most important Umayyad caliph and set in motion a number of significant reforms. Most important was the standardization of administrative language. From that point on, the language used in records and on coins was Arabic instead of Greek, which until that time had been used in the western part of the empire, and Middle Persian (Pahlavi), which had been used in the east. A standardized form of written Arabic was thereby established. The foundation inscription in the interior of the Dome of the Rock in Jerusalem, a glass mosaic frieze, is the oldest extant Arabic monumental inscription. It is at the same time the earliest material evidence of Qur'ān verses. The Dome of the Rock (*Qubbat al-ṣakhra*), which marks the site of the Prophet Muḥammad's ascension to heaven, bears the foundation date of 691. Its inscription addresses non-Muslims, especially Christians, strongly admonishing them to adopt the strict monotheism of Islam. The meaning of this oldest Islamic monumental construction is disputed. One possible motive was the desire to have something comparable to the splendid Christian Church of the Holy Sepulcher; another might have been the dynasty's wish to demonstrate its own power. 'Abd al-Malik initiated a comprehensive construction program for the project, which was completed by his son and successor al-Walīd I (705–715): The al-Aqsa Mosque (*al-masjid al-aqṣā*, "the farthest mosque," as referred to in the Qur'ān, sura 17:1) was built along the axis of the Dome of the Rock, although it has not survived in its original form. The Umayyad Mosque, which was modeled on this, still exists in Damascus at the site of the Church of St. John, the former Jupiter temple. The buildings of the residence of the Prophet in Medina, in whose inner courtyard he was buried, were replaced by a new, magnificent mosque. The main mosque in al-Fusṭāṭ (Old Cairo) was also rebuilt. With these projects, in which Syrian-Byzantine and Coptic artists played an important role, 'Abd al-Malik and al-Walīd created the seminal examples of Islamic monumental architecture and Islamic architectural decoration.

The conquests continued under the rule of the Umayyads. Although an initial siege of Constantinople (Istanbul)
failed in 674–678 and a sea operation against Constantinople in 717–718 was equally unsuccessful due to the
Byzantines' use of Greek fire, broad regions in both the
west and the east were conquered. In 711, an army of Arabs
and Berbers led by Ṭāriq crossed the Strait of Gibraltar, the
rock beside which henceforth was known as *Jabal Ṭāriq,* or
"Ṭāriq's Mount," ending the rule of the Visigoths on the
Iberian peninsula. At the same time Arab troops advanced
into the Indus delta in present-day Pakistan. In present-day
Uzbekistan, Bukhara was conquered in 710 and Samarqand
in 715. While the Arabs did take the most remote Iranian
city, Chach (Tashkent) in 751, this victory ultimately weakened the conquest movement. Even the incursion of a
Spanish-Arab force into France, widely discussed in
Europe, was brought to a halt between Tours and Poitiers by
Charles Martel in 732 and appears in fact to have been
nothing more than a foray for spoils, targeting the wealthy
St. Martin's Abbey in Tours. In the end, France was not
conquered, even though Roussillon and parts of Languedoc
and Provence were temporarily subject to Arab rule. The
counter-movement by Christian forces to reconquer the
Iberian Peninsula (*Reconquista*) already began under
Charlemagne.

The final decade of Umayyad rule was characterized
for the most part by weak and short-lived caliphates as well
as by internal conflicts. The last significant ruler, Hishām
(724–743), one of ʿAbd al-Malik's many sons, managed to
hold the empire together. Central power was maintained
from the Pyrenees to central Asia. The Caspian Gates, the

passes at the eastern end of the Caucasian foothills, were fortified against a Turkish invasion from the northern steppes. Like his father and brother, Hishām was also a great builder. Numerous "desert castles" of the Umayyads can be traced back to him; they were used for controlling the Bedouins as well as for the agricultural development of the desert steppes and for hunting lodges. The ruins of Qasr al-Hayr al-Sharqī northeast of Palmyra clearly have the dimensions of a palace city. A wealth of stucco carvings has been preserved from Khirbat al-Mafjar in the Jordan valley, not far from Jericho, including a statue of the caliph (currently kept in the Rockefeller Museum in Jerusalem).

The Umayyads maintained their domestic rule through alternating support from northern and southern Arabian tribes. The Islamic *umma* had never been able to overcome the regional differences. The "Arab empire" ultimately fell, in part because it was unable to integrate the growing circles of people who wanted to be part of the *umma*. Islam claims to be egalitarian: All Muslims are said to be equal before God. In reality, however, not only did older tribal structures with their particular loyalty relationships remain intact, but new groups that joined the *umma* had difficulty asserting themselves over the established elites. In addition to the Meccan emigrants (*muhājirūn*), there were the Medinan "helpers" (*ansār*), followed by the Meccans who had retained their pagan beliefs to the end and the Arab Bedouin tribes that had been won over or subjugated and then integrated into the *umma*. And finally there was a growing number of converted non-Arab Muslims, who had a client relationship with the ruling Arab elites and were therefore called *mawālī* ("clients"). The dehgans, the Persian knightly nobility, quickly converted to Islam almost en masse, bringing their vassals and tenant farmers with them. As auxiliary military troops and as local authorities and tax collectors, they were indispensable to the Arabs and were thus allowed to retain their old privileges, although the Arab aristocracy refused to grant them equal status.

Arab tribal units in dispute with the central government over the distribution of spoils and tax revenues incited a rebellion, in alliance with the Iranian *mawālī*, which started in the most remote northeast corner of Iran in 747 and ended in 750 with the conquest of Iraq and the taking of Damascus. This opposition was also backed by Shi'ite groups, who regarded the Umayyads as parvenus and believed that the 'Alids, the descendents of Muḥammad's cousin and brother-in-law 'Alī, were the sole legitimate successors to the Prophet. Later Arab historiography has accused the Umayyads of lacking religious legitimacy, claiming that they debased the caliphate into a secular kingdom (*mulk*), although this is a religiously colored judgment that historians need not accept. The caliphate of the Umayyads of Damascus was one of the most splendid epochs in Arab history. Court literature and monumental architecture reached an apex and the political power of the Umayyad caliphate, which reached from southern France to the Indus, was never again achieved. The fall of the dynasty brought the dissolution of the caliphate only 120 years after the death of Muḥammad.

# The 'Abbāsid Caliphate
# of Baghdad

With the fall of the Umayyads in 750, which is referred to as the "'Abbāsid revolution," a dynasty came to power that would occupy the caliphate for more than half a millennium, until the Mongol invasion of 1258. The 'Abbāsids were the descendants of 'Abbās, an uncle of Muḥammad, and were thus closely related to the Prophet – in contrast to the Umayyads. Muḥammad's direct blood descendants, the 'Alids, who initially supported the overthrow of the Umayyads, were again left empty-handed. Their supporters, the "party" (Shī'a), now became a fixed part of the opposition.

The revolutionary army that had brought down the old regime through its march from central Asia to Iraq and on to Syria and Egypt was comprised primarily of discontented Arabs. Although the new dynasty was Arab and Qurayshi, like its predecessor, the exclusivity of the "Arab empire" could never be reestablished. Persian "clients" had played a significant role in the coup, and men from their ranks began assuming important positions in the army, administration, royal court, and in spiritual life. A geographical shift, which included the establishment of a new capital, accelerated this process. The new rulers remained in Iraq and, after some consideration, decided to establish a new imperial residence and palace city near the old town of Baghdad on the west bank of the Tigris, calling it Madīnat al-Salām, the "City of Peace." Al-Manṣūr (754–775) was

the second 'Abbāsid caliph. Around 758 he started building
a circular grounds based on a Persian model, with a palace
and mosque in the center. At the perimeter, inside the surrounding wall, there were government offices (dīwāns) and
residences for officials and functionaries. The army was
quartered outside the city. The Round City of Manṣūr,
which has disappeared without a trace, was completed in
762. Markets soon developed at the four arterial roads leading out of the city. These grew into suburbs, so that the
palace facility quickly expanded into an actual city. The
caliph and his successor also built a number of castles on
both banks of the Tigris in 773, which served as residences
instead of the Round City. Under Caliph Hārūn al-Rashīd
(786–809) and his son al-Ma'mūn (813–833), the metropolis encompassed a densely populated area of almost four
square miles with an estimated population of almost one
million. It was the largest and most populous city in the
world at the time.

Around this time, changes became evident in the court
of the Baghdad caliphs. While the Umayyads in Damascus
and in their desert castles acted like powerful Arab tribal
sheikhs, the ceremonies of the 'Abbāsids in Baghdad increasingly assumed the splendor of Great Kings in Middle-
Eastern antiquity. Hidden away in his Round City far from
the masses, the caliph had contact only with privileged people. Like the Sassanid Persian king and the Byzantine emperor, he held audiences concealed behind a curtain, his
rank emphasized by his crown or diadem (tāj), a crown that
hung over his head by a chain (shamsa), or other precious
insignias. In addition to their first names, caliphs assumed
an epithet when they were crowned, such as al-Mansūr (the

Victorious), al-Rashīd (the Upright), and al-Ma'mūn (the Trustworthy). A special feature of 'Abbāsid rule was the emergence of the office of the vizier (*wazīr* = "helper"), who served as a kind of chief administrator, controlling and coordinating the major government ministries (dīwāns) – taxes, army, and chancellery – and directing domestic and foreign policies. Even before the office had been firmly established, the Iranian Barmakid family from the area of present-day Afghanistan – Yaḥyā ibn Khālid and his sons al-Faḍl and Ja'far – exercised almost unlimited power in Baghdad during the first seventeen years in Hārūn's reign, until the caliph forcibly removed them in 803.

The caliphate began to shrink after the 'Abbāsid Revolution. Once Islamic rule became rooted in the provinces, the differences between provincial interests and those of the central government became increasingly apparent. The extremely long distances made communication, and thus direct administrative control of the peripheries, difficult. Baghdad was no longer able to support the armies necessary to hold together the huge empire between the Pyrenees and the Indus.

Rule was regionalized according to two models. The first was the establishment of states independent of Baghdad. Arab warriors on the Pyrenean peninsula refused to recognize the new dynasty. In 756 they took in a fugitive Umayyad prince who had escaped the massacre of his family and who was able to establish himself as the "commander" (*amīr*) of al-Andalus – that is, the Islamic Iberian Peninsula – and pass on his rule to his descendants. In present-day Morocco another refugee, Idrīs, a descendant of the Prophet, was able to gain the support of the Awrāba.

This Berber tribe had occupied the Roman city of Volubilis and helped Idrīs to power. Fez (Fās), founded by Idrīs in 789, was expanded in 808 by his son Idrīs II. Other Arab refugees from Andalusia and Kairouan made the city into the first Arab settlement in the midst of the Berber tribes of the western Maghreb.

The other model was practiced in Kairouan starting in 800. This Arab garrison town in present-day Tunisia was occupied in 761 by an 'Abbāsid army and made a subject of Baghdad. Caliph Hārūn al-Rashīd installed Ibn al-Aghlab, an officer in this army, as a governor and military commander (*amīr*) in 800. He founded a *de facto* independent gubernatorial dynasty, the Aghlabids (800–909). With the approval of the caliph, who remained the nominally recognized commander in chief, Ibn al-Aghlab governed over the central Maghreb and Sicily, which was conquered between 827 and 878. The emir paid the caliph an annual tribute and, as a sign of the caliph's supremacy, agreed that he be named at the invocation to close Friday sermons (*khutba*) and on coins (*sikka*). Similar dynasties headed by governors nominally subject to Baghdad were later established in Egypt as well as in eastern Iran and central Asia, greatly limiting the actual power of the caliphs in Baghdad. The conquests came to a halt and, despite numerous campaigns, Byzantine Asia Minor could not be conquered in the name of Islam.

# Al-'Arabiyya: High Arabic Language and Literature

Baghdad bookseller Ibn al-Nadīm compiled a "catalog" (*fihrist*) in 988, indexing all the authors he knew and their works. He reported that more than one hundred shops of book scribes and booksellers could be found on a single lane of the bazaar in the capital of the caliphate and that he knew of a Baghdad bibliophile who hoarded the manuscripts of six generations of learned authors in a chest: on parchment, Egyptian papyrus, Chinese paper, and leather scrolls, all of which had been marked with the name of the author and certified. Ibn al-Nadīm listed more than six thousand book titles in his "catalog," which was by no means limited to Muslim authors. He was particularly interested in Greek philosophers.

The Islamic conquests not only expanded the horizons of the Arabs immensely, but also provided them with access to new technologies. Following a battle between Arab troops and Chinese border guards at the River Talas (in present-day Kyrgyzstan near the border to Kazakhstan) in 751, it was discovered that several paper producers were among the Chinese prisoners of war, who had been settled in Samarqand. Paper production soon became a local industry in eastern Iran and was brought to Baghdad by al-Faḍl, a Barmakid, in 794, quickly spreading westward from there. Paper was one of the prerequisites for the incredible production of Arabic literature that began in the ninth and

tenth centuries. Another was the existence of the metropolis of Baghdad and the court of the caliph, which served not
only as a crossroads and gathering point for influences from
the four corners of the known world, but also as a place
where science and literature were valued and promoted.

Arabic literature of the 'Abbāsid period developed
above all from religious writings. An unprecedented
amount of information, which until that time had been
passed down primarily in oral form, was collected and put
down in writing. During the final years of the Umayyad
period, Ibn Isḥāq (died ca. 767) of Medina had already
compiled the hagiography (*sīra*) of the Prophet Muḥammad. His work has survived in an abridged edition by Ibn
Hishām of Basra (died ca. 830). Al-Wāqidī (747–823), a
protégé of Caliph Hārūn al-Rashīd and the Barmakid
Yaḥyā, collected the chronicles of Muḥammad's military
expeditions and campaigns (*al-maghāzī*). His secretary Ibn
Sa'd (784–845) compiled the biographies of the Prophet
and his companions, as well as those of the most important
personalities of subsequent generations, into what is today
a nine-volume work. All of these authors were "clients,"
*mawālī*, that is, non-Arab Muslims. Ibn al-Kalbī of Kūfa
(737–821), whose *Book of Idols* includes extensive information about ancient Arab gods and their shrines and rites,
lived in Baghdad for a time under the caliph al-Mahdī
(775–785).

*Kitāb al-kharāj,* a treatise on taxation written for Caliph
Hārūn al-Rashīd by Abū Yūsuf (died in 798), a Baghdad
judge, marks the beginning of Arabic legal writings. Abū
Yūsuf was a student of the great Iraqi legal scholar Abū
Ḥanīfa of Kūfa (died in 767), whose mausoleum in Bagh-
dad remains a Sunnī pilgrimage site to the present day. The

Sunnī legal schools (singular *madhhab*), which continue to exist even today, emerged from the student circles of Abū Hanīfa, the Medinan Mālik (died in 796), the Palestinian al-Shāfiʿī (767–820), who died in Egypt, and Ibn Ḥanbal (780–855) of Baghdad and were a prerequisite for the flourishing, extensive production of Islamic legal writings, which today fill entire libraries with their fundamental treatises, commentaries, and supercommentaries.

A short time later the traditionaries also started their collections. At first they compiled the oral traditions, usually short, anecdotal reports about the sayings and decisions of the Prophet Muḥammad, which had become increasingly important in legal, theological, and political debate beginning around 700. They reviewed the sayings according to a criteria of authenticity they themselves had developed and recorded them systematically in written form. The most notable collector of these traditions, or *Hadīth* ("events"), was al-Bukhārī (810–870), a scholar of Persian descent from central Asia, who traveled to Baghdad, Mecca, and Egypt "in search of knowledge" (*fī ṭalab al-ʿilm*). The Sunnīs regard his *Saḥīḥ* ("The Authentic"), containing 2762 hadiths, as the most important religious work after the Qurʾān. The other five Sunnī standard collections of the Prophet's traditions from this era emerged in a similar way, by means of extended travels in order to collect such materials. By and large they were written in Arabic by Iranian or central Asian men. In addition to the Qurʾān and its commentaries, it was primarily these collections of traditions and legal works that allowed classical High Arabic to spread to the remotest corners of the caliphate after having been standardized in Basra and Baghdad.

This growing interest in the history and early period of

Islam helped to strengthen the sense of cohesion among Muslims, whether they were of Arab descent or not. The first recountings of historical events occurred orally in the form of individual tidings (*khabar*), which were then recorded during the 'Abbāsid period in written form in chronological collections, as was done for the sayings of the Prophet as well. The oldest preserved chronicle is one by Khalīfa ibn Khayyāt (died in 854), a Basran. The history of the Arab-Islamic conquests was compiled in Baghdad by al-Balādhurī (died in 892), a man of Persian descent. The zenith of early 'Abbāsid historiography is *Ta'rikh al-rusul wa al-muluk* (*The History of Prophets and Kings*), a chronicle of the world from creation to the author's present, written by the Iranian Ṭabarī (839–923). This mammoth, thirteen-volume work follows his travels to Syria and Egypt using older collections in Baghdad, providing most of our knowledge about early Islamic history.

In addition to these works related to Islam, the belles lettres also developed. This genre was unambiguously secular in nature and was written and read not by the religious scholars (*'ulamā'*), but by the courtiers and officials of the dīwāns, the "secretaries" (*kuttāb*). The apex of courtly poetry can be found in the poems of Abū Nuwās (died in 815), a Persian "client" at the court of Hārūn al-Rashīd and his son al-Amīn, who despite his Persian background was and continues to be celebrated by Arabs as one of their greatest poets, although his verses, which rebound in wine, women, and song, certainly have not found the approval of pious religious scholars. The most significant writer of entertaining secular prose (*adab*) which was often based on translations from Middle Persian is al-Jāḥiz (776–869), a member of a "client" family from Basra. His satires and *Kitāb al-bukhalā'* (published in English as both *The Book of Misers* and *Avarice and the Avaricious*), his polemics and his encyclopedias, such as *Kitāb al-ḥayawān* (*The Book of Animals*), remain peerless examples of Arab prose even today. Finally, it was during the era of Hārūn al-Rashīd and the Barmakids in Baghdad that the oldest Arabic core of *1001 Nights* was written.

This rich literary life gave rise to High Arabic, or *'Arabiyya,* as Arabic grammar is also a product of 'Abbāsid Iraq. The first important Arab grammarians and lexicographers, Sībawayh (died 786) and al-Khalīl (died 791), lived and worked in Basra. Although this interest in grammar originally arose from a religious desire to understand enigmatic passages in the Qur'ān as precisely as possible, a purely scholarly interest in the subject quickly developed as well. The Basra school, in contrast to the Kūfa school, attached great importance to standardizing the language, seeking to adapt the rules of the proper, high language, or *fusḥa* ("most eloquent, purest"), to the Bedouins' exemplary use of language, which was considered especially pure. Classical *'Arabiyya,* the high language, emerged between the eighth and tenth centuries in Iraq from the mutual influences of spoken language, literature, and standardized grammar. Even today it continues to unite all Arabs.

# The Arab Reception
# of Antiquity

High Arabic, which assumed its standardized form in Baghdad and Basra, was also understood by educated classes in Samarqand and Bukhara, in Cordoba and Toledo, regardless of whether they were of Arab descent or not. 'Arabiyya offered a means of communication that was used from the Chinese border to the marches of France, facilitating a cultural exchange that the world had seen only once before, during the Hellenist age. Arabic now took the place of Greek, as Islam replaced Hellenism. Although Arabs were able to conquer neither Asia Minor nor Constantinople and Greece, three of the most important Hellenist metropolises did come under their control: Seleukeia on the Tigris, Antiocheia (Antioch), and Alexandria. Alexandria no longer had the central role in science that it had occupied well into the fifth century, but the heritage of antiquity was still very much alive throughout the eastern Mediterranean realm, and it was eagerly appropriated by Arabs. The story that the second caliph, 'Umar, destroyed the library of Alexandria is merely a legend.

According to tradition, the Caliph al-Ma'mūn (813–833) reported that Aristotle once appeared to him in a dream: "A man with light, reddish skin, a high forehead, thick eyebrows, a bald head, dark blue eyes, and handsome features was sitting at a lectern." The caliph turned to the great scholar and questioned him. Encouraged by this encounter, he then began collecting Greek manuscripts and having them translated into Arabic. This legend is a symbolic representation of an actual process that continued over several generations. Aramaic-speaking Christians – who comprised the vast majority of the caliph's subjects in the Fertile Crescent – were particularly responsible for the survival and transmission of the heritage of antiquity. Much of Greek literature had already been translated into Aramaic, and translations into Arabic were usually completed through this intermediate step. The first known translator into Arabic was a Christian, Yaḥyā (Yuḥannā) al-Bitrīq ("Patrikios"), who translated numerous medical works as well as Ptolemy's *Tetrabiblos,* purportedly commissioned by Caliph al-Manṣūr (754–775). His son, who was also named Yaḥyā, converted to Islam and was the protégé of a vizier of the caliph al-Ma'mūn. The younger Yaḥyā started translating the works of Aristotle: *On Heavens, Meteorology, History of Animals, Politics,* and the basic work on logic, the *Organon.* He also translated Plato's *Timaeus,* which investigates the nature of the physical world.

In 830, al-Ma'mūn opened his famous *Bayt al-ḥikma,* the House of Wisdom, which was not a university, as is sometimes claimed, but a library hall, whose constantly growing inventory of manuscripts was accessible to scholars. The caliph also sponsored translations into Arabic. A Syrian Christian, Yūḥannā ibn Māsawayh, was the first director of this institute. He was succeeded by Ḥunayn ibn Isḥāq (Latinized as Johannitius), son of a Christian apothecary from al-Ḥīra, the ancient capital of the Lakhmids on the Euphrates. He is said to have learned Greek in Alexandria and improved his Arabic in Basra. As a young doctor he entered into service for al-Ma'mūn and remained active under Caliph al-Mutawakkil (847–861). Ḥunayn is the most important translator of the Baghdad School. He translated from Greek primarily into his native Aramaic, and less often into Arabic. He is responsible for the Arabic translation of numerous treatises of Galen and other ancient physicians such as Hippocrates, Rufus of Ephesus, and Paul of Aegina. He also translated works of the pharmacologist Discorides, the geographer and astronomer Ptolemy, the mathematician Archimedes, and Plato and the Neoplatonists Porphyrios and Alexander of Aphrodisias. Ḥunayn died in 873, but the Baghdad school of translation continued into the tenth century, supported by caliphs, viziers, and other high-ranking officials. In 991 or 993, Shapur ibn Ardashir, the Persian vizier of Caliph al-Rādī, founded a House of Knowledge (*dār al-'ilm*) in the Baghdad suburb of al-Karkh. It contained a library with more than ten thousand volumes and was also open to foreign scholars staying in Baghdad.

Arab interest in Greek texts was selective. Only works of prose were translated, in particular those dealing with scientific or philosophical subjects. Literature – epics, drama, and lyric poetry – was completely absent. Most of Plato's dialogues remained untranslated as well. Aristotle, in contrast, was regarded as "the philosopher" par excellence; and everything that came after him – especially the extensive works of Plotinus and the Neoplatonists – was associated with him. The Greek words *philosophos* and *philosophia* were borrowed in Arabic as *faylasūf* and *falsafa*, as were countless terms from the fields of medicine, botany, pharmacology, and astronomy.

The significance of the Arab reception of antiquity is twofold. In the first place, it enriched and expanded intellectual life in the Islamic world. On this basis, a philosophy arose that was independent and Arabic – albeit only "Islamic" to a limited extent. Its first representative was al-Kindī (ca. 800–870), the descendant of an Arab family from Kūfa, who was a protégé of the caliphs al-Ma'mūn and al-Mu'taṣim (833–842) and a teacher to one of the latter's sons. Kindī's system was greatly influenced by Aristotelian and Neoplatonist thought. The philosopher al-Fārābī (872–950), a Turk from Transoxania, also resided in Baghdad and later in Syria. The physician and philosopher Ibn Sīnā (Latinized as Avicenna, 980–1037) was born in Bukhara and lived and taught in many cities in Iran. His central texts, *Al-Qānūn (The Canon of Medicine)* and the philosophical *Kitāb al-Shifā' (The Book of Healing)*, came to be standard works, not only among Arabs, but soon in the Christian western world as well. The religious scholars (*'ulamā)* of Islam always suspected that Greek philosophy was heretical, although they often employed Aristotelian logic in theological disputes. The natural sciences, on the other hand, were adopted without reservation and developed further. The "ancient sciences" (*al-'ulūm al-qadīma*) were added to the canon of the religious – that is, Islamic – sciences as a matter of course.

The Arab reception of antiquity, however, proved to be as important for the Christian Western world as it was for the Arabs themselves. While monastery libraries did contain Latin texts, Greek literature existed at most in Latin translation. The mediating role played by the Arabs here was invaluable. Texts from antiquity translated into Arabic found their way to western Europe, above all via the Iberian peninsula. After Charlemagne took Barcelona in 801, the creation of the Spanish March (Marca Hispănica) in Catalonia brought the Franks in close contact with the "Saracens," as Christians called Muslim Arabs. The name comes from the Greek term *Sarakenoi*, an Arab tribe on the Sinai Peninsula. Gerbert d'Aurillac, a scholar and cleric who later became Pope Silvester II (999–1003), spent three years in his youth studying in the Catalonian bishopric of Vic and in the nearby Ripoll monastery. There he used Arabic sources to develop his knowledge of mathematics and astronomy, using primarily astronomical instruments such as the astrolabe and the armillary sphere. The Christian reconquest of Toledo in 1085 by King Alphonse VI of Castile created another site where Europeans encountered Arabic literature. The circle of Archbishop Raimund I (1126–1151) was responsible for extensive translations from Arabic into Latin, performed by learned clerics from all over Europe. In addition to Michael Scot and Robert of Ketton (Robertus Ketenensis), Herman of Carinthia, also known as Herman Dalmatin, worked there as well. Peter the Venerable, the abbot of Cluny, encouraged Robert to prepare the first Latin translation of the Qur'ān, a project that was completed in 1143. While the conquest of Jerusalem during the first crusade in 1099 had sparked interest in Islam, scholarly interest independent of the church's missionary aims emerged quickly. Aside from the Qur'ān, Robert also translated Al-Khwārizmī's *Algebra* into Latin in 1145. Central among those works of antiquity that reached the Christian Western world through Islamic Spain were those dealing with mathematics and astronomy. Arab-

Islamic scholars also produced independent contributions of their own, such as the astronomical tables of the Spaniard Maslama al-Majrītī ("of Madrid," died ca. 1007), which were rendered into Latin in 1126 by English scholar and cleric Adelard of Bath. About fourteen years later, the tables of the elder al-Battānī (Albategnius), which were based on observations made in Mesopotamia around 900, were translated by Plato of Tivoli. Gerhard of Cremona translated the *Toledan Tables,* which are based on observations by many Muslim and Jewish astronomers of Spain, including al-Zarqālī (Arzachel). Copernicus cited Albategnius and Arzachel in his major work *De revolutionibus orbium coelestium (On the Revolutions of the Heavenly Spheres),* focusing on their corrections of Ptolemy.

The Andalusian Aristotelian Ibn Rushd (Latinized as Averroēs, 1126–1198) of Cordoba exercised perhaps the greatest influence on Western philosophy. After his extensive oeuvre was translated into Latin, it triggered a wave of Aristotelianism throughout Western Europe. It was in fact through Averroēs that the Western world was introduced to Aristotle, and even Thomas Aquinas was forced to critically address the Latin Averroism.

# Arabic Numerals
# and the Zero

During his studies in Vic and Ripoll in Catalonia from roughly 967 to 991, Gerbert d'Aurillac, later Pope Silvester II, was one of the first Western scholars to become familiar with "Arabic" numerals and how to do arithmetic with them. The Romans, in contrast to the Greeks, had also used a numerical system, but it was poorly suited for arithmetic computation. The Arabs, on the other hand, had a much more practical and versatile tool for writing numbers, composed only of glyphs for the digits one to nine and the zero. It is the same system – except for a few graphic modifications, in particular a ninety-degree rotation – that continues to be used throughout the world today as "Arabic numerals." The Arabs themselves referred to this method of numerical computation as "Indian arithmetic," which suggests that they presumed the system originated in India. What was unique about this system was the use of decimal positions and the related use of a special sign as a placeholder, the zero – *sifr* in Arabic, "empty" – which corresponds to the words *cipher* or *zero*. The Sumerians and Babylonians also used a decimal place value system and eventually even developed a sign for zero, but their system was never popularized. The Indian system had probably already spread to Iran during the late Sassanid dynasty. In India itself, the astronomer Aryabhata (ca. 476) had worked with nine ciphers, and the mathematician Brahmagupta

(598–665) had developed arithmetic rules that used a zero. The Iranian Muḥammad al-Khwārizmī (from Khwārizm, the inland delta of the Oxus/Amu Darya, south of the Aral Sea) is responsible for the general widespread use of the system. In 820 he wrote his fundamental work *Al-Khwarizmi on the Hindu Art of Reckoning*, which describes the basic arithmetic operations and setting up of equations. The treatise introduced the system and thus made it practicable throughout the Arab world. The work became known in the West in its Latin translation as *De numero Indorum* and in an adapted form as *Liber Algorismi de pratica arismetrice*. The Latinized form of Khwārizmī is *Algorismus,* which led to the coining of the mathematical term "algorithm." Another work by Khwārizmī was even more significant: *al-Mukhtaṣar fī ḥisāb al-jabr wal-muqābala* (*The Compendious Book on Calculation by Completion and Balancing*). *Al-gabr* or *al-jabr* – literally the "setting" of a dislocated bone – actually refers to the completion or transposition of terms from one side of an equation to the other, whereas "balancing" refers to what we normally call "reduction." When Robert of Chester (Robertus Castrensis) translated this work in 1145 under the Latin title *Liber algebras et almucabola* and a short time later Gerhard of Cremona prepared an improved translation entitled *De jebra et al-mucabola,* the way was paved not only for "Hindu reckoning" in the West, but also the term for it: algebra.

# Arabization and Islamization

The caliphate established the framework for two related but clearly distinct processes: linguistic Arabization and religious Islamization, which did go hand in hand with one another, but occurred at different tempos and with varied success in the various countries. Neither process was ever definitively concluded.

Arabic, the language of the Qur'ān and thus of divine revelation, became the language of all religious and juristic writings. Under Caliph 'Abd al-Malik (685–705) it became the sole official language; under the 'Abbāsid caliph of Baghdad it was also established as the language of scholarship, spoken by scholars and the educated from Samarqand to Toledo and from the Caucasus to Yemen. In addition, during the conquest period the Arab army had carried their language to distant garrisons, where it initially existed in scattered linguistic enclaves, such as Old Cairo in Egypt or Kairouan in present-day Tunisia, isolated from the surrounding indigenous language environments.

On the Arabian Peninsula, the North Arabic of the Ḥijāz rapidly replaced Old South Arabic. North Arabic, which is now generally referred to simply as Arabic, is also spoken in Yemen today. Old South Arabic has survived only in small communities there: Mehri on the mainland and Soqotri on the island of Socotra in the Indian Ocean. Both of these languages have preserved the grammatical structures of Old South Arabic, but their vocabularies are now North Arabic to a great degree.

Within the Fertile Crescent, Arabic eclipsed Aramaic, which had been the local language since about 1000 BCE, spoken by all groups in the population regardless of their religious faith. It showed particular resistance to change as the language of the literature and liturgy of the Christian churches – the Syrian Jacobite as well as the Nestorian Church in the former Persian empire. Aramaic is spoken even today by Christians in Syria in the area around Ma'lūlū north of Damascus and among the "Assyrian" or "Chaldean" (Nestorian) Christians in the border triangle of Syria, Iraq, and Turkey.

Iran, on the other hand, resisted Arabization. Although there as well, Arabic was the language of Islamic literature, philosophy, and science, the Semitic language, which is starkly distinct from Indo-Germanic Middle Persian, was never adopted by the Iranian populace. Although powerful Arabic-speaking colonies were established in the aftermath of the conquest, (New) Persian nevertheless became the national language of literature beginning in the tenth century, initially for lyric and epic poetry, and soon afterward for secular prose as well. Vizier al-Bal'amī produced a Persian translation and edited version of Ṭabarī's great chronicle of the world in 963, and around 995 Ferdowsi wrote the *Shāh-nāmeh (Book of Kings)*, which became the Persian national epic. Ibn Sīnā (Avicenna) also wrote scientific prose in Persian and verse in both Arabic and Persian. In preserving its national language and traditions, Iran remained outside of the Arab world.

In Egypt, the use of Arabic was long limited to the al-

Fustāt (Old Cairo) military camp and a number of garrisons such as Alexandria or Aswān, whereas in rural regions the old languages of the pharaohs were spoken in their most modern form, Coptic (Arabic *qiftī* or *qubtī,* meaning "Egyptian"), and maintained as the language of literature and liturgy of the Coptic church. Because Arabic, rather than Greek, was introduced as the official, administrative language and was the only language the authorities permitted, it soon became the spoken language as well, especially among the educated classes. Today Egypt is an Arab country; Coptic is used only in church liturgy and is no longer understood even by Christians.

Libya and the Maghreb comprised the Latin, western part of the Roman Empire. Latin was the language of the urban populace and the Catholic Church. Large segments of the population, peasants and Bedouins alike, however, spoke those languages referred to jointly as "Berber" – literally, "barbarous." There had been a steady decline in the number of Roman cities in North Africa since the third century, causing the Latin-speaking urban population to diminish. Consequently, the Arabs encountered only moderately urbanized landscapes when they conquered the region at the end of the seventh century. Here, too, al-Qayrawān (Kairouan), the military settlement from the period of conquest, and smaller urban garrisons were the locus of Arabization. While the military was continually supplemented and reinforced with advancing troops, the rural population remained Berber and retained their own languages. The first major immigration of entire Bedouin clans and tribes did not occur before 1050, when the government in Cairo took the tribal branches of the Hilāl, Sulaym, and Maʿqil, who had become nomadic in Upper Egypt east of the Nile, relocated them across the river, and unleashed them on the apostate Maghreb. In 1052 the Bedouin armies defeated the emir of Kairouan at Jabal Haydarān in southern Tunisia and, as a contemporary chronicler noted, inundated the entire country "like a swarm of locusts." This marked the beginning of an unremitting flow of immigrant Arab Bedouins into the Maghreb, as the various tribes and clans followed their relatives from the Sinai and the Arabian Peninsula. The actual extent of Bedouin devastation in the former Roman Africa, Numidia, and Mauritania is disputed among scholars. While the immigrating Arab tribes destroyed neither cities nor roads and bridges, their advance resulted in the unambiguous displacement of Berber nomads, especially the Zenāta tribe, from Algeria's high plateau, which became grazing areas for Arab Bedouins. The Berbers were forced into the mountains, where they continue to live today as farmers and seminomads. Whereas only remnants of Berber-speaking peoples can still be found in Libya and Tunisia, the Kabyles (from Arabic *qabīla,* "tribe") in Algeria make up thirty percent of the population. The westernmost region of present-day Morocco was the least Arabized; here the Berber-speaking population survived primarily in the high mountains of the Atlas range and the Rif, where they comprise about forty percent of the population today. The Bedouin invasion reached as far south as Mauritania. The Arabic dialects of the Maghreb are those of the immigrant Bedouins.

The Iberian Peninsula remained largely Latin-speaking, even under Islamic rule. Only a segment of the immigrants were Arabs; over the course of the centuries, Berbers made up a much larger proportion. Nevertheless, *al-Andalus*, as the entire peninsula was called (presumably a Visigothic word), was part of the Arab world. The southern half of the peninsula was most strongly influenced by the foreign religion, culture, and language, due in part to the Christian *Reconquista* advancing from the north. Whereas Barcelona returned to Christian rule as early as 801, Toledo in 1085, and Zaragoza in 1118, Cordoba remained Islamic until 1236, Sevilla until 1248, and Granada until 1492. The linguistic influence on Spanish (Castilian) can be recognized even today in the numerous borrowings from Arabic. While the rivers in the north have retained their ancient names: Ebro, Duero/Douro, and Tajo/Tejo, those in the south have Arabic roots, as is evident in their compounding with the word *al-wādī:* Guadalupe, Guadiana, Guadalete, Guadalquivir (*al-Wādi al-kabīr,* "the great river").

Sicily (*Siqilliya*) was part of the Arab world for a much shorter length of time. The Tunisian Aghlabids' conquest of the Byzantine island lasted from 827 to 878. Palermo (*Bālarm*), the seat of the Arab emir, was called *al-Madīna* ("the city"); Taormia became *al-Mu'izziyya.* Numerous locations have retained their old Arabic names, such as Marsala (*Marsā 'Alī*) and Caltabellotta (*Qal'at al-ballūṭ,* "fortress of the oak"). Even the Arabic name for Mount Etna, *al-Jebel* ("the mountain"), has been incorporated into the local name for the mountain, Mongibello. Linguistically the island appears to have been largely Arabized. In any case, Greek disappeared entirely when the island was re-Christianized and then completely Latinized following the Norman conquest (1060–1091).

The process of religious Islamization should be distinguished from that of linguistic Arabization. Although the two were parallel developments, there are important distinctions between them.

In Iran and Iraq, the Zoroastrian "state church" of the Sassanids perished with the fall of the Persian empire. The fire temples were destroyed or fell into ruin. This development was probably the result of the rapid conversion to Islam by the dehgans, the Persian knightly nobility. When almost the entire aristocracy converted en masse to the new religion, the rest of the populace followed. It is certainly significant that – in contrast to the Christian churches – the priestly hierarchy here simply ceased to exist. The "magicians" (*majūs*), as the Arabs referred to the Zoroastrians, were able to enjoy the status of *dhimmīs,* since they were monotheists and considered "People of the Book," as were Christians and Jews. A large portion of Zoroastrian scripture was not codified until the early Islamic period, especially under the 'Abbāsid caliphs. All of this, however, did not prevent the almost complete disappearance of Zoroastrianism. Only small communities have survived to the present, primarily in central and eastern Iran. There is also a Parsi (i.e., Persian) minority on the Indian subcontinent.

In contrast, the Nestorian church, which was officially recognized in the Persian empire, continued under caliphate rule. The primate of the church, the Catholicos, established his seat in the newly founded city of Baghdad, playing an important role at the court of the caliph as the officially recognized head of his church. Remnants of the Nestorian church, which calls itself the "Assyrian" or "Chaldean" church, are present today especially in northern Iraq and across the borders to Turkey and Iran. There are numerous Christian churches in Mosul on the Tigris, which is the seat of both a Jacobite bishop, or maphrian, and the Chaldean (Nestorian) metropolitan. The Jews, who had been residents of the country since the Babylonian captivity (597 or 586 BCE), were of course also "People of the Book." The Babylonian Talmud originated here. During the Sassanid dynasty the seat of the Jewish exilarch or "head of the exile" (Arabic *Ra's al-jālūt*), from the lineage of David, was in Ctesiphon. The exilarch later resided in Baghdad, where – like the Nestorian Catholicos – he was an esteemed member of the caliph's court.

In contrast, followers of the religion founded by Mani (215–277), which started in Iraq, were persecuted and systematically murdered by Muslims. The Manichaeans were dualists and therefore were regarded with suspicion by the strictly monotheistic Muslims. The severe persecution by the 'Abbāsid caliphs between 780 and 795 destroyed Manichaeism. The seat of their leader – originally in Babylon – was moved in the late tenth century to Samarqand, where many Manichaeans had immigrated. Manichaeans are known to have still been living in central Asia into the fourteenth century, where their trail disappears. Numerous Gnostic sects and groups that were often simply referred to collectively as Manichaeans suffered a similar fate in Iraq. Only a small Baptist sect of the Mandaeans has survived in the marshy regions of southern Iraq.

As former provinces of the Roman-Byzantine empire, Syria, Lebanon, Palestine, and the Emirate of Transjordan – always referred to by Arabs as a single country, *al-Shām* – were Christian lands with Jewish and Samaritan minorities. They long retained this status even under the Muslim Arab rule, and to the present have maintained both the Monophysite Syrian ("Jacobite") and the Greek Orthodox ("Melkite") churches with their patriarchs, metropolitans, and bishops, and numerous churches and monasteries. The Church of the Holy Sepulcher in Jerusalem was always in Christian hands – except for a short interim between 1009 and 1020 under the Fāṭimid caliph al-Ḥākim. The Maronite church of Lebanon, named after the Syrian monk Maron (ca. 400), did not become independent until the eighth century under Islamic rule. A Uniate church, the Maronites are today the largest Christian group in Lebanon with their own patriarch.

In Egypt, the Arab-Islamic conquest ended the predominance of the Greek-Orthodox (Melkite) church, thereby alleviating the indigenous Monophysite Coptic (that is, Egyptian) church from extreme hardship. From then on the Coptic patriarchs of Alexandria led the Christians not only of Egypt, but also of Nubia, Sudan, and Ethiopia (Abyssinia). The new Arab metropolis of al-Fusṭāṭ (Old Cairo) became a bishop's seat. Egypt's population remained largely Christian, probably into the fourteenth or fifteenth century. Though the precise point in time cannot be determined, the scales began to tip as a result of a steady influx of Muslims – soldiers, officials, and Bedouins – and the attractiveness of Islam as the prevailing religion and the religion of the rulers. There was also occasional gentle pressure from above, especially on Coptic officials, who had dominated tax administration for centuries. Today the Coptic segment of the Egyptian population is estimated at about ten percent.

Christianity in the Maghreb – in contrast to Egypt and the Middle East – disappeared entirely, along with the Latin language. The Roman Catholic church offered less resistance, perhaps in part due to the gradual dwindling of Roman cities since late antiquity. The city of Thamugadis (Timgad) in present-day Algeria was already destroyed by Berbers in 485. The last bishop of Sitifis (Sétif) was mentioned in 525; the last one of Cuicul (Djemila), in 553. All of this happened long before the Islamic conquest, which perhaps merely continued, or even accelerated, a process that had been going on for centuries. In the late tenth century there were still forty-seven bishoprics in the Maghreb, fourteen of them in the southern part of present-day Tunisia. In 1095, however, Pope Leo IX lamented in a letter to the bishop of Carthage that "in all of Africa" only five bishoprics were still occupied. A short time later the Catholic church as an organization must have vanished entirely from the Maghreb, although St. Louis IX, King of France, did encounter a few Christians in Carthage on his crusade in 1270.

Al-Andalus, the Iberian peninsula, is a special case insofar as the Christian *Reconquista* started here immediately after the Islamic conquest. As a result, Islamic influence on the peninsula was gradually forced southward and in the thirteenth century limited to present-day Andalusia. The situation of the non-Muslim minority was no different here than in North Africa and the Middle East. Islam was the prevailing religion; Christians and Jews enjoyed the protected status of *dhimmīs*. There is no evidence that the atmosphere here was particularly tolerant or liberal in comparison to Asia Minor and the Middle East. The "Alhambra

Islam" frequently invoked by present-day authors is more utopian fantasy than historical reality. Nevertheless, minorities here were not treated more harshly than they were elsewhere. There were Jewish and Christian viziers and high-ranking officials here, as well as non-Muslim scholars.

The *Reconquista* had different consequences in the regions of Spain and Portugal that returned to Christian rule. In the eastern kingdom of Aragón the nobility was more tolerant with its new Muslim subjects, well aware of the economic repercussions their expulsion or extermination would bring. In contrast, the influence of the church and the orders of knighthood – the most important supporters of the conquest movement – prevailed in Castile, where policies of complete re-Christianization through forced baptism or expulsion were enacted. When Granada was conquered in 1492 by the "Catholic Kings" Ferdinand and Isabella, this policy was implemented throughout all of Spain under the influence of Cardinal Cisnero. There were revolts by Arabs and Berbers of Andalusia who were forced to convert but secretly remained faithful to Islam. This led to the decrees of 1609 to 1614 by which King Philipp III expelled all of the "Moriscos" from the peninsula. With them – almost 300,000 people – Islam and Arab influence disappeared entirely from the Iberian peninsula. Aside from Sicily, this was the most significant loss the Arab world was forced to accept.

# The Mamluks

In the ninth century, an innovation developed in Baghdad under the 'Abbāsids that had enormous military, social, and political consequences for the Islamic world: the emergence of the military caste of the Mamluks.

The Arabic word *mamluk* is a passive participle of the verb "to own." A Mamluk therefore is someone owned by someone else, a slave. The word came into use for a new kind of soldier. This phenomena is specific to the Islamic world and exerted a decisive influence there far into the modern era. When Napoleon landed in Egypt in 1798, he was confronted by an army of Mamluks.

It was Caliph al-Mu'taṣim (833–842), a son of Hārūn al-Rashīd, who in 815 was the first to purchase Turkish slaves from central Asia when he was a prince. He gave them military training and used them as soldiers in his guard. In 832 he already had a core group of 4000 slave soldiers; after acceding to the throne he continued to buy slaves on a grand scale. They came from the nomadic Turkish tribes of central Asia, that is, from present-day Uzbekistan, Turkmenistan, and Kazakhstan, and were sold primarily at the market in Samarqand, where they were purchased by agents of the caliph. The young men, removed from their families and homeland, developed a personal loyalty to their new owner. Unlike the Arab soldiers, who had previously comprised the armies of Islam, they had no tribal ties. The new troops, however, proved to be

70

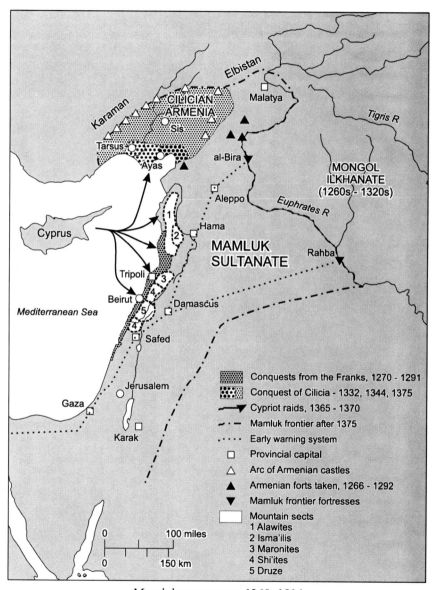

*Mamluk supremacy, 1260–1516*

From William Harris, *The Levant* (Princeton: Markus Wiener, 2005)

such an impediment in the metropolis of Baghdad and so
onerous to citizens that in 836 the caliph established
Sāmarrā, a new residence on the Tigris about seventy-five
miles northwest of Baghdad, for himself and his new army.
The next seven successors also resided there, expanding the
Turkish army and the city, whose ruins extend today about
thirty miles along the banks of the Tigris, making it one of
the world's largest archaeological sites.

The new army soon developed a dynamic of its own.
The soldiers imported as slaves were set free after a certain
period of time and were then able to rise to the ranks of
officers and generals or obtain positions in offices at court
or become provincial governors. Al-Muʻtaṣim ensured that
soldiers were supplied with Turkish slaves as wives, so that
the troops increased in number not only through purchases
but through births as well. In Sāmarrā itself the army must
have ultimately comprised about 20,000 men.

The disadvantages of this system, inherent to all praeto-
rian guards, soon became apparent: The first generation of
liberated slaves attained high offices and distinctions and
began acting as kingmakers. They installed and deposed
caliphs at will, even murdering them on occasion. When the
ʻAbbāsid caliphate threatened to sink into anarchy, Caliph
al- Muʻtamid decided to move the court back to Baghdad
in 892.

This new type of military continued to prevail, although
it was never used exclusively. There were always units of
free mercenaries as well from all over the world: Kurds,
Iranian Daylamites from the southern shores of the Caspian
Sea, Berbers or Arab Bedouins as light auxiliary troops.
The Mamluk type of soldier, however, dominated not only

the military, but also the political world – not only in Sā-marrā and Baghdad, but in Syria and Egypt too. Soon the kingmakers became kings themselves. In many countries, including Afghanistan and India, former slaves and their descendants assumed power and founded Mamluk sul-tanates. The most important of these was the Egyptian sul-tanate, which will be discussed below. In Spain and North Africa, the soldier slaves were not of Turkish, but of east-ern European descent and were sweepingly referred to as "Slavs" (*ṣaqāliba*, sing. *ṣaqlabī*). They were brought pri-marily from across the Adriatic Sea.

The emergence of the Mamluks is significant primarily because for centuries they provided the Arab world with military and political elites who were of non-Arab origin and who, even if they adopted the Arabic language, retained an awareness of their foreign traditions. In the last millen-nium up to the present day, it has been more an exception than the rule that reigning houses in the Arab world were of Arab descent.

# The Arab World from 900 to 1500 CE

al-Ḥarīrī, Maqāmāt: *Travelers arriving at a village (VII / 13th century)*

The year 909 CE marks an epochal year in the history of Islam. A caliphate was established in Tunisian Kairouan in that year that for the first time could challenge and rival the 'Abbāsid caliphate in Baghdad on a long-term basis. The Fāṭimid dynasty, which claimed (albeit disputedly) to be direct descendants of Muḥammad's daughter Fāṭima and Caliph 'Alī, was able with the support of the Berbers to assume control of present-day Algeria. In 910, 'Abdallāh al-Mahdī, who had previously campaigned for himself in the underground, appeared openly in the city of Kairouan and assumed the title of caliph. His caliphate (909–934) was the first of an extremely successful dynasty that challenged not only the religious and political claims of the 'Abbāsids in Baghdad to be Muḥammad's heirs; the Fāṭimids' Shi'ite Isma'īlī sect of Islam also offered a religious alternative to the ruling Sunnīs. In 929, the Umayyad emir of Cordoba 'Abd al-Raḥmān III (912–961) also assumed the title of caliph. This meant that three "successors" – two Sunnīs and one Shi'ite – each claimed the exclusive heritage of the Prophet Muḥammad. The disintegration of the caliphate, which had in fact been long in the making, was now officially sealed.

# Iraq

Mesopotamia, the land of the Tigris (*Dijla*) and the Euphrates (*al-Furāt*) rivers, consisted of two different landscapes for Arabs: the actual *al-'Irāq* – the name probably means "low lands" or "flat country" – in the southeast; and *al-Jazīra*, the "island," in the northwest between the middle reaches of the two rivers. The military camps of al-Baṣra and al-Kūfa, which had been established by Arabs, and the caliphate capital of Baghdad were located in Iraq. After the founding of Baghdad, Seleucia-Ctesiphon (*al-Madā'in* or "the cities" in Arabic), the ancient royal city of the Parthians and the Persians, diminished increasingly in significance. Babylon had already disappeared as a city even before the Islamic conquest. The metropolis of the north was Mosul (*al-Mawṣil*) on the Tigris, across from the ancient ruins of Nineveh.

As the seat of the 'Abbāsid caliph, the metropolis of Baghdad long remained the center of the Islamic world. After the turmoil in Sāmarrā and the emergence of the western caliphate, however, the political significance of the caliphs in Baghdad increasingly declined. While the 'Abbāsid caliph in Baghdad continued to rule without interruption until the Mongol invasion in 1258, only isolated representatives of this dynasty actually governed themselves and then only as a kind of Iraqi territorial prince. The Baghdad caliphate was repeatedly subject to the tutelage of military "patrons," who usurped political power and –

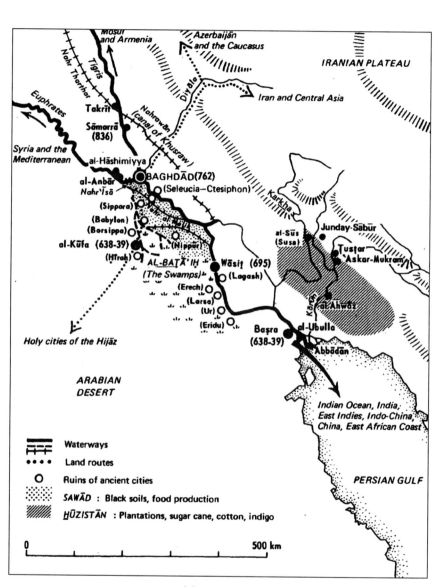

*Mesopotamia*

From *The Golden Age of Islam*

equipped with formal legitimation from the caliphs – exercised the real power for them. The focus of such rule lay primarily in Iran. Iraq was often little more than a western province of Iran.

The first patrons of this kind were the Būyids (932–1055), a widely branched Iranian condottiere family that established a series of dominions (Shiraz, Isfahan, Hamadan, Kerman) in western Iran and also seized power in Baghdad in 934. For 110 years, Būyids administered a protectorate over the caliphates, formally as commanders-in-chief (*amīr al-umarā'*) of the army, but in reality as sovereign rulers. They did not even eschew assuming the ancient Persian title of great king or emperor (*Shāhānshāh*, "king of kings"), which is completely antithetical to Islam. While the caliph had always been a Sunnī, the Būyids were Shi'ites and vigorously promoted members of this faith. A large portion of the Shi'a religious writings arose under their aegis. The burial places of their imams, which had been pilgrimage sites for Shi'ites for centuries, were expanded into magnificent shrines and received elaborate endowments: the grave of 'Alī in al-Najaf near Kūfa; the grave of the third imam (the Prophet's grandson al-Ḥusayn) near Karbalā'; the double grave of the seventh and ninth imams in al-Kāẓimiya in the north of Baghdad as well as the graves of the tenth and eleventh imams in Sāmarrā; and the site at which the twelfth imam is supposed to have disappeared into "occultation" and from which he is expected to return.

The Būyids were overthrown by the Seljuqs, a Turkish dynasty that had forayed into Iran as the leaders of a wandering tribe of Turkish nomads from Central Asia. In 1038, their leader Toghril Beg had himself proclaimed sultan in eastern Iran, transforming the word *sulṭān*, which actually means "ruler," into a title. As the protector of Sunnī Islam, he compelled the Baghdad caliphs to officially recognize him and then appeared in Baghdad in 1055 with his followers to accept this recognition. The capital of the "Great Seljuq" Empire, however, was Isfahan in Iran, while Baghdad was left to the powerless caliphs.

With the Seljuq dynasty, Turks or Turkmen appeared for the first time in the Islamic world not as imported military slaves, but as larger tribal groups. A steady flow of Turkish tribes now moved westward through northern Iran. In 1071, the Turks succeeded where Arabs had continually failed: After defeating the Byzantine Emperor Romanus IV Diogenes at Manzikert (present-day Malazgirt north of Lake Van), the Seljuqs overran what had been Greco-Christian Asia Minor.

Although Baghdad lost its political significance under the Seljuqs, it remained a cultural center with enormous appeal and influence, particularly after the Seljuq vizier Niẓām al-Mulk (1065–1092), an Iranian, established a madrasa, a legal, theological institution of higher education based on Iranian precursors, and appointed the famous Sunnī theologian and mystic al-Ghazālī (1058–1111) as the institution's first professor. A large number of similar institutions quickly arose in Baghdad. The Mustanṣiriyya, founded by Caliph al-Mustanṣir in 1233, is today Baghdad's best-maintained monument from the pre-Mongol era. The work by the Sunnī jurist and preacher al-Khaṭīb al-Baghdādī (1002–1071) offers an excellent example of intellectual life in the caliphate capital during this period. His

*Chronicle of Baghdad* (*Ta'rīkh Baghdād*) – actually a lexicon of scholars – comprises fourteen volumes with entries on no less than 7,831 people active in the intellectual life of the city.

Even after the gradual disintegration of the Seljuq empire, Baghdad remained a strategic object in particular for eastern rulers, even if individual caliphs such as al-Nāṣir (1180–1225) were occasionally able to exercise their own rule on a regionally limited basis. The invasion of the Mongols, however, brought all of this to an end. In 1235, Hulagu Khan, grandson of Genghis Khan and brother of the Mongolian Great Khan Mongke, was ordered to subjugate the caliphate. When Caliph al-Musta'ṣim (1242–1258) refused to comply with official demands to support the Mongols with an army, the Mongols overran Iran from the Oxus (Amu Darya) and attacked Iraq. In January 1258, the Mongols were outside Baghdad. The caliph, his vizier, and the Nestorian Catholicos – Hulagu's mother was Christian – attempted in vain to negotiate. On February 10, the Mongols forced their way into the city and began to burn, murder, and plunder. The caliph and many of his dignitaries and family members were strangled. Thus the caliphate, the succession of the Prophet Muḥammad, came to an end. Although the Catholicos and numerous mosques and madrasas were spared, the city itself did not recover from this blow until the nineteenth century. Iraq was incorporated into the Mongol Empire. Mongol rulers in Iran, the Il-Khan and their successors, quickly converted to Islam, but they resided in Iran and adopted Iranian Islamic culture. In Iraq, they were always regarded as foreign occupiers.

# Syria/Palestine

Arabs commonly treat the territories of present-day Syria, Lebanon, Jordan, Israel, and Palestine as a unity they call *Bilād al-Shām*, the land to the left or land of the north, in contrast to Yemen, the land to the right or to the south. In political terms, however, this territory was divided into small cantons by its mountains and had never formed a unified whole, even under Islam. When regionalized political rule was established in the ninth century, the southern part – Palestine, Transjordan, and southern Syria including Damascus – was tied to the respective emirs ruling in Egypt, whereas northern Syria with its emerging metropolis of Aleppo (*Ḥalab* in Arabic) constituted an emirate onto itself under the dynasties of Bedouin origin, the Ḥamdānids (945–1004) and the Mirdasids (1023–1079). The Islamic emirate of Aleppo usually paid tribute to the Christian Emperor in Byzantium, although sometimes it was ruled as a joint Byzantine-Egyptian condominium, functioning as a buffer state between the Christian and the Islamic worlds. During this era, three Arab Bedouin groups exerted the decisive political pressure on the western horn of the Fertile Crescent. From the Transjordan, the Tayyi pressed across the Jordan River into Palestine in pursuit of grazing land, booty, and the recognition of their Sheiks as provincial governors; in the center, the Kalb pushed the Palmyrenes out of the oasis of Damascus; in the north, the Kilāb moved into Aleppo, which they ultimately also ruled as Mirdasid emirs.

This division of the region appeared to become firmly established when Turkish Seljuqs invaded Asia Minor from Iraq in 1071, expanding their rule into northern Syria, while the south remained under control of the Fāṭimids in Cairo. The first Crusade, however, altered this in a completely unforeseen manner. In June 1098, Crusaders conquered Seljuq Antioch (Antakya). On July 15, 1099, they took Fāṭimid-controlled Jerusalem and engaged in a terrible massacre of the Muslim population. Four western, Roman Catholic states were established: the county of Edessa with its epicenter east of the Euphrates; the Norman Principality of Antioch; the county of Tripoli under the Count of Toulouse at the foot of Mount Lebanon; and the Kingdom of Jerusalem – the most important of the four – with its alternating Lotharingian (later Lorraine) and French ruling houses.

The foreign rule of the "Franks" (*al-ifranj*), which lasted almost a century, met with no unified resistance from the Muslim side. Ibn al-Athīr (1160–1233), a historian from Mosul, complained bitterly about the disunity of the Muslims in his world chronicle *al-Kāmil fī al-ta'rīkh* (The Complete History). However, neither the Fāṭimid caliphs in Egypt nor the caliphs in Baghdad and their Seljuq protectors were in fact capable of preventing the transformation of Palestine, Lebanon, and large parts of Syria into Christian feudal domains.

Resistance was organized only when the emir of Mosul, Zengi (1127–1146), son of a Turkish Mamluk, was able to destroy the first of the four Crusader states by taking Edessa in 1144. His son and successor Nūr al-Dīn ("Light of Religion," 1146–1174) established his residence in Aleppo

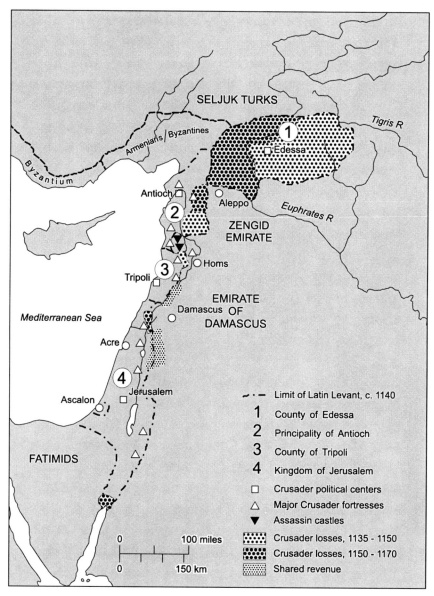

*Crusader alignment, 1130–1170*

From *The Levant*

and successfully continued the war against the Crusaders. In 1154, he was able to occupy Damascus, where a Seljuq emir ruled, without a fight. Then he attempted to bring Egypt under his military control, in rivalry with King Amalric I of Jerusalem. His success marked the end of Crusader rule. Yūsuf ibn Ayyūb, whose epithet was *Ṣalāḥ al-Dīn* ("Righteousness of the Faith," *Saladinus* in Latin), was a Kurdish military leader under Nūr al-Dīn. He assumed power in Cairo in 1171 with the aid of the Syrian army, bringing down the Fāṭimid caliphate. After Nūr ad-Dīn's death in 1174, Saladin, as he was known in the West, proclaimed his independence from Aleppo and began to expand his power from Egypt to Transjordan, Syria, and northern Mesopotamia, and on to Mecca and Medina and Yemen. In a letter to Baghdad, Saladin justified his actions against the Muslim rulers there by pointing to the necessity of uniting Muslims in a just war or *jihād* against the infidels. The caliph provided him with a diploma of investiture for Egypt and Nubia, Arabia, Palestine/Syria, and the entire Maghreb, thereby legitimating Saladin's military conquests. After 1177, the new sultan adopted the title "Restorer of the Empire of the Commander of the Faithful" (that is, of the Baghdad caliph). The three remaining Crusader states were surrounded for the first time by a united Islamic empire, which would soon crush them. On July 4, 1187, Saladin's army defeated the Crusaders led by King Guy de Lusignan at Hattin (*Ḥiṭṭīn*) near the Sea of Galilee. Within a few months, Saladin had conquered almost all of Palestine. Jerusalem capitulated on October 2, 1187. After this, Syria/Palestine was united politically with Egypt.

# Egypt

After the Arab-Islamic conquest in 641–42, Egypt became a province of the caliphate. Its emirs resided in the Arab military camp of al-Fusṭāṭ (or Fusṭāṭ Miṣr) in the south of what later became Cairo. The land was ruled by hereditary dynasties for two brief periods of time. The Turk Aḥmad ibn Ṭūlūn (868–884) from Sāmarrā was the first governor of the Tulunid dynasty, which ruled until 905. The Ibn Tulun mosque, which he erected next to his palace complex, still exists today. The Ikhshīdids ruled Egypt from 935 to 969. Their first governor, Muḥammad al-Ikhshīd, had also been a Turkish general.

However, Egypt did not become the center of a truly independent empire until 969, when after a series of failed harvests, epidemics, and other catastrophes the notables of al-Fusṭāṭ decided to transfer rule to the Shiʻite Fāṭimid caliph of North Africa, the fourth Fāṭimid ruler al-Muʻizz (955–975), who sent an army of Berbers and "Slavs" led by the freedman Jawhar. The army marched into Egypt in 969 and immediately began building a new capital city north of al-Fusṭāṭ, which the caliph entered from Tunisia in June 973. The new palace city was named "The Victorious of Muʻizz" (*al-Qāhira al-Muʻizziyya*). Under the rule of the Egyptian Fāṭimids (969–1171), Cairo (*Qāhira*), with its new Friday mosque the Al-Azhar (The Brilliant), became one of the largest metropolises of the Arab world, soon to rival Baghdad in size and importance. The fall of the

'Abbāsid caliphs in Baghdad remained the declared goal of
the Shi'ite counter-caliphs in Cairo. Egypt's Muslim population – which was still a minority in comparison to Coptic
Christians – remained Sunnī even under the Shi'ite dynasty.

Control over the holy sites of Mecca and Medina, with
the attendant responsibility for protecting the annual pilgrimage (*hajj*), fell to the Egyptian Fāṭimids almost automatically. In contrast, they were forced to fight a hard battle for control of Palestine/Syria and even then were able to
assert control only temporarily, particularly in Aleppo.
Thanks to a rebellious Turkish general, Friday prayers for
the caliph in Cairo were held in Baghdad for an entire year,
1059, before the Seljuqs were able to re-occupy the city.
The Shi'ites were never able to restore this kind of unity to
the caliphate. In the west, Cairo ruled at least nominally
over what is today Libya and Tunisia and large parts of
Algeria (where the Zīrid Berbers ruled the Maghreb for

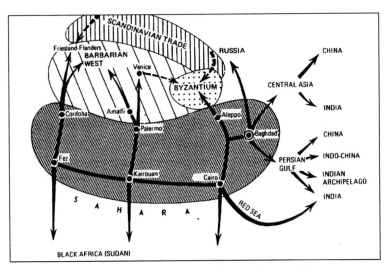

*Trading connections of the Muslim world*

From *The Golden Age of Islam*

Cairo as a kind of viceroy), as well as over Sicily, whose emirs regularly had themselves reaffirmed in Cairo. Due to its control of the Red Sea and Yemen, Egypt became the hub of world trade at the time between the Indian Ocean and the Mediterranean. Immense wealth flowed into the country from this, as well as from surplus agricultural production, high-quality textiles, and the export of alum, a mineral in great demand, also in Europe, for tanning leather and which was mined as a state monopoly. Under the Fāṭimids, Italian maritime trading cities became active in the Levant – first Amalfi and Pisa, and later Venice and Genoa. This trade reached its apex during the Crusades.

The loss of the Maghreb in 1044 when the Zīrids established their independence did not weigh all too heavily against these Fāṭimid successes. The dynasty, however, did experience a serious internal crisis during the era of the Crusades. It lost not only its Syrian-Palestinian provinces, but was also occupied a number of times by armies of the King of Jerusalem, becoming a protectorate of the Crusaders. However, the fall of the Fāṭimids and Saladin's reestablishment of Sunnī orthodoxy in 1171, along with his subsequent unification of Cairo, Damascus, and Aleppo proved to be prerequisites for a resumed, even greater expansion of Egyptian power.

Saladin's victory over the Crusaders at Hattin in 1187 brought almost all of Palestine, including Jerusalem and the Syrian coast, under Muslim control again. The Franks led by King Richard the Lionheart of England and King Philip II (Philip Augustus) of France did retake Acre in 1191, and Emperor Friedrich II was even able to negotiate a restitution of Jerusalem from the Egyptian Sultan in 1229 without

a struggle, so that only the Temple Mount with the Dome of
the Rock and the al-Aqṣā Mosque remained in the hands of
the Muslims. This intermezzo, however, lasted only until
1240.

The Saladin dynasty, the Ayyūbids (named after Saladin's father, Ayyūb = Job), was a dynastic ruling alliance.
All the princes of the original Kurdish family were given
provinces and ruled in continually changing constellations
from Yemen to northern Mesopotamia. Cairo and Damascus remained the centers of Ayyūbid rule.

Sultan al-Ṣāliḥ Ayyūb (1240–1249), a great nephew of
Saladin, reinforced the Mamluk troops in Cairo through
extensive purchases of Turkish war slaves, establishing the
Baḥrī (River) Regiment, which was named after their bar-
racks on Roda Island in the Nile. This elite troop took advantage of French King Louis IX's crusade against Cairo
in 1249 to remove the Ayyūbid dynasty. One of the Mamluk
officers, the Turk Aybak, proclaimed himself Sultan and
established Mamluk rule over Egypt, Palestine/Syria, and
the holy shrines, which lasted until 1517. The Turkish
Mamluks enjoyed several spectacular successes, which
legitimated their usurped rule and bolstered their reputation
as champions of Sunnī Islam. On September 3, 1260, at the
"Spring of Goliath" ('Ain Jālūt) near Nazareth, they defeated the Mongols, whose vanguard had already pushed
through up to Gaza. In 1261, the important Mamluk Sultan
Baybars (1260–1277) named an 'Abbāsid prince, who had
fled from the Mongols, "caliph" in Cairo. However, like his
successors prior to 1517, this caliph had no real power and
had only to "install" the respective Mamluk sultan. Baybars, who sought to complete Saladin's work, was also able

to conquer the castles of the Ismāʿīlī assassin sects along the Syrian border between the Crusaders and the Muslims. In almost annual campaigns, the already diminished territory of the Crusaders was continually reduced further. Baybars re-conquered Caesarea, Ashkelon, Jaffa, Haifa, and Antioch. Under Sultan Qalāwūn, the city of Tripoli in Lebanon fell in 1289. In May 1291, his son al-Ashraf Khalīl was able to take Acre, the final base of the Crusaders on the Levant coast.

The rule of the Mamluks in Cairo (1250–1571) was one of the most remarkable and successful examples of state building in the Arab world. The Malmuk military aristocracy was, as Jerusalem historian David Ayalon writes, a "one-generation aristocracy": Only Mamluks brought in from outside – initially of Turkish and beginning in the fourteenth century of Circassian descent – could ascend the military hierarchy and ultimately become sultan. Their children were forced, in principle, to take up civil professions. Many of them became scholars, who produced the abundant religious and secular literature we have about the Mamluk era. Despite the non-Arab origins of this elite, Egypt remained an Arab country, and it was almost certainly during the Mamluk period that Muslims for the first time constituted a majority of the population. This era still today has an influence on the city of Cairo. While work on the citadel began under Saladin, the majority of the mosques, madrasas, and mausoleums in the city can be traced back to endowments by Mamluk sultans and officers. Even after the Ottomans conquered Egypt, the Mamluk military aristocracy continued to lead the country.

# The Maghreb and al-Andalus

No independent state developed in premodern times in what is today Libya. The two urbanized regions there in antiquity – the five cities of the Greek Pentapolis with its main city of Cyrene (Cyrenaica) and the three cities of the Roman Tripolis, Oea, Sabratha, and Leptis Magna – were separated by a great distance. While the former was administered primarily by Egypt under the name of al-Barqa, the latter lay within Kairouan's sphere of influence.

Under Arab rule, the former Roman provinces of Africa and Numidia were combined to form the region of Ifrīqiya, which encompassed not only Tripoli and present-day Tunisia but all of northeastern Algeria as well, including Constantine, Bône, and Bougie. The Arab city of al-Qayrawān (Kairouan), originally a fortified military camp, replaced the abandoned city of Carthage as the urban focus of the region, becoming a significant center for religion and the arts and sciences. Under the Aghlabid dynasty (800–909), which was nominally subject to Baghdad, Kairouan acquired a metropolitan character. The mosque of Emir Ziyādat Allāh I (817–838), which was completed in 836 and still exists today, became a model of architecture and architectural decoration for the entire region. The palaces and parks in Raqqāda (six miles south of Kairouan) have been uncovered by contemporary archeologists in extensive excavations.

The Aghlabids were driven out of Algeria by a Berber army in 909. A year later, the Fāṭimid 'Abdallāh al-Mahdī proclaimed himself caliph in Kairouan. This Ismā'īlī-Shi'ite dynasty brought the Maghreb ("the West" in Arabic) into open conflict with the Sunnī caliphate of the 'Abbāsids in Baghdad. A new palace city, al-Mahdiyya, was built on the coast of a rocky peninsula, and another palace, al-Man-ṣūriyya (directly south of Kairouan), was erected later. After the peaceful assumption of power in Egypt in 969, the fourth Fāṭimid caliph al-Mu'izz settled in the newly found-ed city of Cairo in 973, leaving the Maghreb to his viceroy, the Zīrid Berber prince from Algeria, who moved into the abandoned Fāṭimid palaces.

When the Zīrids renounced their allegiance to Cairo in 1044 and returned to Sunnī Islam, recognizing the distant Baghdad caliph, it triggered an emigration westward by Arabic Bedouin tribes between 1050 and 1052 (see page 63), marking the beginning of the Arabization of southern Tunisia and the central Algerian steppe.

In Arabic, Morocco is called *al-Maghrib al-Aqṣā*, "the farthest west." Six successive Muslim dynasties have ruled Morocco up to the present. These dynasties have consis-tently drawn their power from indigenous Berber tribes, even if they themselves have for the most part been Arabs from the Middle East and Asia Minor. The model for this form of rule, which is typical for Morocco, was established by a political refugee, Idrīs, who was a direct descendant of Muḥammad's grandson al-Ḥasan. Idrīs established his rule around the old Roman city of Volubilis in 789, supported by the Awrāba, a Berber tribe. Idrīs's mausoleum in nearby Moulay Idriss remains a kind of national shrine for Moroc-

cans even today. His son Idrīs II (793–828) expanded the
city of Fez (*Fās*), which had been founded by his father,
into a metropolitan center of Arab rule (see page 45). The
Kairouan (al-Qarawiyyīn) Mosque in Fez became the country's religious and intellectual center.

Following the fragmentation of Idrīsid rule into a dozen
local entities, the Tunisian Fāṭimids and the respective
rulers in al-Andalus battled over control of Morocco. The
country was then unified by Ibn Yāsīn, a pious man who
had founded a monastery-like Islamic fortress or ribāṭ in
southern Morocco. Warriors of the Sanhāja, a Berber people from the western Sahara whose men wore blue veils,
gathered around Ibn Yāsīn and formed the militia of the
"Ribat people" (*murābiṭūn*, in the Spanish derivative
*Almorávides*), which was quickly able to conquer all of
Morocco and the coast up into the area around Algiers. In
1062, their secular prince Yūsuf ibn Tāshfīn (1061–1106)
founded Marrakech (Marrākush, in Spanish *Marruecos*,
from which the current name Morocco is derived) as his
capital, which, in contrast to Arab-influenced Fez, was a
city of Berber-African character.

Yūsuf ibn Tāshfīn crossed the Strait of Gibraltar with an
Almoravid army in 1086 to intervene in al-Andalus. The
caliphate of Cordoba had ceased to exist in 1031, and the
Islamic sphere of power there had splintered into more than
a dozen regional "party kingdoms" (in Arabic, *mulūk al-
ṭawā'if*; in Spanish, *Reyes de Taifas*) in Malaga and Sevilla,
Cordoba, Valencia, Toledo, and Zaragoza, and others. This
period of numerous small courts was very rich in cultural
terms. Poetry, science, and the arts blossomed. The al-
Ja'fariyya Palace (in Spanish, *Aljafería*) near Zaragoza tes-

tifies even today to the magnificence of the *ṭā'ifa* princes. They were unable, however, to resist to the rising Christian *Reconquista*. The intervention of the Almoravids unified the dwindled al-Andalus once more under the Berber dynasty of Morocco. The advance of King Alfonso VI from León and Castile in 1085, however, led to the definitive loss of Toledo.

The Almoravids were strict Sunnīs. The reform movement of Ibn Tūmart (Berber for Ibn 'Umar), the Berber holy man from the High Atlas, opposed the Almoravids' dogmatic and legally ossified understanding of Islam and probably their customs as well, which were unfamiliar to Arabs, such as men rather than women wearing veils. Ibn Tūmart was able to win over the Masmūda farmers from the high mountains, who called themselves "The Monotheists" (*al-muwaḥḥidūn*; in the Spanish derivative *Almohades*), and came down from the High Atlas to topple Almoravid rule. When Ibn Tūmart – who was revered as the Mahdī ("The Rightly Guided One") sent from God – died in 1130, one of his students, 'Abd al-Mu'min (1130–1163), assumed leadership of the religious movement (regarded as heterodox by Sunnīs) and called himself caliph, successor, to the Mahdī Ibn Tūmart. This was the first time a non-Arab ruler assumed this sacred title, which until this time had been reserved for members of the Quraysh tribe from Mecca. After 1145, the Almohads subjugated all of al-Andalus that remained Muslim and defeated King Alfonso VIII of Castile at Alarcos (west of today's Cuidad Real) on July 18, 1196. It was the last important Muslim military victory against the Christian Spaniards. The entire Maghreb up to Tunis and Tripoli also came under Almohad rule; in particular the Bedouin Hilāl tribe was subject to this centralized rule.

The Almohad court was influenced by the culture of Cordoba. Especially the architecture of the epoch testifies to the predominant influence that the so-called "Moorish" art of Andalusia had on Morocco and Algeria. The great mosques of the Almohads, the Mosque of Tinmal in memory of Mahdī Ibn Tūmart in the High Atlas (1153), the Great Mosque of Tlemcen in Algeria (1136), the Kutubiyya (Booksellers') Mosque in Marrakech (around 1150–1196), the enormous mosque of Rabat including its unfinished minaret, the Ḥassān Tower (around 1190), the Great Mosque of Sevilla with its minaret, which today serves as a bell tower for the cathedral (1195; in Spanish, *la Giralda*, "the weathervane"), and the Torre de Oro (Tower of Gold) (1220) on the Guadalquivir River in Sevilla were all products of the Almohad epoch.

The court of the second Almohad caliph Abū Yaʿqūb Yūsuf (1163–1184) became a center of scholarship and literature. He sponsored the astronomer, physician, and writer Ibn Ṭufayl (ca. 1100–1185) from Cadix, whose *Ḥayy ibn Yaqẓān* (Alive, Son of Awake) was the most important philosophical romance of Arabic literature: the story of a young man who grows up alone on a deserted island and who must develop his insights and capacities solely through his own intellect and reason. Translated into Hebrew as well as Latin (under the author's name Abubacer), the novel continued to be influential into the modern era in Europe. Ibn Ṭufayl drew young intellectuals from al-Andalus into his circle, including the jurist and Aristotelian philosopher Ibn Rushd (Averroës), who was born in Cordoba in 1126 and became a protégé of Caliph Abū Yaʿqūb Yūsuf. Ibn Rushd served the Caliph as a judge in Sevilla, Cordoba, and Marrakech (1183), where he then succeeded Ibn Ṭufayl as court physician. Under Caliph Abū Yūsuf Yaʿqūb (1184–1199), Ibn Rushd fell out of favor in 1195, and all of his philosophical writings were burned. However, after being banished for a brief period of time, he was rehabilitated and allowed to return to Marrakech, where he died in 1198. Ibn al-ʿArabī (1165–1240), the most important Arab mystic, also struggled with the intolerance of Almohad religious scholars. Born in Murcia, Ibn al-ʿArabī left the Almohad Empire in 1204, finding refuge in Damascus after an extended journey.

The Almohads abandoned their heterodox religious doctrine voluntarily. In 1230, Caliph Idrīs al-Maʾmūn personally renounced the Almohad doctrine on the pulpit (minbar) of Marrakech cursed the Mahdī Ibn Tūmart, and proclaimed the return to Sunnī Islam. Even before the Almohads were defeated at Las Navas de Tolosa by a coalition of Christian kings from northern Spain, their decline was imminent. The cities of southern Spain now fell to the Christians in rapid succession, including Cordoba in 1236 and Sevilla in 1248.

Up to the end of the fifteenth century, three Muslim states determined the fate of the Maghreb and Andalusia. From Tunis, the dynasty of the Ḥafṣids – founded by the Almohad governor Abū Ḥafṣ, a student of the Mahdī Ibn Tūmart – ruled all of Ifrīqiya, that is, Tunis and eastern Algeria, between 1228 and 1574. The Banū Merīn (Merinids), a nomadic Zenāta Berber clan, came to power in Morocco and western Algeria. In 1216, they advanced from the

Sahara to Morocco, occupying Marrakech in 1269. Like their predecessors, Merinid rulers were the heirs of Moorish culture and the art of Andalusia. They also adopted the eastern institution of the madrasa, the legal, theological institution of higher education. The magnificence of Moorish architectural decoration, which had arisen in Cordoba, reappeared in the madrasas of the Merinid in Fez, Marrakech, and Meknes. The Merinids, however, no longer intervened in al-Andalus. Only the Nasrid dynasty in Granada (1230–1492), which attempted to maneuver between Moroccan rulers and Christian powers, remained Islamic. In 1492, the palace of the Nasrids, the Alhambra (*al-Ḥamrā* = "the Red"), fell into the hands of the "Catholic Kings" Isabella of Castile and Ferdinand V of Aragon. It is not wholly fortuitous that the fall of Granada was contemporaneous with Columbus's mission and the discovery of the new world and thus with one of the dates marking the dawn of the modern era.

The historian Ibn Khaldūn (1332–1406) developed a theory about the rise and fall of Muslim empires based on the vicissitudes of Moroccan-Andalusian dynasties. Ibn Khaldūn was the scion of an old Arab family, which was originally from Ḥaḍramawt but had already settled in Sevilla in the eighth century, and later in Ceuta and Tunis, where Ibn Khaldūn was then born. The scholar led a checkered life, traveling to numerous minor courts in North Africa and then to Granada, before he ended up in Cairo, where he served in a number of positions as a judge, although he was also jailed repeatedly during this time. He began his historical work on the Berbers with an extensive "prolegomena" (*Muqaddima*) investigating the laws of historical events.

According to the work, clan solidarity (*'aṣabiyya*) of tribal associations makes up the powerful driving force for the development and expansion of political power, and the inevitable weakening of such solidarity in urban settings ultimately leads to dynastic decline. Ibn Khaldūn is often considered the "first sociologist," and in fact his highly original work, which comprises three volumes in modern book form, is unparalleled in medieval literature.

# The Arab World from 1500 to 1800 CE

*Waterwheels at Hamah, Syria*

From Charles Issawi, *The Middle East Economy: Decline and Recovery*
(Princeton: Markus Wiener, 1995)

There is a widespread perception that in the early modern era and even in the late Middle Ages the Arab world – and the Islamic world as a whole – experienced a developmental rupture that is best described by terms such as "stagnation" or "decline." Muslims, according to this argument, failed to undergo particular developments that were fundamental for the history of Europe – the Reformation, the French Revolution, and the industrial revolution – and for this reason have remained "backward." This failure supposedly left Muslims both defenseless against European colonial intervention and unprepared for modernity (to which they are said to react with uncertainty and violence even today). A variety of different factors are mentioned as possible or ostensible causes for this "decline and stagnation," including the ossification of religious doctrines in Sunnī Islam during the late Middle Ages, the European discovery of the Americas and of sea routes to India with the accompanying shift in the world trade routes, and the lack of communal self-administration and self-reliance in Middle Eastern cities.

In a series of recent studies, historians have demonstrated that at least the thesis of general economic decline needs to be modified. In the sixteenth century, the Ottoman Empire possessed an expanding and tautly organized central state, which had abolished numerous borders and thus established an economic region and trade routes that it was quite capable of securing. Coffee trade across the Red Sea, which resulted in an economic boom especially for Egypt, compensated for the shift of the spice trade to routes around the Cape of Good Hope, which were controlled by Europeans. Silk production in the Levant also remained competitive for quite some time.

Nevertheless, it is indisputable that the age of discovery ushered in an epoch of unparalleled European global dominance. Almost the entire Islamic world gradually came under the political, military, or economic control of European nations. This fate, however, was not limited to the Islamic world. It also occurred in the Indian subcontinent, Southeast and East Asia, as well as in North and South America. It is therefore hardly possible to hold Islam responsible for this development. What instead requires explanation is the precise, unprecedented dynamic that allowed Europeans to subjugate the rest of the world. There is as yet no convincing and generally accepted account of this.

The Crusades can be regarded as a prelude to this development. They represent the first attempt by western Europe to resolve internal demographic, social, and economic problems through measures taken beyond its own borders. It is certainly no coincidence that ascendant trade municipalities such as Pisa, Venice, and Genoa, with their dynamic bourgeois merchant elite, were both the driving force and the benefactors of the "armed pilgrimages" to the Holy Land. The age of discovery also marked the beginning of the expansion of European interventions in North Africa and Asia. The Portuguese occupied Ceuta as early as 1415 and Tangiers in 1471. After taking Granada in 1492, Spain also sought to control the North African coast across the Strait of Gibraltar. However, the aspiring Ottoman Empire proved to be a worthy opponent for the Spanish monarchy.

# The Fertile Crescent under Ottoman Rule

By the beginning of the fourteenth century, the small Turkish principality of the Ottoman (*'Uthmān*) clan in northwestern Asia Minor had rapidly developed into an important territorial state. In 1357, the Ottomans were able to establish a foothold on the Balkan Peninsula, crowning their conquests with the capture of Byzantine Constantinople in 1453. While all of this took place outside of the Arab world, Arabs were directly confronted with the new empire in the early sixteenth century. Sultan Selim I brought down the Mamluk dynasty in Syria and Egypt. After the victory over the Mamluks at Marj Dābiq north of Aleppo in August 1516, the sultan occupied all of Syria and Palestine and then, in 1517, Egypt too. The Sharif of Mecca immediately sent him the key to the Ka'ba.

Under Selim's successor Suleyman I (the "Magnificent") (1520–1566), Iraq was also incorporated into the Ottoman Empire. In 1534–35, Azerbaijan with its capital city of Tabriz and northern Iraq with Baghdad were occupied, and in 1546, the south with Basra as well. In 1552, the Ottoman army expanded into the eastern coast of Arabia, where the province of (Sanjak) al-Ḥasā (around Hofūf) was established. The Ottomans were able to assert their maritime predominance through two naval bases, one in Basra on the Persian Gulf and the other in Suez (*Suways*) on the Red Sea. Ottoman Turkish rule over the Arab countries of

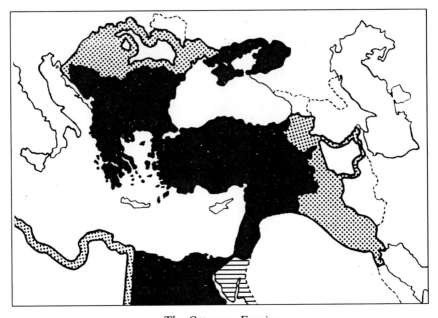

*The Ottomon Empire*

From *The Middle East Economy: Decline and Recovery*

the Fertile Crescent continued for the next four centuries until the empire finally collapsed during the First World War.

Turkish rule certainly had some positives aspects. The urban economy prospered, particularly in the trade center Aleppo. Damascus and above all Baghdad flourished again, after having endured numerous campaigns from Iran following the Mongol invasion. Centralized power in Istanbul, which remained unbroken in the sixteenth century, was maintained through strong governors (pashas), tax collectors, judges, and foreign garrison troops recruited in part from the Balkans. The unified legal system, codified under Sultan Sūleyman – whom the Turks called the "Legislator"

(*Qānūnī*) – and a tightly organized and highly efficient cadastral registration and tax assessment system were introduced everywhere. At the beginning of the seventeenth century, however, the reins began to loosen. The united elite, which as merchants and landowners had traditionally dominated economic and religious-intellectual life, began to (successfully) demand participation in political life. In Iraq, the governor Hasan Pasha (1704–1723) established his own de facto independence through his private army of Georgian and Circassian Mamluks, bequeathing his power to his son Ahmad Pasha (1723–1747). After this, outright Mamluk rule in Baghdad and Basra was established, which was tolerated and recognized by Istanbul and would continue until 1831. A similar situation developed in Mosul. In Syria, the local al-'Aẓm family played a comparable role from 1725 to 1807 as local governors recognized by the central government. Their palace in Damascus still testifies today to their wealth and magnificence. The pasha of Sidon, Ahmad al-Jazzār (1775–1804), whose fortress in Acre even Napoleon Bonaparte was unable to capture, ruled in a similarly independent manner.

The loosening of central power in the Ottoman Empire in favor of local and regional princes, however, did not automatically signify economic decline. While the empire itself was thrown into a serious crisis, the semi-autonomous provinces of the Arab world were able to thrive economically. As always, the Bedouins remained a disruptive factor, pushing repeatedly into settled territories in Syria/Transjordan as well as in western Iraq.

# The Arabian Peninsula

In 1516-17, the Turkish Ottomans conquered Syria, Palestine, and Egypt, which meant that the Ḥijāz along with the cities of Mecca and Medina were also subject to the Sultan of Constantinople. In 1517, the Sharif of Mecca sent the key to the Kaʿba to Sultan Selim I and in return was confirmed in his office. From this point on, the Ottoman Sultan bore the title "The Custodian of the Two Holy Shrines" (*khādim al-ḥaramayn*), a title given to Egyptian Mamluk sultans prior to this (and used today by the king of Saudi Arabia). The sultan was now responsible for the support and care of the holy sites of Islam as well as for the organization and protection of the annual pilgrimage, the hajj, with pilgrim caravans from Damascus and Cairo.

Given its variety of starkly differing geographies, Yemen was not exactly predestined for political unity. Separate minor dynasties had been established in ʿAden, on the plains of Tihāma at the Red Sea, and in the metropolis of the highlands Ṣanʿāʾ. The most permanent force in Yemen was the Zaydī-Shiʿite imamate of northern Yemen with its center in Ṣaʿda, which had been established in the ninth century and remained intact until 1962 – the longest-standing dynasty of the Islamic world. Its territory, however, did change over time. The Zaydīs repeatedly occupied Ṣanʿāʾ, only to lose it and then reoccupy it again. In 1538, the Ottomans began to subjugate Yemen as well. They occupied Ṣanʿāʾ in 1546, compelling the imam to recognize the suzerainty of the sultan in 1552. Over time, however, the Ottomans were unable to sustain their rule, especially after European colonial powers appeared in the Indian Ocean and in the Red Sea – at first the Portuguese, then the Dutch and English. The Turks withdrew from Yemen in 1635.

Oman (*'Umān*) is separated from the rest of the Arabian Peninsula by deserts that long ensured its isolation. Since time immemorial, its coastal residents have been seafarers, who used the monsoons to reach the coasts of East Africa and India, making their living from maritime trade. In the sixteenth century, the Portuguese took control of the ports of Qalhāt and Masqaṭ (Muscat) in Oman as well as port of Hormuz (1514) on the Iranian side of the gulf. Oman remained part of the Portuguese colonial empire for a century and a half. In 1650, local Ya'rubīs were able to retake Masqaṭ. The succeeding Āl Bū Sa'īd dynasty (beginning in 1741) was able to expand its power to the island of Zanzibar off the African coast, giving rise to a remarkable double empire across the Indian Ocean.

In the eighteenth century, a form of political rule was established in the interior of the Arabian Peninsula that has continued, albeit with interruptions, to today: Wahhābism, the religious revival movement that led to the establishment of the Āl Sa'ūd monarchy (in Arabic, *Āl* = family; not to be confused with the article *al-*). The wandering preacher Muḥammad ibn 'Abd al-Wahhāb (1703–1792) sought to reestablish a pure and strict Islam true to its original form by opposing blasphemous "innovations" such as saint veneration, the worship of graves, and the mysticism of the dervish orders. Only the Quran and sayings of the Prophet were supposed to guide Muslims. Support from the tribal leader Muḥammad ibn Saʿūd (died in 1765) ensured the dissemination of Ibn ʿAbd al-Wahhāb's teachings in the oases and among the tribes of central Arabia. As a result, Ibn Saʿūd's son ʿAbd al-ʿAzīz (1765–1803) was able to establish a powerful desert empire. The religious furor of the Wahhābīs was directed against the Sunnīs in Mecca and Medina, as well as against the Shiʿites in Iraqi Najaf and Karbalāʾ. The imam shrines of the Shʿites were destroyed in 1802 by Wahhābīs armies, who also took Medina in 1804 and destroyed the al-Baqīʿ cemetery, where numerous companions of the Prophet and several Shiʿite imams had been buried. However, they did not dare to touch the Prophet Muḥammad's grave, although they did close it off to visitors. The Ottomans were unable to take direct action against these desert warriors. In a series of campaigns from 1811 to 1818, their Egyptian viceroy Muḥammad ʿAlī destroyed this first Saudi kingdom, and in 1815, Ottoman rule over the holy shrines was restored.

# Egypt

The Ottomans conquered Egypt in 1517, transforming it into a province of the Turkish empire. New foreign elites appeared in Cairo, headed by the Turkish governor (*wālī*) who had the rank of a pasha and was accompanied by an army made up of the many nationalities within the Ottoman Empire. Especially the infantry of the Janissary corps (in Turkish, *Yeni Ḵeri*, "new troops") – comprised of Christian children from the Balkans forced into military service – were an increasingly important power factor. Egyptian Mamluks, however, were also employed in a new regiment.

The ties between the Egyptian province and central government in Constantinople were initially very close. However, the reins loosened over the course of time, as was also the case in Syria and Iraq. Access to power opened up again for local elites, as the foreign army was gradually "Egyptianized." In the seventeenth century, a Mamluk faction, the Faqāriyya, was able to rule Egypt for thirty years, limiting the power of the wali. In 1660, a rival faction, the Qāsimiyya, ousted the Faqāriyya. Something approaching a civil war ensued, in which the two sides crippled and almost annihilated each other, opening the way again for foreign intervention. The Janissary corps regiment was now able to control the country for an extended period of time and to defy the governor until the eighteenth century, when rivalry between Mamluk factions arose again. After 1760, Malmluk beys ruled the country, ultimately in a kind of

duumvirate between rivals Ibrāhīm Bey and Murād Bey
(whom Napoleon Bonaparte encountered upon landing in
Alexandria in 1789).

A number of factors (such as the aforementioned coffee
trade) testify to Egypt's prosperity during the time: Cairo's
population doubled (from approximately 150,000 inhabitants in 1500 to about 300,000 in 1700); the city limits were
extended; and a great variety of monumental buildings
were erected during this era – mosques, schools, baths, car-
avanserais (*khān*), and mausoleums. Of the many educational institutions in Egypt, the Al-Azhar Mosque in Cairo
became the most distinguished in the late seventeenth century. Its elected leader, the *Shaykh al-Azhar*, came to be recognized as the foremost legal and religious authority, not
only in Egypt, but throughout the Sunnī world.

# The Maghreb

During the early modern era, the western Mediterranean served as the stage for antagonisms between the Christian maritime powers of Spain and Portugal on the one hand and the Ottoman Empire on the other. Through the use of its fleet, the Ottoman Empire attempted to gain control of the lands at the eastern and western ends of the Mediterranean by assuming the role of the protector of Muslims on the Iberian Peninsula (albeit without success) and in North Africa.

After taking Ceuta in 1415, the Portuguese continued their maritime expansion along the Atlantic coastline, occupying a series of bases on the Moroccan coast after 1458. The Spanish emerged as a naval power in the Mediterranean. The port cities of the North African coast became centers for a privateer war – understood as a *jihād* – against the Christian countries north of the Mediterranean. Booty and ransom were the economic motivations for these "Barbary pirates" of the Maghreb as well as for their Christian counterparts. After a raid by Moroccan corsairs on the Spanish cities of Alicante, Elche, and Malaga in 1505, the Spanish occupied all of the important ports of the Maghreb coast from 1505 to 1511: Marsā l-kabīr (Mers-el-Kēbir), Oran, Mostagānem, Tenes, Cherchell, an island off the coast of Algiers, Bougie, and Tripoli. In response, the Ottoman sultans encouraged and supported the corsairs by sending ships. Four brothers from the island of Lesbos (including the legendary Khayr al-Dīn, also known as Barbarossa) emerged as the leaders of this maritime enterprise against the Christians from 1504 to 1510. After 1516, Algiers (in Arabic, al-Jazā'ir, "the Islands") developed into a virtual corsair state under Khayr al-Dīn, tolerated by the Hafsid sultans of Tunis and supported by the Ottomans. Sultan Selim promoted the corsair to *beylerbey* (Turkish "bey of beys" for the Arabic *amīr al-umarā'*, "leader of leaders") with the rank of a pasha and provided him with troops and artillery. In 1534, he was able to occupy Tunis in the name of the Ottoman sultan. This success led to the intervention of Christian powers – Charles V sent his fleet to Algiers and Tunis in 1535 and Mahdia (al-Mahdiyya) was occupied from 1550 to 1554. In 1571, a Christian coalition of the Holy Roman Empire, the Papacy, and the Republic of Venice defeated the Ottoman fleet by Lepanto (Nafpaktos) near the entrance to the Gulf of Corinth, and in 1573, Don Juan de Austria took Tunis. Both were bitter setbacks for the sultan, but the Spanish were still unable to assume permanent control of the North African coast. In 1574, Sinan Pasha occupied Tunis from Tripoli. Spain decided to abandon the fight. In 1581, King Philip II agreed to an armistice with the Sublime Porte, ending the century-long power struggle and ceding North Africa to the Muslims.

The indirect Ottoman rule established in Tunis and Algiers led to curious polities. The Turkish army and fleet jointly ruled these two "regencies": Officers and captains sat together in the ruling councils (dīwān). In Tunis in 1591, a revolt of forty local officers with the Turkish title of *dey* ("uncle") removed the weak pasha from office. The deys placed one of their own in command, who then appointed the commander of the fleet (*qabtān* = "captain") and the bey, that is, the military officer responsible for collecting taxes from the local tribes of the interior. Throughout the entire seventeenth century, Tunisia was governed by deys, although the actual power gradually shifted to beys, who commanded their own troops. In 1705, there was a putsch by the agha (commander) of the *sipāhī*, the elite mounted force within the Ottoman cavalry divisions: Ḥusayn ibn ʿAlī appointed himself bey and did away with the office of the dey. After 1710, the Husseinite dynasty ruled in Tunis as beys and struggled to transform the former corsair enclave into a modern state.

In Tripoli as well, local militia officers removed the pasha from power in 1603. A similar development also occurred in Algiers: Janissary officers (aghas), who dominated the divan, initially governed alongside the weak pasha. In 1659, the pasha's prerogatives were reduced to a merely honorary title with the Janissary officers rotating in a two-month cycle. After a military revolt in 1671, the deys elected by the militia headed the provincial government, which the Porte recognized as a sovereign state in 1711.

Morocco was the only country of the Maghreb that was able to avoid both Spanish and Ottoman rule, thanks to an Arab family from the south, from Sūs in the backcountry of Agadir. The Banū Saʿd were descendants of the Maʿqil Bedouins, who had immigrated to the Maghreb in the eleventh century. They formed an alliance with a marabout, a local spiritual leader, and in 1511 began to engage in a jihād against the Portuguese (who had occupied Agadir in 1505), subsequently expanding their power to the North over the High Atlas. In 1524, they captured Marrakech,

where Saʿdi graves in the magnificent mausoleum still testify to their power. They were able to take Agadir from the
Portuguese in 1541, occupy Fez in 1549, and conquer cor-
sair-ruled Tlemcen (*Tilimsān*) in western Algeria in 1550.
An invasion by the Portuguese was thwarted in the Battle of
the Three Kings in 1578, which took place at al-Qasr al-
Kabīr (*Alcazarquivir* in Spanish). King Sebastian was defeated and killed in the fighting, as were the Moroccan pre-
tender al-Mutawakkil and the Saʿdi sultan ʿAbd al-Malik.

The Saʿdi dynasty disintegrated after attempting a massive expansion into the Niger region. The Alawites, the
dynasty that continues to rule Morocco today, was able to
achieve the renewed unification of the country. As their
name implies, they are descendents of ʿAlī and Fāṭima, the
daughter of the Prophet Muḥammad, and thus Sharifs (the
Arabic plural is *shurafāʾ*; in French, *chorfa*). Their progenitor was a descendant of the Prophet from the al-Ḥasan line
who had immigrated to the Maghreb from Yanbuʿ on the
Red Sea and settled in Rissani (Risānī) in the Tafilalt oasis
at the eastern foot of the High Atlas in the early thirteenth
century. The Alawite Sharifs ruled the Tafilalt oasis beginning in 1636, and proceeded to conquer the rest of the country from there. After taking Fez in 1666, Moulay (Mūlāy)
al-Rashīd assumed the title of sultan. His brother Moulay
(Mūlāy) Ismāʿīl (1672–1727) succeeded him to the throne
at age twenty-six and was the most significant ruler of the
dynasty. He built Meknes (Miknās) into the new capital city
and into a garrison for his powerful army, which consisted
in part of sub-Saharan Africans, freed slaves, and Christian
renegades. Moulay Ismāʿīl drove first the Spanish out of
al-Maʿmūra and al-ʿArāʾish (Larache) and, after a five-year

siege, the English out of Tangiers, which they had taken from the Spanish in 1622. The sultan was in fact able to subjugate almost all of Morocco, namely, that part of the country required to pay taxes to the central government (the "government lands," *bilād al-makhzan*), including the tribes on the High Atlas and the edge of the desert. In addition, the sultan was able to modernize the army and, like contemporary European countries, sought to institute a kind of mercantile economic policy that would stimulate and direct trade and the economy through directives from above. In doing this, his most important partners were the French King Louis XIV and his minister Jean Baptiste Colbert. The fact that after Moulay Ismāʿīl's death his powerful state was again subject to riots and revolts demonstrates the actual lack of inner cohesion in the largely rural country, which was splintered into Berber and Arab tribal territories.

The "Moriscos," who had been driven out of Spain, contributed significantly to the economic prosperity of the Maghreb in the seventeenth century. In 1563, King Philipp II issued a ban prohibiting Moriscos (who had been forced to convert to Christianity but were in large part still secretly faithful to Islam) from possessing weapons without special authorization; and in 1566 he issued an edict banning Arab clothing and the veil as well as religious ablutions, ordering the surrender of all Arabic books and the exclusive use of the Castilian language within three years. Rioting ensued, particularly in Andalusia, between 1568 and 1571, which was quashed by force. Although many Muslims hoped the Ottoman fleet would intervene, it did not. Between 1609 and 1614, edicts were issued under Philipp III, authorizing the dispossession and expulsion of the

Moriscos. While approximately 25,000 former Muslims remained in the country as Catholics, about 275,000 people
left the Iberian Peninsula, seeking refuge in the various
cities of the Maghreb. This influx brought life to North
African cities, not only economically but also culturally.
The Moriscos' contributions to art, architecture, and folklore are still recognizable in North Africa today.

# The Nineteenth Century

*The opening of the Suez Canal with Empress Eugénie of France,*
*wife of Napoleon III*

From *The Middle East Economy: Decline and Recovery*

# The Mashriq

During the nineteenth century almost the entire eastern (*al-Mashriq*) part of the Arab world – the Fertile Crescent, Egypt, and segments of the Arabian Peninsula – remained part of the Ottoman Empire, even though various autonomous regions sporadically appeared. The Arab countries were therefore subject to decisions made in Constantinople and increasingly to those in other European metropolises as well. They were greatly affected by the crises of the Ottoman Empire, which had to accept significant territorial losses in the Balkans and north of the Black Sea. Just as consequential were the sultans' reform efforts starting in 1792 and the growing political, military, and economic influence of the major European powers.

A summary of all the developments of the Ottoman Empire would exceed the scope of this book; only the milestones of its development can be mentioned here: army reform based on the European model by Selim III (1789–1807) and the violent eradication of the Janissary corps (1826); Gūlhane's reform edict of 1839, the *Hatt-i Sherīf* ("noble edict"), declared in response to pressure from Europe, which for the first time made Muslims and non-Muslims equal before the law; the "reorganization" (*tanẓīmāt*) of the legal and educational systems based on a new reform edict, the *Hatt-i Humayun* ("imperial edict") of 1856; the creation of a civil code, the *Mejelle* ("code," 1870–1876), which applied to the entire Ottoman Empire and continued to be effective after the collapse of the em-

121

pire; and the introduction of a constitution in 1876 and the convening of the first Ottoman parliament in 1877, which, however, was suspended after only two short sessions in 1878 by the autocratic sultan 'Abdul Ḥamīd II (1876–1909).

Prior to the First World War, a consensus existed among the major powers of England, France, Austria, and Prussia/ Germany not to contest the territories of the Ottoman Empire, which in particular was intended to prevent Russia from gaining control of Constantinople and the Balkans. Greek independence in 1829 was the only exception. The European powers even helped the Ottoman government, the Sublime Porte (*Bāb-i ālī*), in securing its rule over the Arab countries, preventing in particular the emergence of a major Egyptian kingdom. In return the Ottomans opened their empire to the trade interests of the major powers, which led the Porte to become increasingly dependent on the Europeans. This development culminated in the Anglo-Ottoman trade agreement of 1838, the empire's bankruptcy in 1875, and the establishment of an international debt administration (*Administration de la dette publique ottomane*) in Constantinople in 1881.

**Iraq.** Mesopotamia, which was largely rural, remained to a great extent a domain of Arab nomads, the Bedouins, into the nineteenth century. In the few urban centers, local dynasties were established, which were then tolerated by the Porte: in the north the Jalālī emirs in Mosul; in the south the Mamluks of Georgian descent in Baghdad, who also controlled the port city of Basra. Nevertheless, the Porte removed the local rulers in 1831 through a military intervention and reinstated the direct administration of Iraq. One of the most significant governors and modernizers was Midhat Pasha (1869–1872), Grand Vizier (1872), and Minister of Justice, and the father of the constitution of 1876, who later became governor of Damascus (1878–1880).

The cities along the Euphrates, al-Najaf and Kerbelā (Karbala), had special status. The two holy Shi'ite shrines, the tombs of 'Alī and his son al-Ḥusayn, had attracted numerous Shi'ite clerics and scholars from Iran in the eighteenth century and developed into centers of Shi'ite jurisprudence and theology. Because the Shi'ites in the two cities remained largely to themselves, the Sunnī Ottomans didn't intervene, but when the Ottoman administration started forcing the nomadic Bedouins of southern Iraq to settle, the Shi'ite clerics found fertile missionizing ground among the tribes that had been only superficially Islamized. Within only a few decades, all of southern Iraq became Shi'ite, and the shrines found a loyal and generous clientele among the tribal sheikhs cum landed gentry. A tight symbiosis, often reinforced through marriage, developed between the clergy of the two shrines and the rural population of southern Iraq, which has continued to today.

**Syria.** The history of Greater Syria (*bilād al-Shām*) started in the nineteenth century with Napoleon's failed advance from Egypt, which was stopped by Ahmad Pasha al-Jazzār's defense of Acre. The Porte maintained its Syrian provinces and was even able to push back the local forces to the benefit of the central government. In Damascus the supremacy of the al-'Azm family ended in 1808. Although Greater Syria came under the control of the Egyptian pasha Muḥammad 'Alī (see page 126) in 1831, he was forced to abandon his conquests in 1840 due to pressure from England and Austria, which had come to the aid of the Ottoman Empire.

Lebanon assumed an exceptional position, having been a refuge for religious minorities since time immemorial. The Maronites controlled the north of the mountainous region; this Christian community was a Uniate church and had maintained close ties to western Christianity and France since the Crusades. Under their emir Bashīr II al-Shihābī (1788–1840), the Maronites established the foundations for their centuries-long dominance in the mountains of Lebanon, especially at the expense of the Druze settling in the southern parts of the mountains, a splinter group that had broken off from the Shiʿite Ismaʿīlīs. Maronite attempts to expand to the south had already resulted in heavy fighting between the two Arab groups several times in the nineteenth century (1841–45, 1860). In response to pressure from France, an autonomous province of Mount Lebanon was established in 1861, albeit without the port cities. With France's protection it continued to exist until the end of the Ottoman Empire. The Arab Christian population (Maronites, Greek-Catholic or Uniate, and Greek-Orthodox) outnumbered the Muslim minorities (Druzes, Sunnīs, and Shiʿites). After the First World War, Mount Lebanon became the nucleus of the Republic of Lebanon, which the Allies wanted to maintain as a Christian state and a European sphere of influence.

**Arabia.** The invasion of Iraqi Kerbelā in 1802 by the Wahhābīs under the leadership of the Saʿūd family, as well as the conquests of Medina in 1804 and Mecca in 1806 (see page 109-110) directly affected the interests of the Ottoman Empire and led the sultan to take the title of "Custodian of the Two Holy Shrines." Egypt's pasha, Muḥammad ʿAlī, was ordered to challenge the Wahhābīs. After expanding his army he was able to retake Mecca and Medina in 1811–13, and in 1818 he even succeeded in capturing and leveling Dirʿiyya in central Arabia, the stronghold of the Wahhābīs and the Saʿūd family. Emir ʿAbdallāh ibn Saʿūd was deported to Constantinople and executed there. Egyptian-Ottoman control of central Arabia, however, could not be maintained in the long term and the Saʿūd family was able to reestablish its control only a few years later, albeit on a local scale. The Ottomans used this opportunity once again to consolidate their rule in the Ḥijāz and along the coast of Red Sea. In 1872, Yemen too was returned to Ottoman control.

The Ottomans were forced to accept the fact that the British had established themselves throughout the Arabian Peninsula. In 1839 the East India Company took control of Aden, an important station along the route to India and a base at the entrance to the Red Sea, although its ultimate significance only became evident after the Suez Canal was built. The tribes of the hinterlands became tied to Britain through treaties. A similar development took place on the Arabian gulf coast starting in the 1820s. The conclusion of a permanent truce in 1853 transformed the "Pirate Coast" into the Trucial States, a British protectorate (since 1971, the United Arab Emirates). Of particular significance was the 1899 Anglo-Kuwaiti agreement between Britain and Sheikh Mubarak. The Porte considered Kuwait the end station of a Baghdad railway that had been in planning since

1888, which was to connect the capital, Constantinople, with the Persian Gulf. Because the railroad was being built by an Ottoman-German consortium, the British feared the German Empire could use this to gain influence at the gulf, so it strengthened its ties with the sheikh family of Āl Sabāh in 1899 through a treaty of protection that de facto released the city-state from the Ottoman Empire. This step would have repercussions in 1990–91 in the Kuwait conflict.

**Egypt.** During the first half of the nineteenth century, Egypt was certainly the most important Arab country. Although the significance of the landing of Napoleon's army in 1798 was greatly exaggerated with respect to the Islamic world in general, for Egypt itself it represented a major turning point. The French army, which was modern as in terms of both structure and weaponry, defeated the Mamluks at the pyramids. For the first time, the Egyptians were confronted with an efficient administration, modern jurisprudence, and modern scientific methods and instruments. Shock and admiration of this innovation are reflected in the diary and chronicle of the Cairo intellectual and scholar, al-Jabartī (1753–1825).

After the British and the Ottomans had forced the French to retreat in 1802, the Porte again appointed pashas as governors in Cairo. A violent coup in 1805 installed Muḥammad ʿAlī, an Arnaut (Albanian) from Macedonia, as pasha. His reign (1805–1848) is considered one of the most notable epochs in Egyptian history. After he had three hundred Mamluks massacred in the citadel of Cairo in 1811, he began building up a modern army and initiated a series of reforms that transformed Egypt for a time into a major power of the eastern Mediterranean and the Red Sea. He brought European technicians, consultants, and instructors to the country, especially from France, and sent students to Paris. Most importantly, Muḥammad 'Alī revolutionized Egypt's agriculture. Cultivation methods were improved, irrigation was expanded, and cultivable land was increased. Production focusing on exports (wheat, rice, sugar cane) was promoted and, finally, starting in 1821 a cotton mono- culture was created, which for a short time brought in rich yields, but also made the economy prone to crises. The state also tried to achieve a monopoly, not only in the area of agriculture, but also in manufacturing and the beginnings of industrial production and in trade.

Through this centrally planned and forcibly imposed economic policy, Muḥammad 'Alī created the basis for a huge army, which grew to over 150,000 soldiers and served as a means of imperial expansion aimed at obtaining raw materials. After defeating the Wahhābīs in Arabia, the Egyptians conquered Sudan in 1820–23, which remained aligned with Egypt until the end of the century. From 1822 to 1827 the Egyptian fleet and army, in agreement with the Porte, intervened in the Greek war of independence. The pasha's goal was to control Cyprus, Crete, and the Pelo- ponnese (Morea), but his fleet was annihilated in 1827 in the Bay of Navarino by the allied fleets of the British, French, and Russians. By invading Syria and Asia Minor in 1831 he started pursuing his own power politics at the expense of the Ottoman Empire. The Egyptians were able to take Greater Syria and Cilicia (with Adana and Tarsus) in 1831–1840. England and Austria, acting in their own self- interest, came to the assistance of the Porte, forcing the

Egyptians to abandon their conquests (except for Sudan). England wanted to prevent the emergence of a major Arabic power that might obstruct its trade interests and could threaten its ties to India.

Muḥammad ʿAlī's Egypt is often compared with Japan during the era of Emperor Meiji (1868–1912), who attempted a similar experiment in forceful modernization and emancipation from European influence, and succeeded. Egypt under Muḥammad ʿAlī was indeed the leading Arab country economically, technologically, and militarily. The fact that it failed here was certainly primarily due to European – especially British – intervention, although the structural weaknesses of the country, which were covered over by the forcibly imposed economic prosperity, certainly also played a significant role.

To some extent as compensation for the shattering of his plans to become a great power, Muḥammad ʿAlī was assured the succession of his sons and grandsons, who were confirmed as pashas by the Porte. His son Saʿīd ruled from 1854 to 1863, followed by his grandson Ismāʿīl, who reigned from 1863 to 1879 and received the title of khedive (Persian *chadīv* = viceroy) from the sultan in 1867. The Suez Canal was planned during the reign of Saʿīd and built from 1859 to 1869. It was a project that led within two decades to the ruin of the Egyptian state finances and the country's loss of independence. In contrast to Muḥammad ʿAlī, who had prevented any and all foreign intervention, his successors opened Egypt up to all European influences and especially to European capital, since they hoped Egypt would thus catch up with the major European powers and allowed to enter their ranks, as reformers of the Ottoman

Empire in Constantinople also hoped at the time. In fact, however, Egypt fell prey to foreign trade and money interests. An international pack of financiers, investors, and speculators exploited the opening of the country and sought their profits in a new El Dorado of the Middle East. Sa'īd Pasha's most egregious error was to let himself be talked into acquiring forty-four percent of the Suez Canal stocks, which threw him deeply into debt. In order to cover his short-term financial obligations he had to take out a long-term government bond on a London bank, for which he mortgaged the tax revenue of the provinces of the Nile delta. Because the debts could not be paid off, they accumulated astronomically under his successor Ismā'īl. On top of that came Ismā'īl's ambitious plans to modernize the country and his attempts to create an Egyptian imperium on the upper Nile and in equatorial Africa, in Eritrea and Abyssinia. More and more long-term government bonds had to be purchased, with growing concessions. The revenue earned by the recently built Egyptian railroad was mortgaged, as was the income of the private domains of the khedives. The astronomical level of the national debt ultimately led to the country's financial ruin in 1876 and the forced appointment of French and English financial controllers (dual control), who were responsible for monitoring all of Egypt's financial affairs. In 1876, the state debt administration came under foreign control with the establishment of the *Caisse de la dette publique*. The same thing happened five years later in Constantinople. A new, so-called "European" government was formed in Egypt in 1878, as an Englishman ran the financial department and a Frenchman became Minister for Public Works.

Now the resistance of the khedives and local officers
and notables was aroused, but the European powers forced
the Ottoman sultan to depose Ismāʿīl and to name his son
Tawfīq (1879–92) as his successor. In early 1882 the opposition, led by Aḥmad ʿUrābī and supported by Egypt's large
landowners and businesspeople, succeeded in taking power
for a short time in Cairo and temporarily forcing out the foreign Mamluk, Turco-Circassian elite. However, as early as
September of that year British troops occupied the country.

# The Maghreb

The fates of the three North African regencies that formally belonged to the Ottoman Empire (Tripoli, Tunis, and Algiers) took a similar course, though with considerable chronological delays. In the phase of dīwān rule, the council (*dīwān*) of officers of the Ottoman fleet and army governed the port city and its environs. This period was followed in all three by the establishment of a dynasty that developed from the dīwān and which over the course of the nineteenth century came under economic and military pressure from Europe and were ultimately forced to give way to direct colonial rule.

This development was first concluded in Algiers. There, the French took advantage of an incident to intervene in 1827. The dey of Algiers is reputed to have hit the French consul with a flyswatter. After a lengthy blockade of the port, French troops occupied Algiers in June-July 1830 and forced the dey, Husayn, to step down. The Bourbon king Charles X was still reigning when the coup occurred, but even the constitutional monarchy of Louis Philippe, the "Citizen King," and, after 1871, the Third Republic continued to control the country under pressure from the military. In the face of vehement resistance, Constantine was taken in 1837, but the Tuat oases in the southwestern corner could not be occupied until 1900.

The dynasty of the beys in Tunis solidified its rule by abolishing the Janissary corps at the beginning of the century, similar to Muḥammad ʿAlī in Egypt. The Mamluk officers of Circassian descent continued to comprise the military and political elite. Tax reform and even the brief experiment with a constitution (*dustūr*) and a parliament (1861–64) – albeit a powerless one – were supposed to modernize the country and relieve the pressure from Europe. But like the situation in Egypt, the policy of purchasing government bonds in Europe led to a growing national debt starting in 1863, and in 1869 a financial commission was appointed to look after the interests of the European creditor nations of France, Italy, and Britain, thereby undermining the state authority. The era of Khayr al-Dīn Pasha (1869–1879), an Abkhas from the Caucasus who sought to modernize the country in the style of the Ottoman tanẓīmāt reforms, instead led to an even greater influx of foreign capital into the country. The situation rapidly worsened and, ultimately, the French occupied Tunisia in 1881 in order to forestall the colonial ambitions of a recently united Italy. Under their protectorate – the bey remained in office – the country now opened to European settlers, especially the French, but also Italians, who immediately started acquiring estates and engaging in agriculture and viticulture in grand style.

In Tripoli the dynasty of the Qaramanli pashas (starting in 1720) had already been eliminated by the Ottomans in 1825, who turned the semiautonomous regency back into a directly administered province. This move was an attempt to counter Egypt's independence efforts under Muḥammad ʿAlī and the French conquest of Algeria. As a result, European influence remained very weak in Tripoli. Not until the Italian conquest of Libya in 1911–12 did it become part of North Africa's colonial framework.

In Morocco, too, direct colonial rule was not established until the early twentieth century. The sultans of the 'Alawid dynasty in fact had control only over the Atlantic coastal plain with the four royal cities of Fez, Meknes, Rabat, and Marrakech, and over a territory that often fluctuated in size and in which the central government was able to levy taxes with the help of loyal tribes. This area was called the *makhzan* (literally "warehouse, magazine") and its size varied according to the momentary political constellation. Powerful regional princes (*qā'id*, "leader") and monastery-like centers (*zāwiya*, "corner, hermitage") run by religious orders (*ṭarīqa*, plural *ṭuruq*) exercised power in certain regions that proved difficult if not impossible for a centralized authority to control. France and Spain agreed in 1904 to divide up the country into spheres of interest. The German Empire had similar ambitions, but these were quashed at the Algeciras Conference in 1906. When in March 1912 the French set up their protectorate covering most of the country, Morocco was divided. The north became a Spanish protectorate and the port city of Tangier obtained international status.

# Strategies against European Intervention: Europeanization, Islamic Renewal, Nationalism

Local elites in the Middle East and North Africa clearly recognized the pressures exerted by the European powers starting in the nineteenth century and correctly assessed the ensuing dangers. There was no scarcity of attempts to resist the growing foreign control. Reforms in the Ottoman Empire, in the largely autonomous Egypt, and in Tunisia sought to institute a forced modernization, or even Europeanization. They hoped in this way to catch up to Europe, which was becoming increasingly powerful – economically, politically, and militarily – and to be accepted into the community of nations as equal partners. This failed to occur due to the Europeans' own interests, which put greater value on opening markets for their own industries than on allowing potential competition to emerge.

The policies pursued by both the Ottoman and the Egyptian governments to open up to Europe nevertheless had positive effects as well. In the Fertile Crescent and in Egypt, the amount of productive agricultural land increased considerably; in Iraq, the increase was even tenfold, as a result of settling the Bedouins. The construction of the first Aswān High Dam on the Nile in 1902 made agriculture independent of the fluctuating peaks in the annual flooding of the Nile. Telegraph networks and railroad lines made vast areas accessible – just a few examples should suffice here: the Baghdad railroad line (1888–1940) and the Ḥijāz line (1900–1908), which connected Damascus and Medina and was intended to continue on to Yemen via Mecca. Steamship navigation connected waterways, which was particularly significant on the Tigris and the Euphrates; the construction of the Suez Canal eliminated the need for maritime trade routes around the Cape of Good Hope. Turkish and Arabic print media emerged. The flip side was that opening up to foreign capital, which largely financed these improvements in infrastructure, came at the expense of local trade, crafts, and agriculture.

European investors and entrepreneurs were not the only beneficiaries of the increased agricultural land area and intensified cultivation; local elites profited as well. A new class of local wealthy bourgeoisie and large landowners developed in the nineteenth century in the agrarian countries of the Middle East. Prior to the upheavals in the 1950s the notables came from these social classes and held political sway. In addition to these groups, who remained attached to the cultural and religious customs of their native roots, an elite developed in all of these countries which was oriented toward Europe and distanced themselves rigorously from the popular masses and their traditional ways of life, especially in the rural areas. This division of society, which of course also includes intermediate stages, has remained characteristic of Middle Eastern societies to today.

Europeanization was opposed especially by those segments of the population that viewed themselves as victims of the process, including the urban middle classes, the farmers, and the Bedouins. Countering the powerful foreign influences with something of their own meant returning to established traditions, especially Islam. Since the foreigners were perceived primarily as Christians, their own self-definition as Muslims was an obvious connecting link. In numerous places, charismatic religious leaders organized resistance, which was open to everyone who saw their status threatened by the rapid social changes.

Armed resistance first formed in places where the colonial power was immediately evident in the form of military troops. Thus the French in western Algeria encountered the resistance from the irregular militias around 'Abd al-Qādir, son of a sheikh of the mystical Qādiriyya order, who in 1832 called himself the "Sultan of the Arabs." The French had recognized him in a number of agreements and treaties as the leader of a partly independent west Algerian state, but when he started to constantly expand his sphere of power and declared *jihād* against all non-believers, the French opposed him with military strength from 1840 to 1847, ultimately forcing his surrender. He spent the rest of his life writing mystical works in exile in Damascus (1883).

The revolt of the Mahdī in Sudan was similarly rooted in the traditions of the mystical orders (*ṭuruq*). The forty-year-old sheikh Muḥammad Aḥmad claimed in 1881 to be "The Rightly Guided One" (*al-mahdī*), the savior and redeemer of Islam sent by God and anticipated by all Muslims. He vowed to expel the non-believers, referring to the British, whose General Charles Gordon had led a merciless regiment from the Sudanese capital of Kharṭūm (Khartoum), expanding Egypt's sphere of power – in reality Britain's – as far as equatorial Africa from 1874 to 1879 in the name of the khedive. The Anglo-Egyptian Convention of 1877 played a significant role in the rise of the Mahdī. The convention abolished slavery in Sudan, which was a powerful blow to the slave traders and holders there. Corresponding to his title, the Mahdī appeared as the renewer of Islam. His supporters called themselves *anṣār*, or helpers, based on the model of the Prophet Muḥammad's supporters in Medina. In the province of Kordofan, an Islamic state headed by the Mahdī emerged. Gordon, who in 1884 was redispatched by London, was killed in January 1885 when the Mahdī's soldiers stormed Khartūm. But the Mahdī also died the same year. The regime of his successor (*khalīfa*) was weakened by famine and internal strife, which allowed the British to regain control of Sudan in 1898. The family of the Mahdī continues to be involved in Sudanese politics even today.

In Libya, it was the Sanūsiyya (Sanusi) Order that took up the struggle against the Italian invaders in 1911. Founded in 1843 by the mystical sheikh Muḥammad al-Sanūsī (1787–1859), the strictly puritanical order, which – similar to the Arab Wahhābīs – recognized only the Qur'ān and the Sunna as foundations of Islam and frowned upon music and dance, established a number of religious centers (*zāwiya*) and was thus able to expand his influence and economic power from the Sirte and Cyrenaica (East Libya) all the way to central Africa, up to Lake Chad and the Wadai mountains. From its center in the Kufra oases (as of 1895), the order controlled the tribes and peasant inhabitants of a vast area. The Sanusi order tenaciously resisted the French in the Sahara and, starting in 1911, the Italians in Libya. Their resistance remained unbroken into the First World War and the Italians were forced to recognize their state.

Libya's royal house developed after the Second World War from the dynasty of the order sheikhs.

Such religiously inspired resistance movements remained limited to certain regions and, with the exception of the Sanusis and the Arab Wahhābīs, were suppressed by the colonial powers' superior military strength. Towards the end of the nineteenth century, however, pan-Islamic ideas also emerged. Their most important advocate was the enigmatic agitator Jamāl al-Dīn al-Afghānī (ca. 1839–1897). He tried to hide his Iranian, Shi'ite family background behind supposedly Afghani – that is, Sunnī – origins. At the court of the king of Afghanistan, in Cairo and then Istanbul and then back to Cairo (1871–1879), in India, London, and Paris, in Russia, Iraq, and Iran, and finally back to Istanbul, he tirelessly spoke out as a teacher, author, and journalist for a strong, modern Islam that would unite the Muslim peoples in their struggle against the Europeans. He shied away neither from conspiring against Muslim monarchs who were submissive toward Europeans, nor from harshly criticizing the backwardness of the traditional Islamic scholars, the *'ulamā'*. Afghānī inspired an entire generation of Islamic modernists around the turn of the century. His most notable student was the Egyptian Muḥammad 'Abduh (1849–1905). The Islamic legal scholar, who was also a journalist, succeeded in winning the support of the khedive 'Abbās II in 1892 to reform the revered Azhar University, which then introduced modern subjects. In 1899 he became Grand Mufti (chief religious jurist) of Egypt. His Islamic modernism is open to various interpretations. It is invoked today by liberal as well as by Islamist ideologues. *Al-Nahḍa*, the "rebirth" or "renaissance," is the collective term

for the movements of the late nineteenth century that proclaimed the revival of an Arabic and an Islamic identity.

Discussion on the future role of Islam in Middle
Eastern society also raised the question of the function of
the caliphate. The Turkish sultans only began using the title
of successor (*khalīfa*) to the Prophet Muḥammad in the
eighteenth century. They adopted the title so they could
appear before the Russian czar as the patron of his Muslim
subjects, since the czar claimed the role of protecting the
orthodox Christians in the Balkans. Although the Ottomans
were neither members of the Quraysh tribe nor even Arabs
at all, they were recognized in Arab countries as the legitimate leaders of the Sunnī *umma*. As the only Muslim state
that was still halfway intact, the Ottoman Empire was the
obvious political frame of reference for the Sunnī Muslims.
At most a kind of Turco-Arabic dual monarchy was considered as a possibility, similar to the Austro-Hungarian
Empire – an idea advocated by the secret society of the
*Qahṭāniyya* (named after the legendary progenitor of the
Arabs, see page 25), founded in 1909 by Syrian officers in
Constantinople.

The mood began to change after a coup brought the
Young Turks to power in Constantinople in 1908. Their
regime pursued a course of forced Turkization of the
empire. The Turkish language was to take precedence in the
army, administration, judiciary, and school instruction; and
Arabic was to be repressed. Even the sanctified Arabic call
to prayer was to be replaced by a Turkish formula. This
Turkish nationalism provoked an Arab nationalism. The
idea of the Arab countries' seceding from the Ottoman Empire was raised and the establishment of an Arab caliphate

was discussed as well. In 1901 the Syrian 'Abd ar-Rahmān al-Kawākibī (1849–1903) published a book in Cairo entitled *Umm al-qurā* (The Mother of All Cities) – referring to Mecca – in which he called for the reestablishment of an Arab caliphate. When in 1924 the Turkish national assembly in Ankara declared the caliphate of the Ottoman sultan abolished, scholar and journalist Muhammad Rashīd Ridā of Syria (1865–1935) called for the reestablishment of the office of the caliph in his treatise *al-Khilāfa aw al-imāma al-'uzma* (The Caliphate or the Great Imamate). As a follower of Muhammad 'Abduh he had immigrated in 1897 to Egypt, where he founded the influential monthly *al-Manār* (The Lighthouse, 1899–1940). Rashīd Ridā proposed that the holders of the office should be determined by the leading scholars of the entire Islamic world: the scholars of the Azhar in Cairo, the Fatih and Süleymaniye mosques in Istanbul, the Zaytūna Mosque in Tunis, and the religious academy in Deoband, in northern India. One of the most promising candidates for the office was the Sharif of Mecca, al-Husayn ibn 'Alī (ca. 1853–1931), who had been appointed in 1909 by the Young Turks as "Custodian of the Two Holy Shrines." As a descendant of al-Hasan, grandson of the Prophet, he was a member of the Quraysh tribe and the Hāshim clan (see page 29) and therefore also legitimated through religious tradition.

Aside from such pan-Islamic ideas that were rooted in al-Afghānī's agitation, a secular Arab nationalism also became apparent. The question of the existence of an "Arab nation" was posed for the first time in the early twentieth century. In 1869 the Ottoman tanzīmāt reformers proclaimed an "Ottoman" nationality, which included all the countless nationalities of the empire, but the artificial construction was disavowed after 1908 as a result of the Young Turks' crass policies of Turkification and disappeared with the collapse of the empire. Arab nationalisms – at first in plural form – broke new ground. Patriotic clubs and secret societies emerged in major cities such as Damascus and Constantinople, where the future shape of an Arab state was discussed. The framework of considerations remained at first limited to Greater Syria and Mesopotamia as the nucleus and the Arabian peninsula – entirely or in part – as an accessory. Egypt, under British control, remained out of reach. There the notion of an "Egyptian nation" had grown in the nineteenth century; with the territorial isolation of the Nile valley and its five-thousand-year history – first brought into public consciousness by Napoleon's expedition – this was certainly not lacking in historical roots. The Maghreb, however, did not even enter the field of vision at first. There was not yet any talk of a pan-Arab nationalism. A secular Arab nationalism, based on the Arabic language and Arab history and culture, without emphasis on the Muslim religion, appeared attractive especially for the Christian minorities. It is striking that numerous representatives of Arab-nationalist ideologies were Christians.

# State Building and Independence in the Twentieth Century

*Gamal Abdel-Nasser*

# The First World War and the Mandatory Period

The decision of the Young Turk regime to enter the First World War on the side of the Central Powers sealed the fate of the Ottoman Empire. In response, the Allies abandoned the policy of supporting the "sick man of Europe" and began planning the partition of the empire. In their correspondence from July 1915 to March 1916, the British High Commissioner in Egypt Sir Henry McMahon promised the Sharif of Mecca Ḥusayn ibn 'Alī the crown of an Arabian kingdom in return for fighting against the Turks. From the outset, however, there were disagreements about the borders of this kingdom. According to the Arab position, the northern border was to run about thirty to forty miles north of the current Syrian-Turkish border and include Cilicia with Adana, Tarsus, and the port of Alexandretta (Iskenderun). The British, however, were adamant that predominantly non-Muslim areas such as Mount Lebanon should not be part of the future Arab kingdom. This was to apply for Palestine as well, where, as British Foreign Secretary Arthur Balfour declared on November 2, 1917, "a national home for the Jewish people" was to be established. However, on May 16, 1916, British diplomat Sir Mark Sykes and French Consul General in Beirut François Georges-Picot had already secretly determined their countries' future spheres of influence in the Fertile Crescent.

In the meantime, Sharif Ḥusayn ibn 'Alī and his sons

Fayṣal and ʿAbdallāh had taken up arms against the Turks in the summer of 1916. On October 29, Husayn ibn ʿAlī assumed the title "King of the Arabs." The British and the French, however, only wanted to recognize him as "King of the Ḥijāz." British Colonel T. E. Lawrence ("Lawrence of Arabia") coordinated attacks on the most important Turkish supply line, the Ḥijāz Railway, and on the Turkish stronghold of al-ʿAqaba, which ended with Husayn triumphantly entering Damascus on October 1, 1918.

The end of the First World War and the Paris peace negotiations raised Arab elites' hopes for imminent independence, in particular since U.S. President Woodrow Wilson had tied the United States' entry into the war with the establishment of the "right to self-determination." As a result, British and French plans to partition the territory could not take place openly. The newly founded League of Nations legitimated their intervention only in the form of preliminary "mandates," which were in fact supposed to prepare those countries for independence.

The Syrian National Congress convened in June 1919 and proclaimed the country's independence on March 7, 1920. The French, however, were not prepared to concede this without a fight. In July 1920, the French defeated the troops of the Sharif's son Fayṣal and in September secured statehood for Lebanon, that is, the Christian—Maronite-dominated Mount Lebanon, which was expanded to encompass coastal cities, including Beirut, thereby cementing the partition of Lebanon and Syria.

In 1920, Shiʿite clerics in Iraq called for a revolt against the British, who had taken power in the country three years earlier. The uprising was quashed in 1921. The British installed Faisal – son of the "King of the Ḥijāz" – as king,

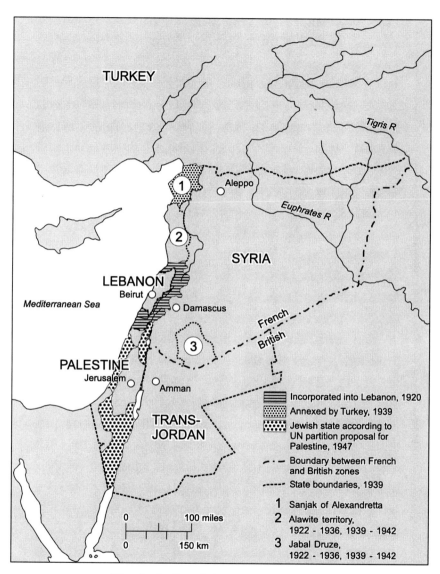

*The Anglo-French Levant, 1920–1947*

From *The Levant*

while Fayṣal's brother 'Abdallāh had to content himself
with the title "Emir of Transjordan." Jordan became formally independent in 1923, but remained under British
mandate. Instead of the hoped-for "Kingdom of the Arabs,"
the Hashemites were given only three limited territories,
two of which remained under British influence. Despite its
formal independence, Iraq in particular remained closely
tied to British interests through the Anglo-Iraqi treaty of
October 1922. The British also retained direct control of
Palestine, where the Balfour Declaration – to create a
"home for the Jewish people" – was supposed to be implemented. As indicated in a statement by Colonial Minister
Winston Churchill, the British were apparently considering
a binational state dominated by non-Muslims similar to
Maronite-Druze Lebanon. Jewish immigration to Palestine
meanwhile continued. In July 1922, the mandate of the
League of Nations came into force.

The Hashemites were also the losers on the Arabian
Peninsula against the Saudis (*Āl Saʿūd*) of Najd. In 1902,
the young 'Abd al-'Azīz "Ibn Saʿūd" recaptured Riyadh,
thereby initiating the gradual reestablishment of a Saudi-
Wahhābī kingdom. He occupied al-Ḥasā, the eastern province of the Ottoman Empire on the Persian Gulf, in 1912,
and conquered 'Asīr, the mountainous landscape south of
Mecca, in 1920. Although al-'Azīz was initially forced to
recognize Ottoman suzerainty and content himself with the
title of provincial governor in 1914, the titles he assumed
illustrate his inexorable rise. In 1915 he declared himself
"Emir of Najd," and in 1921, "Sultan of Najd and Its
Dependencies." His political power was based on the military settlements he had established in 1913, which were

comprised of Bedouin tribes he had settled and won over to Wahhabism and that formed a secret religious fraternal organization known as *al-Ikhwān* or "the Brotherhood," which he used in battle whenever necessary. After the Turkish National Assembly in Ankara declared the caliphate of the Ottoman sultan abolished in March 1924, a conflict emerged with the Sharif of Mecca Ḥusayn ibn ʿAlī. The Sharif assumed the title of caliph, in response to which Ibn Saʿūd sent his Ikhwān to Mecca, which he entered in December 1924. On January 8, 1926, Ibn Saʿūd had himself declared "King of the Ḥijāz and Sultan of Najd." The British recognized Ibn Saʿūd's independence in 1927, and his state was officially named "The Kingdom of Saudi Arabia" in 1932.

Zaghlūl Pasha (Saʿd Zaghlūl), a graduate of Azhar University and a lawyer by profession, led the struggle for independence in Egypt. He was the leader of a delegation (*wafd*) to London that sought unsuccessfully to negotiate the abrogation of protectorate status. The delegation also traveled to the Paris Peace Conference but there as well efforts remained fruitless. Zaghlūl's arrest and exile triggered rioting in Egypt that ultimately led the British to end the protectorate status, which was officially abolished in 1922. Egypt became a constitutional monarchy in 1923. Khedive Ismāʿīl's son was crowned King Fuʾād I, but the British retained military control over the country. Until his death in 1927, Saʿd Zaghlūl, head of the Wafd party and briefly Prime Minister, sought to limit the king's autocracy. In 1936, an Anglo-Egyptian treaty regulated the rights of the former protectorate power and continued to allow British troops to be stationed at the Suez Canal.

# The Salafiyya and the
# Muslim Brotherhood

Like its rival the *Wafd* party, the Muslim Brotherhood
(*al-Ikhwān al-muslimūn*) in Egypt opposed the royal court
and its politics. The brotherhood was founded in 1928 by
Ḥasan al-Bannā (1906–1949), a primary school teacher
who had belonged to various religious associations before
establishing the brotherhood. With Bannā as "Supreme
Guide" (*al-murshid al-'āmm*), the Muslim Brotherhood
was organized according to a strict discipline. Modeled on
mystic Sufi orders of the past, it developed into a modern
mass movement with about half a million members in
Egypt after the Second World War and numerous offshoots
in the mandate territories. The goal of the organization was
a total "Islamic order" (*al-niẓām al-islāmī*), that is, a political, social, and economic order based exclusively on the
Qur'ān and the Sunna. The details of this order remained
vague, as al-Bannā's missives and journal contributions
were rather abstract, as were the principles established at a
general conference held in Cairo in 1939. While the basic
precept was undisputed, namely, that the traditional Islamic
legal order of the Sharī'a should be reintroduced, it remained unclear what form this uncodified – and in principle uncodifiable – order should take.

The Muslim Brotherhood is the oldest and most successful of the various modern organizations that force
Islam into an ideological corset and a self-sufficient organi-

zational form for the purpose of achieving political and, above all, social aims and that can be designated as "Islamism" – as it is a modern ideology – in distinction to traditional Islam. The Muslim Brotherhood was the heir to those intellectuals who founded the Salafiyya movement around the turn of the century, an ideology that propagated an idealized conception of an original Islam, the golden era of "the pious predecessors" (*al-salaf al-ṣāliḥ*) – that is, the Prophet Muhammad, his first four successors, and their companions – as a model for the present. In particular the publicist Rashīd Riḍā (see page 140) can be seen as a pioneer of this idea. Islam as a total system regulating all domains of life "is at once a religion and a state order" (*al-Islām dīn wa-dawla*). While this ideological postulate largely ignores the facts of Islamic history, it has nevertheless proved extremely effective as a slogan: "Islam is the solution" (*al-Islām huwa al-ḥall*) to all political and social problems. Like the founders of the Muslim Brotherhood, the supporters of the movement have largely been members of the middle class and farmers, groups on whose behalf the organization has intervened when the state lacked either the will or the means. The brotherhood seeks to provide food and education as well as a technical infrastructure for the rapidly growing and barely urbanized populace in larger cities. After a member of the Muslim Brotherhood assassinated Egyptian prime minister Nuqrāshī Pasha in 1948, the movement was banned and went underground. Ḥasan al-Bannā was killed by the political police in 1949.

# The Palestine Question

The British Balfour Declaration, which affirmed "the establishment in Palestine of a national home for the Jewish people," remained unfulfilled even a number of years after the First World War. Many Arabs were alarmed by increased Jewish immigration. Between 1932 and 1935, the Jewish population in Palestine rose from seventeen to twenty-seven percent. There had already been repeated riots and clashes in the 1920s. The polemic became increasingly heated and assumed religious tones. In 1933, Rashīd Riḍā declared that anyone who sold land to the British or to Jews was a traitor to Islam, and in 1935, the Mufti of Jerusalem Amīn al-Ḥusaynī issued a *fatwa* or legal pronouncement, which, in a free interpretation of Qur'an 33:72, designated Palestine as the "possession (*amāna*)" divinely entrusted to Muslims. The Nazi persecution of Jews and the global depression contributed to increasing Jewish immigration and an intensification of the conflict. Militant groups formed. The first revolt of Palestinian Arabs against the British mandate began in 1936 and ended when the Second World War started in 1939. In 1937, the British Peel Commission presented a partition plan that sought to limit the future Jewish state to Galilee and the coastal area down to south of Tel Aviv with Jerusalem and the port of Jaffa remaining part of the mandate territory. There were Arab conferences on Palestine in 1931 and 1937 addressing the future of the country, but neither was able to achieve any palpable success.

# The Second World War and the Establishment of the Arab League

Many Arabs sympathized with the Axis powers during the Second World War. This was due in part to the enmity Arabs felt toward Great Britain and France as colonial powers as well as to concerns about continued Jewish immigration to Palestine. Fascist organizations arose sporadically, and anti-Semitic currents – in fact foreign to traditional Islam – also became evident. The British curbed Jewish immigration in 1939, and in May 1941 Foreign Secretary Anthony Eden even declared his support for future Arab unity. However, de Gaulle's government in exile granted independence to Lebanon in 1943 and to Syria in 1945, thus sealing the permanence of their partition. For the duration of the war, France and England retained their control of Arab countries.

The impending Allied victory raised the possibility of independence for the remaining Arab countries as well as issues of Arab unity, especially that of Palestine's place in the Arab world. For this reason, increased preparations for liberation were made even during the war. After preparatory negotiations in Alexandria in 1944, Egypt, Transjordan, Lebanon, Syria, Iraq, and Saudi Arabia, all of which were already formally independent, approved the Pact of the League of Arab States in Cairo on March 22, 1945. (North)

Yemen joined on May 5, and the charter came into force on May 11. The goal of the pact was to promote economic, cultural, and social cooperation among Arab countries. It obligated all members to a foreign policy that did not contravene the interests of other member states and that affirmed the right of Arabs to Palestine.

### Membership in the Arab League

| | | | |
|---|---|---|---|
| 1945 | Egypt, Jordan, Lebanon, Syria, Iraq, Yemen, Saudi Arabia | 1971 | Bahrain, Qatar, United Arab Emirates, Oman |
| 1953 | Libya | 1973 | Mauritania |
| 1956 | Sudan | 1974 | Somalia |
| 1958 | Tunisia, Morocco | 1976 | Palestine (represented by the PLO) |
| 1961 | Kuwait | 1977 | Djibouti |
| 1962 | Algeria | 1993 | Comoros |
| 1967 | South Yemen | | |

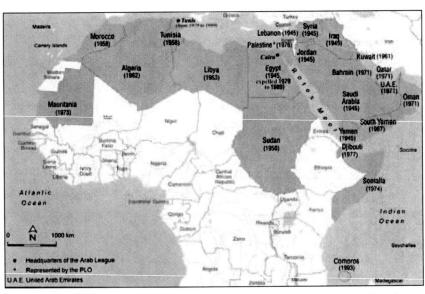

*The member states of the Arab League with the year of entry of each*

# The Founding of Israel and the First Middle East War

In 1947, the United Nations presented a partition plan for the future of Palestine. Arab states, however, refused to recognize this plan and voted against it at the UN General Assembly. Consequently, Great Britain announced that at midnight on May 15, 1948, it was abandoning its mandate for Palestine. In Tel Aviv on May 14, 1948, David Ben-Gurion proclaimed the state of Israel. Troops from member states of the Arab League responded by advancing on the following night. This intervention by Arab allies, who were poorly organized both militarily and politically, ended in a debacle. When a ceasefire was declared on January 7, 1949, Israel had made territorial gains considerably beyond the UN partition plan. The ceasefire line, which in Jerusalem ran directly west of the city wall in the old city, remained the de facto border between the Jewish state and its Arab neighbors for almost twenty years. The West Bank with East Jerusalem went to Jordan, while the Gaza Strip went to Egypt.

The catastrophe (*al-nakba*) was enormous. Flight and expulsion (about sixty percent of the 1.4 million Arab residents of the former mandate territory emigrated), dispossession, and the destruction of more than four hundred Arab villages by Jewish settlers laid the foundation for a conflict that continues even today and to which no end is in sight. There is no political development, no conflict in the Middle East that is not in some way affected by the Palestine conflict.

# Ba'th Party and Nasserism

The major ideologies of the nineteenth and twentieth centuries – liberalism, socialism, communism, and fascism – all had their supporters in the Arab world as well. Following the Second World War, Arab nationalism, which had previously assumed a more regional form ("Egypt for Egyptians"), took on pan-Arab tones. The establishment of the Arab League indicated the direction of future developments. People spoke of a single "Arab nation," defined in particular through a common language, history, and culture, and no longer through Islam. It was above all Christian authors from Syria and Lebanon who laid the theoretical foundations for secular Arab nationalism (Pan-Arabism). This is evident, for example, in the fact that in 1940 two Syrian teachers, the Christian Michel 'Aflaq and the Muslim Ṣalāḥ al-Dīn al-Bītār, founded the *Ba'th* ("resurrection" or "renaissance"), a socialist party opposing the power of the wealthy bourgeoisie and large landowners. It did not take long before additional leftist nationalist groups merged with the party. The declared goals of the Ba'th were Arab "unity, freedom, and socialism." The party was oriented around a secular nationalist ideology, in which Islam was regarded as merely one part of a common cultural Arab heritage.

While the Maghreb states initially remained under French rule, there was a series of revolutions in the eastern part of the Arab world directed against the ruling elite: the land-owning class (which had arisen in the nineteenth century), the wealthy bourgeoisie, and the established dynasties. These revolutions were triggered above all by unresolved social problems, as well as by the failure of old elites with regard to the Palestine issue and their collaboration with the former colonial powers (which continued to exert influence in the area). Leaders of the revolutionary movements were frequently officers, who themselves came from the middle classes and found support there.

A series of military coups began in Syria in 1949, resulting in successive military dictatorships. However, the actual decade of revolts occurred between 1952 and 1962. It was during this period that the remaining Arab countries obtained their independence. In Egypt, the "Free Officers," including Gamāl ʿAbd al-Nāṣir (Nasser, 1918–1970), brought down the regime of King Fārūq (1936–1952) in 1952. In Syria, after the parliamentary system was reinstituted in 1954, the Baʿth had their first great election victory. The party was the driving force behind the experimental unification with Egypt (see page 158). In the same year, a long guerrilla war against the French began in Algeria. By 1962, approximately 20,000 French and 1,000,000 Algerians had lost their lives in the conflict. The Algerian independence struggle mobilized people far beyond Algeria and the Arab world. It came to be seen as the paradigm for liberation movements throughout the Third World. The "Independence" party (*Istiqlāl*) was founded in Morocco in 1944. The popular Sultan Muḥammad V (1927–1958) led the national movement. The French exiled him to Madagascar in 1953, but due to the rioting in the country they were forced to bring him back, and grant-

ed Morocco full independence on March 2, 1956. On that
same day, Habib Bourguiba (*Bū Ruqaiba*), a lawyer, assumed leadership of the New Constitutional Party (Neo–
Destour, see page 132) in Tunisia. In Iraq, King 'Abdallāh
was deposed and murdered in a putsch by Colonel Qassim
(*al-Qāsim*). In Yemen, there was a coup by the army against
the Zaydī imam al-Badr in 1962; the proclamation of a
republic led to a civil war that lasted eight years. Last to fall
was the monarchy in Libya. Here young officers, led by
Colonel Mu'ammar al-Qaddafi (born in 1942), deposed
King Idrīs from the dynasty of the Sanusi sheikhs in 1969.
In the same year, the military led by Colonel Ja'far
Numayrī assumed power in Sudan.

During Nasser's presidency (1954–1970), Egypt assumed the leading political role in the Arab world. Nasser
was successful in a number of actions that greatly enhanced
his prestige, even far beyond Egypt's borders. The first of
these was his treaty with the British in 1954 regarding the
definitive withdrawal of their troops. The nationalization of
the Suez Canal in July 1956 did lead to the final military
intervention by France and Great Britain in alliance with
Israel in October and November of that year, but this was
brought to a halt by the two superpowers, the United States
and the Soviet Union. On February 1, 1958, Nasser announced that the Syrian Ba'th Party had agreed to a union
between Egypt and Syria as the "United Arab Republic"
(UAR), which Yemen – at the time still governed by the
imam – formally entered. This union was supposed to be
the seed of a united Arab nation. A joint National Assembly
was formed in 1960. Only a year later, however, the Syrians, who felt dominated by the Egyptians, withdrew from

the union following a rightist coup. When revolutionary officers in Yemen brought down the imam in 1962 and proclaimed a republic, Nasser took their side and supported the revolutionaries in the subsequent civil war from 1962 to 1969, especially with his air force.

The United States sought to contain the Soviet Union and keep it out of the Indian Ocean and away from Middle Eastern oil reserves by means of the Baghdad Pact of 1955 (between Turkey, Iraq, Iran, and Pakistan), the Middle East Treaty Organization orchestrated by Britain and the United States. Nasser initially attempted to lead the Non-Aligned Movement, but then increasingly sought support from the Eastern bloc, which helped to finance the enormous new Aswan High Dam. Iraq, Syria, Libya, Algeria, Somalia, and South Yemen (which became independent in 1967) all relied on support from the Soviet Union and on intimate economic, military, and political cooperation with the Eastern bloc.

# The Six-Day War
# (June 1967)

Nasser's star began to wane when he overestimated his own power and engaged in a war with Israel to liberate all of Palestine. Palestinian exiles in Kuwait – including Yasir Arafat (1929-2004) – founded the Fatah Organization (*al-Fath*, "the victory") in 1959. In January 1965, the organization called for an armed struggle against Israel. The Syrian Ba'th party's support of the Fatah Organization led Nasser to worry about his reputation as leader of the Arab nation; although inadequately armed he took the reins of a movement that threatened to slip out of his control. He provoked a war by occupying the Sinai Peninsula and demanding the withdrawal of UN troops. Like the war of 1948–1949, the Six-Day War (June 5–10, 1967) ended in a military disaster for the Arab side. Israel took not only East Jerusalem (the old city), which had been in Jordanian control, but also the entire West Bank and the Gaza Strip, where a Jewish settlement policy was introduced that has subsequently been supported or tolerated by all Israeli governments.

This defeat marked the demise of Nasserism, the failure of an ideology of nationalist, pan-Arabist, and socialist ideas. Nasser's death in 1970 bolstered Islamic movements and groups throughout the world.

# The Sadat Era (1970–1981): The October War, the Infitāḥ, and the Oil Crisis

In 1971, Egyptians approved the new liberal constitution (which nonetheless granted the president extensive powers) presented by Nasser's successor Anwar al-Sadat (al-Sādāt). In October 1973, Sadat sent troops across the Suez Canal in a surprise attack, though the victory was quickly neutralized by the United States' intervention. Nevertheless, Egypt regained the Sinai, and the Suez Canal was opened again in 1975. Sadat paid for this partial success by turning to the West politically, ending Egypt's socialist experiment, and liberalizing the economy, in short, by "opening" (*infitāḥ*) the country to Western capital. In 1977, Sadat made a surprise trip to Israel, prayed in the al-Aqṣā Mosque, and spoke before the Knesset. On March 26, 1979, Egypt became the first Arab country reach a peace agreement with Israel at the U.S. Camp David, which included the recognition of their shared border. A "rejectionist front" formed by other Arab countries opposed the peace agreement, and Egypt's membership in the Arab League was suspended from 1979 to 1989.

One consequence of the October War of 1973 – known as the Yom Kippur War in Israel and the Ramaḍān War among Arabs – was the so-called oil price revolution. The founding of the Organization of Petroleum Exporting Countries (OPEC) in 1960 marked an attempt to counterbalance the power of multinational oil companies. The oil embargo of 1973-74, which was agreed to in Vienna as a political weapon, led to unparalleled price increases: The cost of a barrel of oil increased tenfold. This led to an unprecedented flow of capital into the oil exporting countries, particularly Saudi Arabia. The oil embargo was not successful in terms of foreign policy, as consumer nations were able to turn to their own resources to reduce consumption and to develop alternative energy sources. In terms of domestic politics, this influx of capital did more to cement existing political structures than to change them. Saudi Arabia, as a distributor of petrodollars, was now able to exercise a certain hegemony over the other Arab countries, especially those without oil reserves and those bordering on Israel. The Saudis used their influence to strengthen Islamist movements, first and foremost the Muslim Brotherhood, as well as regional tribal leaders, for example in (North) Yemen and South Yemen, thereby weakening leftist revolutionary movements and parties.

The Islamic revolution in Iran in 1978–79 toppled the pro-American regime of the Shah and led to the establishment of the Islamic Republic of Iran under Āyatollāh Khomeinī. It also fueled the hopes of Arab Islamists that similar coups would be possible in their own countries. On November 20, 1979, a group of approximately five hundred Saudi sectarians proclaiming the return of the awaited Mahdi occupied Islam's most sacred shrine, the Masjid al-Ḥarām mosque with the Ka'ba in Mecca. Authorities were able to overpower them only after a two-week siege. The murder of Sadat during a parade in Cairo on October 6, 1981, was also the work of militant Islamists from Upper Egypt. Between 1983 and 1985, Sudanese dictator Colonel Numayrī, who was supported by the Muslim Brotherhood, experimented with implementing Islamic law, introducing penal and tax codes based on the Sharī'a.

# The Lebanese Civil War (1975–1990) and the Iran-Iraq War (1980–1988)

For the regimes of most Arab countries, the 1970s, 1980s, and 1990s proved to be a period of unprecedented stability. In July 1968, the Iraqi Ba'th party led by General Aḥmad Ḥasan al-Bakr ousted President 'Ārif in a bloodless coup and assumed control of the country for the next thirty-five years. Colonel Qaddafi came to power in Libya in 1969 after bringing down the monarchy and continues to rule the country even today. In 1970, then Syrian minister of defense Ḥāfiẓ al-Asad participated in a coup and established a Ba'thist regime, which his son Bashar has continued after Asad's death in 2000. The assassination of leading politicians did not affect this stability. In Egypt the transition from Sadat to President Ḥusnī Mubārak (born in 1928) in 1981 brought no fundamental political changes. The murder of King Faisal in 1975 shook the Saudi monarchy as little as did the transition from his successor Khālid to King Fahd in 1982. The Hashemite king Hussain ruled Jordan from 1952 to 1999, King Ḥasan II ruled in Morocco from 1961 to 1999, and Sultan Qābūs has governed Oman since 1970. The FLN (*Front de libération nationale*), which led Algeria's war for independence against France and came to power after independence was achieved in 1962, has also successfully cemented its power. Habib Bourguiba, who had ruled Tunisia after independence in 1956, was removed in 1987 by the former prime minister General Zīn El-ʿĀbidīne Ben ʿAlī (born in 1936), a change of power that also took place within the ruling elite.

This stability was attained almost universally by the cementing of existing power relations and the rigorous use of police and secret service. In Syria, President al-Asad violently suppressed the opposition of the Muslim Brotherhood. More than 10,000 people are said to have died in the bombing of the city of Ḥamāh. The governments of Egypt, Jordan, and Morocco have, in contrast, attempted to integrate the Islamist opposition through concessions and limited, controlled government participation.

Despite their nationalist, pan-Arabist ideology, the Baʿth regimes in Syria and Iraq had only narrow regional power bases. Ḥāfiz al-Asad was supported especially by the Alawites, a small Shiʿite religious community in the Syrian coastal range (not to be confused with the Alevis in Turkey). Many Alawite men have made a career in the Syrian military, particularly in the air force. Saddam Hussein (born in 1937), who took control of the Iraqi Baʿth party in 1979, ruled the country with the help of the Tikrīt clan, a circle loyal to him with its roots in and around Tikrīt, Saddam's native city on the Tigris. This regional and narrowly limited power base and a political agenda organized primarily around securing its own rule have made both Baʿth regimes completely incapable of effectively representing pan-Arab interests and have also brought them into open rivalry with each other more than once.

Lebanon, in contrast, has been unstable. An unwritten "national pact" has existed here since independence in

1943, regulating the separation of power in the legislative and executive branches according to precisely balanced percentages of the different religious groups. It gave Christians, especially the Maronites, political advantage over Druzes, Shi'ites, and Sunnīs. However, consensus on this proportionality disintegrated in the 1970s as a result of demographic displacements caused primarily by the influx of Palestinians, as well as growth in the Shi'ite population in southern Lebanon. As the government had lost virtually all control over the south of the country, fighters of the Palestinian Liberation Organization (PLO), founded in 1964 in response to the defeat in the Six-Day War, were able to settle here among the primarily Shi'ite population after being driven out of the West Bank, establishing training camps and engaging in attacks on villages on the Israeli side of the border.

Open civil war erupted in Lebanon in 1975. The PLO was the spearhead for the Muslim minorities here, who sought to break the Christian dominance that had been firmly established since the nineteenth century. The Syrian military intervened on the side of the Muslims, an action that the Arab League then legitimated through a retrospective mandate in the summer of 1976. After the Islamic Revolution in Iran in 1979, the Shi'ites in southern Lebanon became increasingly radicalized. Their militant organization Hezbollah (*Hizbu' llāh*, "party of God") joined in the struggle against Israel. This led to a military intervention by Israel in 1982–83, which ended with the occupation of Beirut, a renewed but brief invigoration of Christian forces, and the expulsion of the PLO from southern Lebanon. PLO leader Yasir Arafat went into exile in Tunisia. The general exhaustion of the embattled militias prepared the way for negotiations, which led to a peace plan under the aegis of the Arab League in Ṭā'if, Saudi Arabia in the fall of 1989. The plan was supposed to end the civil war and establish a new political basis in the country. At the end of 1990, the Ṭā'if Agreement was enforced by Syrian troops and written into the constitution.

After the Islamic Revolution led to a regime change in Iran in 1979, Iraqi president Saddam Hussein believed that he could now assert Iraq's old claims to the mouth of the Shatt al-'Arab (the confluence of the Tigris and Euphrates rivers) and to the Iranian border province of Khūzestān, an area rich in oil with a predominantly Arab population. For the United States and its Western allies, Saddam's war against the new Iranian regime offered a welcome opportunity to retaliate against an enemy that had subverted an important pillar of American alliance building in the Middle East, and they provided the Iraqis with support. This war in the Persian Gulf region lasted eight years (1980–1988) and ended in a stalemate. Initially pushed back by Iranian troops, the Iraqis were subsequently able to regain territory. When the Iranian leader Khomeinī was forced to accept a ceasefire, the prewar borders at Shatt al-'Arab were reestablished.

# The 1990s: The First Intifāda and the Gulf War

Mikhail Gorbachev's policy of perestroika beginning in 1986 and the collapse of the Soviet Union in 1990 marked the dissolution of antagonisms between the Soviet Union and the United States. The Cold War had allowed the Arab states to seek support from one superpower or the other according to their needs. The United States was now the sole superpower that Arab governments had to come to terms with.

The end of the opposition between East and West also rendered Palestine superfluous as a substitute battleground for the superpowers. It was now possible for the United States and the Soviet Union to work together for a solution to the conflict in the West Bank and the Gaza Strip. There had been strikes and heavy rioting in these areas in late 1987. This first *Intifāda* ("uprising") continued throughout 1988 and 1989. The central committee of the PLO, which was still in exile in Tunis, declared Yasir Arafat president of an "Independent State of Palestine." Israel took part in top-secret talks with the PLO in Oslo, and official negotiations were held under the aegis of the United States and the Soviet Union in Madrid in October 1991. These negotiations were facilitated by the election of the Labor Party in Israel and the formation of Yitzhak Rabin's government in the summer of 1992. A limited autonomy on the basis of the formula "Land for Peace" was ultimately negotiated on

August 19, 1993. Initially for Gaza and Jericho, it was supposed to be gradually expanded. Israel and the PLO agreed to recognize each other. The agreement, which was signed in Washington in the presence of President Bill Clinton on September 13, 1993, appeared finally to provide the foundation for lasting peace in the Middle East. Arafat, Prime Minister Rabin, and Foreign Minister Shimon Peres were awarded the Nobel Peace Prize in 1994.

In the meantime, however, U.S. involvement in the Middle East had acquired a new dimension when, in August 1990, Saddam Hussein occupied Kuwait and claimed its oil reserves as compensation for his expenditures in the Iran-Iraq War. The independent country of Kuwait, a member state of the United Nations, was proclaimed a province that had historically belonged to Iraq. Saddam hoped that in alliance with Syria and Yemen he could break Saudi Arabia's hegemony and gain access to oil reserves along the Persian Gulf. However, if Saddam had thought that the United States would tacitly support or tolerate this move, he was grievously mistaken. Supported by a United Nations resolution, the United States forged an alliance of twenty-eight nations, including most Arab countries, even Syria. Only Libya, Jordan, and the PLO sided with Iraq. After the ultimatum expired in January 1991, American and allied troops defeated the Iraqi army in the fourteen-day operation called Desert Storm, which was launched from Saudi territory. Coalition forces, however, neither advanced to Baghdad nor toppled the Ba'th regime. Saddam Hussein was even able to violently suppress a Shi'ite uprising in the south of the country in 1991 and to retaliate with mass executions without any reaction by the victors. The economic

sanctions imposed by the United Nations seriously damaged the economic infrastructure of the country and hit the
civilian population the hardest. The victors also erected no-
fly zones north of the 36th parallel and south of the 33rd
parallel in order to protect the Kurds and the Shi'ites from
further reprisals. Iraq's constant obstruction of UN weapon
inspectors, who were supposed to prevent Iraqi production
of nuclear, biological, and chemical weapons, soon brought
Saddam Hussein into renewed conflict with the United
States.

# 7

# The Beginning
of the
Twenty-first Century

*Baghdad 2006*

# The Second Intifāḍa

In the summer of 2000, talks between the PLO and the Israeli government of Ehud Barak resumed under the aegis of the United States, nourishing hopes for a final peace in the Israel-Palestine conflict. But Camp David II was an utter failure, especially – although details were never officially made public – regarding the issues of the fixing of the border, the problematic right of return for displaced Palestinians, and the question of Jerusalem. The Arab enclaves in East Jerusalem would have remained separated from the Palestinian state and interspersed with Jewish settlements. On the Ḥaram al-Sharīf – the Temple Mount of the Jews – the Palestinians would have had owned the al-Aqṣā Mosque and the Dome of the Rock, but not the ground on which they stood. Yasir Arafat rejected Barak's offer as unacceptable for the Palestinians. Then the provocative appearance on the Temple Mount by Ariel Sharon, then right-wing leader of the opposition, on September 28, 2000, triggered the Second Intifāḍa, which led to an extraordinary escalation of the conflict, with a series of suicide attacks by the radical Islamist Palestinian organizations *al-Jihād al-islāmi* and *Ḥamās* ("enthusiasm, zeal"; actually an acronym for Islamic Resistance Movement) and military reprisals by Israel, during which 'Arafāt was temporarily besieged in his headquarters in Ramallāh. The "road map" proposed in 2003 by U.S. president George W. Bush in cooperation with the United Nations, the European Union, and Russia, which

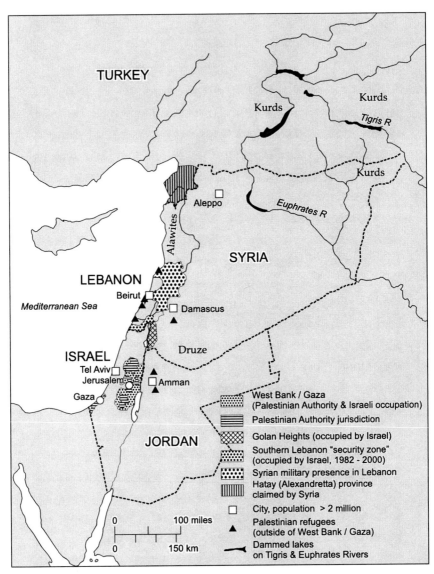

*The contemporary Levant, 2000*

From *The Levant*

was intended to lead to a final peace, was quickly removed from the negotiating table. Even though the Jewish settlements in the Gaza Strip have been removed, the resolution of the conflict seems more distant than ever. The electoral victory of the radical Islamist Ḥamās in the Palestinian territories and the Israeli army's attack on the positions of the Hezbollah militias (Shi'ites supported by Iran) in southern Lebanon in the summer of 2006 dangerously intensified the situation.

# The Iraq War

The attacks on the World Trade Center and the Pentagon on September 11, 2001, by nineteen terrorists of Arab descent led to a provisional reorientation of U.S. Middle East policies, the ultimate effects of which remain to be seen. A second military intervention in Iraq was part of considerations by the U.S. government from the very beginning. Various justifications were offered for attacking Saddam Hussein's Ba'th regime: Saddam's alleged production of weapons of mass destruction; support for the terrorist organization Al-Qā'ida ("the basis") of Usāma bin Lādin, which was responsible for the attacks of September 11; and regime change in Iraq to start the process of democratization in the entire region. Only the last of these carries any real weight. The U.S. government evidently planned to restructure the entire region. The attack by U.S. and British units, this time from bases in Kuwait, started on March 20, 2003, and toppled Saddam Hussein's regime with the capture of Baghdad on April 9. Saddam himself managed to escape, but was apprehended on December 13. Many senior officials were arrested or turned themselves in. Civil authority was initially placed under American civilian administration, which was responsible for the country's reconstruction. The armies of the victors, meanwhile reinforced by Poland and other allies, remained in the country.

Whether or not Iraq can be pacified is largely dependent on the position of the Shi'ite population, which makes up about sixty-five percent of the total Iraqi population. If the autonomous Kurds are not included in these statistics, then the Shiʻites comprise seventy-five percent of the Arab population, compared to twenty-five percent Arab Sunnīs. Even in the capital of Baghdad, which lies within the so-called Sunnī Triangle, the Shiʻites have probably long since become a majority of the population. The influx of refugees from the south following the Iran-Iraq War of 1980–88 have transformed the suburbs of al-Kāẓimiyya in the north, with its Shiʻite shrine, and the former Saddam City in the east (now named Sadr City, *Madīnat al-Ṣadr,* after a Shiʻite Āyatollāh murdered at the behest of Saddam), with their two to three million residents, into Shiʻite strongholds. These could play a significant role in a conflict for power in the future Iraq. Although Āyatollāh as-Sīstānī, leading cleric of the Shiʻite university complex in Najaf, supports non-violent resistance in the time-honored quietist tradition of senior Shiʻite clergy – in contrast to the young Muqtadā as-Ṣadr, who organizes armed militias in Sadr City – the Shiʻites oppose foreign occupation forces in general, which coincides with the Sunnī opposition. A national resistance in which Arab identity carries more weight than religious affiliation is starting to form. Any order imposed on the people from the outside without their approval would remain unstable. But no matter how the experiment ends, the occupation and subjugation of a major Arab country by the United States has opened up a completely new chapter in the history of the Arabs.

The Arab countries between the Atlantic and the Tigris are today considered part of the "crisis belt," which extends even farther to include Iran, Afghanistan, and the Indian subcontinent, all the way to southeast Asia. The centers of conflict in this part of the world are indeed numerous. Violent coups, wars, and civil wars have followed one after another since the end of the Second World War. The perpetual conflict around Palestine seems far from resolution. Again and again, oil reserves in several Arab countries provide grounds for foreign powers to intervene politically or militarily in pursuit of their own interests. And let us not forget that for a period of time the entire Arab world, with the exception of central Arabia, was subject to more or less direct European colonial rule; that is a trauma that still has enormous aftereffects today and continues to feed anti-Western attitudes. Especially the foundation of Israel, a state of European emigrants, is viewed within this context as a source of outrage as long as the Palestinians are not allowed to have their own country. On top of this are the immense demographic and economic problems and the unresolved questions of the future political order. The models of the dictatorial or patrimonial regimes and the traditional monarchies that have prevailed until now are competing with the ideas of democratic constitutions and with drafts for Islamist state and social systems, as favored by the Muslim Brotherhood. The Arab countries have meanwhile become fully integrated into the framework of the global economy and world politics. Their internal policies will have to adapt to that. The momentous upheavals that began with the "Arab Spring" of 2010 and 2011 certainly represent the beginnings of such an adaptation.

# Primary Source Readings from the History of the Arabs

Selected and Edited by
Luke Yarbrough and Oded Zinger

# Introduction

In this appendix, readers will find excerpts from primary sources that complement Professor Halm's succinct narrative. These passages have been chosen to give students a glimpse of the vast and richly textured mosaic of texts that have been generated by and about the Arabs, and to encourage them to explore further. A special effort has been made to present texts of a sort that many history sourcebooks leave aside—particularly literature, cultural history, and society as viewed from below—without losing sight of the political and religious orientations of the dominant textual traditions. Although the majority of the selections are translated from the Arabic, it must not be forgotten that the history of the Arabs is interwoven with those of their neighbors. Accordingly, readers will encounter passages written originally in Persian (e.g., Reading 12), English (e.g., Reading 19), French (e.g., Reading 23), German (e.g., Reading 25), and Hebrew (e.g., Reading 39); passages that concern the Arabs only indirectly (e.g., Reading 22); and passages written in Arabic by people who would not call themselves Arabs. We have felt it important to acknowledge that this book, a representation of the Arabs' history from without, stands in a long tradition of such representations. Conversely, Arab writers have often represented others in ways that made sense to them (e.g., Readings 14 and 28). This said, our primary intention has been to choose representative, lively, and readable passages translated from the Arabic: pre-Islamic poetry, the Qur'an, *hadith*, classical literature, autobiography, historical writing, economic analysis, speeches, *fatwas*, modern short stories, and much more. Excerpts are necessarily short, and reflect the tastes of the compilers. Other scholars would of course make very different selections.

Primary sources, no matter how carefully chosen, are never easy to understand. The texts that follow were written by people far removed from the times, places, and cultures in which this book will be read. As a result, these texts must be studied very carefully. They demand an imaginative leap that only the reader can make, and a willingness to understand other perspectives without passing judgment. Yet the effort has its reward, for these primary sources allow us to enter, however briefly, the lives of people who lived in times and places quite distant from our own. Nonetheless, we are often able to empathize with their ideas, fears, and aspirations. These texts are also the rough building-blocks from which all historical writing is constructed. They can always be reinterpreted and rearranged to produce fresh understandings of the past, by students as well as professionals.

The readings are organized according to the chapters of the book. In cases where a reading pertains to a particular subsection, the reading is preceded by the title of that subsection. Each reading receives a brief introduction. The introduction provides basic information about the text and its author, as well as a few questions to guide the reader. Reference is made throughout to

Professor Halm's text, in the form "(text p. X)." Where we have omitted words from a passage, this is signaled in the form "[...]." Asterisks [ * * * ] between paragraphs indicate a major break in the text, signaling that the following passage is from an altogether different section of the same book.

Occasionally a translation taken from another source has been altered slightly. For the original translation, full text, and additional context to each passage, readers are invited to refer to the References at the end of this appendix.

We would like to thank Markus Wiener, Michael Cook, David Grossman, Jessica Marglin, Yaron Ayalon, Rime Wassim, Katharina Ivanyi, and Rachel Neufeld. The compilers alone are, however, solely responsible for any errors.

# Primary Source Readings

## READINGS FOR CHAPTER 1
## PRE-ISLAMIC ARABIA

## 1. A medieval historian on nomadic and sedentary peoples

### Ibn Khaldun

Ibn Khaldun (text pp. 98-99) is one of the most original thinkers in the Islamic tradition and is widely considered the father of sociology and the philosophy of history. Ibn Khaldun was born in Tunis (1332 CE) to an Arab family and died in Cairo (1406 CE). In his youth he received a thorough education in the Islamic sciences (Qur'an, *hadith*, jurisprudence and, later, theology and philosophy). For most of his life, Ibn Khaldun held various appointments in the courts of rulers in Tunis, Fez, Granada, Bougie and Cairo, and was deeply involved in the regular court intrigues. Alternating between top positions in government and spells in prison, towards the end of his life he found himself dedicating more of his time and energy to his intellectual pursuits, which often reflect the experience he had acquired in politics and the service of power. Ibn Khaldun's greatest work was "the *Muqaddima*," an introduction to a universal history. In this introduction, Ibn Khaldun introduces what he calls "a new science" which does not examine only "what happened," but explores the forces that guide human history, and especially the

From Ibn Khaldun, 'Abd al-Rahman, *The Muqaddimah: An Introduction to History.* Trans. F. Rosenthal (Princeton: Princeton University Press, 1981). Copyright © 1958, 1967 by Princeton University Press. Reprinted by permission.

**rise and decline of empires. As can be seen in the reading below, Ibn Khaldun gives great weight to geographical, social, econom- ic and ethnic factors in what he conceives as the natural cycle of dynasties and empires. At the very heart of his thought is the relationship between nomadic and sedentary peoples. Notice the characteristics he attributes to nomadic (Bedouin) and to seden- tary people. Is the interaction between sedentary and nomadic populations constructive or destructive? What is Ibn Khaldun's explanation for the success of the Arab-Islamic conquests?**

## Both Bedouins and sedentary people are natural groups.

It should be known that differences of condition among people are the result of the different ways in which they make their living. Social organization enables them to co-operate toward that end and to start with the simple necessities of life, before they get to conveniences and luxuries. Some people adopt agriculture, the cultiva- tion of vegetables and grains (as their way of making a living). Others adopt animal husbandry, the use of sheep, cattle, goats, bees, and silkworms, for breeding and for their products. Those who live by agriculture or animal husbandry cannot avoid the call of the desert [Ibn Khaldun uses "desert" here to mean uncultivated land or bad lands], because it alone offers the wide fields, acres, pastures for animals, and other things that the set- tled areas do not offer. It is therefore necessary for them to restrict themselves to the desert. Their social organi- zation and co-operation for the needs of life and civi- lization, such as food, shelter, and warmth, do not take them beyond the bare subsistence level, because of their inability (to provide) for anything beyond those (things). Subsequent improvement of their conditions and acqui- sition of more wealth and comfort than they need, cause them to rest and take it easy. Then, they co-operate for things beyond the (bare) necessities. They use more food and clothes, and take pride in them. They build large houses, and lay out towns and cities for protection. This is followed by an increase in comfort and ease, which leads to formation of the most developed luxury customs. They take the greatest pride in the preparation of food and a fine cuisine, in the use of varied splendid clothes of silk and brocade and other (fine materials), in the construction of ever higher buildings and towers [...] Here, now, (we have) sedentary people. "Sedentary people" means the inhabitants of cities and countries, some of whom adopt the crafts as their way of making a living, while others adopt commerce. They earn more and live more comfortably than Bedouins, because they live on a level beyond the level of (bare) necessity, and their way of making a living corresponds to their wealth.

[...]

**Bedouins are prior to sedentary people. The desert is the basis and reservoir of civilization and cities.**

We have mentioned that the Bedouins restrict themselves to the (bare) necessities in their conditions (of life) and are unable to go beyond them, while sedentary people concern themselves with conveniences and luxuries in their conditions and customs. The (bare) necessities are no doubt prior to the conveniences and luxuries. (Bare) necessities, in a way, are basic, and luxuries secondary and an outgrowth (of the necessities). Bedouins, thus, are the basis of, and prior to, cities and sedentary people. Man seeks first the (bare) necessities. Only after he has obtained the (bare) necessities, does he get to comforts and luxuries. The toughness of desert life precedes the softness of sedentary life.

[...]

## Bedouins are closer to being good than sedentary people.

Sedentary people are much concerned with all kinds of pleasures. They are accustomed to luxury and success in worldly occupations and to indulgence in worldly desires. Therefore their souls are colored with all kinds of blameworthy and evil qualities. [...] Bedouins may be as concerned with worldly affairs as (sedentary people are). However, such concern would touch only the necessities of life and not luxuries or anything causing, or calling for, desires and pleasures [...] As compared with those of sedentary people, their evil ways and blameworthy qualities are much less numerous. They are closer to the first natural state and more remote from the evil habits that have been impressed upon the souls (of sedentary people) through numerous and ugly, blameworthy customs.

This is obvious. It will later on become clear that sedentary life constitutes the last stage of civilization and the point where it begins to decay. It also constitutes the last stage of evil and of remoteness from goodness.

[...]

## Bedouins are more disposed to courage than sedentary people.

The reason for this is that sedentary people have become used to laziness and ease. They are sunk in well-being and luxury. They have entrusted defense of their property and their lives to the governor and ruler who rules them, and to the militia which has the task of guarding them. They find full assurance of safety in the walls that surround them, and the fortifications that protect them. No noise disturbs them, and no hunting occupies them. They are carefree and trusting, and have ceased to carry weapons. Successive generations have grown up in this way of life. They have become like women and children, who depend upon the master of the house. Eventually, this has come to be a quality of character that replaces natural (disposition).

The Bedouins on the other hand, live separate from the community. They are alone in the country and remote from militias. They have no walls and gates. Therefore, they provide their own defense and do not entrust it to, or rely upon others for it. They always carry weapons. They watch carefully all sides of the road. They take hurried naps only when they are together in company or when they are in the saddle. They pay attention to every faint barking and noise. They go alone into the desert, guided by their fortitude, putting their trust in themselves. Fortitude has become a character quality of theirs, and courage their nature. They use it whenever they are called upon or an alarm stirs them.

**The reliance of sedentary people upon laws destroys their fortitude and power of resistance.**

Not everyone is master of his own affairs. Chiefs and leaders who are masters of the affairs of men are few in comparison with the rest. As a rule, man must by neces-

sity be dominated by someone else. If the domination is
kind and just and the people under it are not oppressed
by its laws and restrictions, they are guided by the
courage or cowardice that they possess in themselves.
They are satisfied with the absence of any restraining
power. Self-reliance eventually becomes a quality natural to them. They would not know anything else. If, however, the domination with its laws is one of brute force
and intimidation, it breaks their fortitude and deprives
them of their power of resistance as a result of the inert-
ness that develops in the souls of the oppressed [...] For
this (reason), greater fortitude is found among the savage
Arab Bedouins than among people who are subject to
laws. Furthermore, those who rely on laws and are dominated by them from the very beginning of their education and instruction in the crafts, sciences, and religious
matters, are thereby deprived of much of their own fortitude. They can scarcely defend themselves at all against
hostile acts. This is the case with students, whose occupation it is to study and to learn from teachers and religious leaders, and who constantly apply themselves to
instruction and education in very dignified gatherings.

   [...]

The restraining influence among Bedouins tribes
comes from their *shaykh*s and leaders. It results from the
great respect and veneration they generally enjoy among
the people. The hamlets of the Bedouins are defended
against outside enemies by a tribal militia composed of
noble youths of the tribe who are known for their
courage. Their defense and protection are successful
only if they are a closely knit group of common descent.
This strengthens their stamina and makes them feared,

since everybody's affection for his family and his group is more important (than anything else). Compassion and affection for one's blood relations and relatives exist in human nature as something God put into the hearts of men. It makes for mutual support and aid, and increases the fear felt by the enemy.

[...]

**Arabs can obtain royal authority only by making use of some religious coloring, such as prophecy, or sainthood, or some great religious event in general.**

The reason for this is that because of their savagery, the Arabs are the least willing of nations to subordinate themselves to each other, as they are rude, proud, ambitious, and eager to be the leader. Their individual aspirations rarely coincide. But when there is religion (among them) through prophecy or sainthood, then they have some restraining influence in themselves. The qualities of haughtiness and jealousy leave them. It is, then, easy for them to subordinate themselves and to unite (as a social organization). This is achieved by the common religion they now have. It causes rudeness and pride to disappear and exercises a restraining influence on their mutual envy and jealousy. When there is a prophet or saint among them, who calls upon them to fulfill the commands of God and rids them of blameworthy qualities and causes them to adopt praiseworthy ones, and who has them concentrate all their strength in order to make the truth prevail, they become fully united (as a social organization) and obtain superiority and royal authority. Besides, no people are as quick (as the Arabs) to accept (religious) truth and right guidance, because their natures have been preserved free from distorted habits and uncontaminated by base character qualities.

[...]

For all these (reasons), the Arabs are by nature remote from royal leadership. They attain it (only) once their nature has undergone a complete transformation under the influence of some religious coloring that wipes out all such (qualities) and causes the Arabs to have a restraining influence on themselves and to keep people apart from each other, as we have mentioned.

This is illustrated by the Arab dynasty in Islam. Religion cemented their leadership with the religious law and its ordinances, which, explicitly and implicitly, are concerned with what is good for civilization. The caliphs followed one after another. As a result, the royal authority and government of the Arabs became great and strong. When Rustum [the commander of the Persian army that fought against the Muslims during the Islamic conquests] saw the Muslims assemble for prayer, he said: "Umar eats my liver. He teaches the dogs how to behave."

Later on, the Arabs were cut off from the dynasty for generations. They neglected the religion. Thus, they forgot political leadership and returned to their desert. They were ignorant or the connection of their group feeling with the people of the ruling dynasty, because subservience and lawful (government) had (now) become strange to them. They became once again as savage as they had been before. The epithet "royal" was no longer applicable to them, except in so far as it (continued to) apply to the caliphs who were (Arabs) by race. When the caliphate disappeared and was wiped out, governmental power passed altogether out or their hands. Non-Arabs took over the power in their stead. They remained as Bedouins in the desert, ignorant of royal authority and political leadership. [...] When the Arabs forgot the religion, they no longer had any connection with political leadership, and they returned to their desert origins. At times, they achieve superiority over weak dynasties, as is the case in the contemporary Maghrib. But their domination leads only to the ruin of the civilization they conquer, as we have stated before.

*Arabia in the Hellenistic Period;*
*Arabia between Byzantines and Persians*

## 2. The nomads of Arabia in Antiquity

### Diodorus Siculus, al-Mas'udi

**The fact that Islam arose in the towns of western Arabia can obscure another fact: that much of the peninsula was home to nomadic or transhumant herders. Great travelers and traders, the nomadic Arab peoples had frequent contacts with their neighbors to the north: Syrians, Greeks, Persians, and others. It is to such contacts that we owe the first description below, by the first-century BCE historian Diodorus Siculus. He may be using here an account composed by one of the generals of Alexander the Great. His description seems to refer to the Nabateans (text p. 9). While Arabia was not as uniformly hostile to civilization as this passage claims, the description does capture some of the perquisites of desert life. The second passage, by the tenth-century writer al-Mas'udi, represents an idealized vision of the free and noble desert nomad. Such visions of the past were useful to**

From Hoyland, Robert, *Arabia and the Arabs: From the Bronze Age to the Coming of Islam* (London; New York: Routledge, 2001).

**Arabic speakers who moved from Arabia into the Fertile Crescent, where they encountered peoples who possessed distinct identities of their own. Stressing their unique connection to the Arabs of the desert helped Arabic speakers to claim distinct and durable identities and thus avoid assimilation. Idealized as it may be, this account reflects widespread understandings of the nomadic life before and after Islam. What might be some of the drawbacks to this lifestyle? If you were a settled ruler on the fringes of Arabia, how would you foresee dealing with neighbors such as these?**

They live in the open air, claiming as native land a wilderness that has neither rivers nor abundant springs from which it is possible for a hostile army to obtain water. It is their custom neither to plant grain, set out any fruit-bearing tree, use wine, nor construct any house; and if anyone is found acting contrary to this, death is his penalty. They follow this custom because they believe that those who possess these things are, in order to retain the use of them, easily compelled by the powerful to do their bidding. Some of them raise camels, others sheep, pasturing them in the desert .... They are exceptionally fond of freedom; and whenever a strong force of enemies comes near, they take refuge in the desert, using this as a fortress; for it lacks water and cannot be crossed by others. But to them alone, since they have prepared subterranean reservoirs lined with stucco, it furnishes safety. (Diodorus Siculus)

An Arab skilled in oratory was sent to [the Persian emperor] Khosro, who asked him about the Arabs, why they lived in the desert and chose the nomadic life. The Arab replied: 'O king, they are masters of their land rather than mastered by it, and they have no need for fortification walls, since they can rely on trenchant blades and pointed lances for their protection and defence.' ... 'And what is the Arabs' main sustenance?' 'Meat, milk, date-wine and dates.' 'And what are their qualities?' 'Might, honour, magnanimity, extending hospitality to the guest, providing security to the client, granting refuge to the weak, repaying favours and dispensing generosity. They are travellers of the night, masters of the stealth attack, denizens of the desert, the good hosts of the wilderness. They are accustomed to temperance and averse to subservience; they practise vengeance, disdain ignominy, and preserve their honour.' (al-Mas'udi)

*Old Arabic Language, Poetry, and Script*

# 3. Arabic poetry

### 'Antara ibn Shaddad

**Poetry, memorized and performed publicly for a variety of purposes, was cultivated by the Arabs long before Islam (text pp. 18-19). Poets were more than entertainers. Their verses were used as propaganda in inter-tribal warfare, and as a means of legitimizing and influencing local rulers. The following excerpt, attributed to the sixth-century poet-warrior 'Antara, touches on several common themes. The ever-present hand of fate (ll. 1-2), battle exploits (ll. 3-5, 9-14), and fine horses (ll. 6-8) are obvious interests, but others can be discerned: travel by night, a landscape of rocks, mountains, wastes, hillocks, and sands, and the market culture, among others. The poet's attention shifts easily from topic to topic. Arabic poetry tended to place greater**

From Arberry, A.J., *Arabic Poetry: A Primer for Students* (Cambridge: Cambridge University Press, 1965).

value on an exquisitely fashioned individual line than on the coherent interconnection among the lines of a poem. Of the poet little is known. He was the child of an Arab father and an African mother, and figured as the hero of many a later legend. What are the cultural values that come through in this poetry? How do these values compare with the ones described by Ibn Khaldun (Reading 1 above)?

1. Make war on me, O vicissitudes of the nights, (now) on my right hand and now on my left,
2. And labour to be hostile to me and to thwart me; by Allah! you have never occupied my mind.
3. I have a high purpose firmer than a rock and stronger than immovable mountains,
4. And a sword which, when I strike with it ever, the useless spearheads give way before it,
5. And a lance-point which, whenever I lose my way in the night, guides me and restores me from straying,
6. And a mettlesome steed that never sped, but that the lightning trailed behind it from the striking of its hooves.
7. Dark of hue (it is), splitting the starless night with a blackness, between its eyes a blaze like the crescent moon,
8. Ransoming me with its own life, and I ransom it with my life, on the day of battle, and (with) my wealth.
9. And whenever the market of the war of the tall lances is afoot, and it blazes with the polished, whetted blades,
10. I am the broker thereof, and my spear-point is a merchant purchasing precious souls.
11. Wild beasts of the wilderness, when war breaks into flame, follow me from the empty wastes;

12. Follow me, (and) you will see the blood of the foe-
    men streaming between the hillocks and the sands.
13. Then return thereafter, and thank me, and remember
    what you have seen of my deeds,
14. And take sustenance of the skulls of the people for
    your little children and your whelps.

# READINGS FOR CHAPTER 2
# ARABIA AND ISLAM

*Arabia on the Eve of Islam; The Prophet Muhammad*
## 4. The Qur'an

**Muslims consider the Qur'an (text pp. 28-31) to be the direct
speech of God, revealed through the Prophet Muhammad to its
Arabic-speaking audience. The Qur'an occupies a place of special importance not only for Muslims, but for all speakers of
Arabic. Its language has unique power to evoke, and affected,
directly or indirectly, all Arabic prose that followed. In fact, the
book's "inimitability" (*i'jaz*) became an item of faith for
Muslims. Because of this, no translation can capture the full
effect of the original. The Qur'an treats a variety of topics,
using subtly different vocabulary and style, which accord in part
with the development of its concerns over the roughly two
decades during which it came to the Prophet. The following
excerpts hint at four of these concerns. The first passage, from
the second *sura* ("The Cow"), alludes to tensions with other
monotheists, and reinterprets their sacred histories for new purposes. Here the Qur'an substitutes Ishmael (Isma'il, thought to
be a progenitor of the Arabs) for Isaac, the son of Abraham.**

From Abdel Haleem, M.A.S., trans., *The Qur'an: A New Translation* (Oxford; New
York: Oxford University Press, 2004).

The "House" in this passage is usually understood to refer to the Ka'ba in Mecca, toward which all Muslims are to pray five times daily. The second passage comes in the fourth *sura* ("Women"), and bespeaks the Qur'an's concern for equity and justice, as established by the tenets of the sacred law revealed in the book. How might one go about deriving law from passages such as these, as Muslim jurists would do in the centuries following the Qur'an's revelation? The third, fourth, and fifth passages are complete *sura*s that occur near the end of the Qur'an, which is ordered roughly from longest to shortest *sura*. They treat, respectively, the Prophet's ethical concerns and the consolation that he received from God at times of frustration, his desire to dissociate from those who did not accept his message, and a radically monotheist theology that clashed with the Christian doctrine of the Trinity. Other prominent concerns in the Qur'an include God's impending judgment, and the Prophet's own role in warning his people about it. What can you infer about the book's target audience from these passages?

## The Cow (2), 120-30

The Jews and the Christians will never be pleased with you unless you follow their ways. Say, 'God's guidance is the only true guidance.' If you were to follow their desires after the knowledge that has come to you, you would find no one to protect you from God or help you. Those to whom We have given the Scripture, who follow it as it deserves, are the ones who truly believe in it. Those who deny its truth will be the losers. Children of Israel, remember how I blessed you and favoured you over other people, and beware of a Day when no soul can stand in for another. No compensation will be accepted from it, nor intercession be of use to it, nor will anyone be helped. When Abraham's Lord tested him with certain commandments, which he fulfilled, He said,

'I will make you a leader of people.' Abraham asked, 'And will You make leaders from my descendants too?' God answered, 'My pledge does not hold for those who do evil.' We made the House a resort and a sanctuary for people, saying, 'Take the spot where Abraham stood as your place of prayer.' We commanded Abraham and Ishmael: 'Purify My House for those who walk round it, those who stay there, and those who bow and prostrate themselves in worship.' Abraham said, 'My Lord, make this land secure and provide with produce those of its people who believe in God and the Last Day.' God said, 'As for those who disbelieve, I will grant them enjoyment for a short while and then subject them to the torment of the Fire—an evil destination.' As Abraham and Ishmael built up the foundations of the House [they prayed], 'Our Lord, accept [this] from us. You are the All Hearing, the All Knowing. Our Lord, make us devoted to You; make our descendants into a community devoted to You. Show us how to worship and accept our repentance, for You are the Ever Relenting, the Most Merciful. Our Lord, make a messenger of their own rise up from among them, to recite Your revelations to them, teach them the Scripture and wisdom, and purify them: You are the Mighty, the Wise.' Who but a fool would forsake the religion of Abraham? We have chosen him in this world and he will rank among the righteous in the Hereafter.

## Women (4), 1-11

In the name of God, the Lord of Mercy, the Giver of Mercy

People, be mindful of your Lord, who created you

from a single soul, and from it created its mate, and from
the pair of them spread countless men and women far
and wide; be mindful of God, in whose name you make
requests of one another. Beware of severing the ties of
kinship: God is always watching over you. Give orphans
their property, do not replace [their] good things with
bad, and do not consume their property with your
own—a great sin. If you fear that you will not deal fairly with orphan girls, you may marry whichever [other]
women seem good to you, two, three, or four. If you fear
that you cannot be equitable [to them], then marry only
one, or your slave(s): that is more likely to make you
avoid bias. Give women their bridal gift upon marriage,
though if they are happy to give up some of it for you,
you may enjoy it with a clear conscience. Do not entrust
your property to the feeble-minded. God has made it a
means of support for you: make provision for them from
it, clothe them, and address them kindly. Test orphans
until they reach marriageable age; then, if you find they
have sound judgement, hand over their property to them.
Do not consume it hastily before they come of age: if the
guardian is well off he should abstain from the orphan's
property, and if he is poor he should use only what is fair.
When you give them their property, call witnesses in; but
God takes full account of everything you do.

Men shall have a share in what their parents and closest relatives leave, and women shall have a share in what
their parents and closest relatives leave, whether the lega-
cy be small or large: this is ordained by God. If other relatives, orphans, or needy people are present at the distribution, give them something too, and speak kindly to
them. Let those who would fear for the future of their

own helpless children, if they were to die, show the same concern [for orphans]; let them be mindful of God and speak out for justice. Those who consume the property of orphans unjustly are actually swallowing fire into their own bellies: they will burn in the blazing Flame.

Concerning your children, God commands you that a son should have the equivalent share of two daughters. If there are only daughters, two or more should share two-thirds of the inheritance, if one, she should have half. Parents inherit a sixth each if the deceased leaves children; if he leaves no children and his parents are his sole heirs, his mother has a third, unless he has brothers, in which case she has a sixth. [In all cases, the distribution comes] after payment of any bequests or debts. You cannot know which of your parents or your children is more beneficial to you: this is a law from God, and He is all knowing, all wise.

## The Morning Brightness (93), 1-11

In the name of God, the Lord of Mercy, the Giver of Mercy

By the morning brightness and by the night when it grows still, your Lord has not forsaken you [Prophet], nor does He hate you, and the future will be better for you than the past; your Lord is sure to give you so much that you will be well satisfied. Did He not find you an orphan and shelter you? Did He not find you lost and guide you? Did He not find you in need and make you self-sufficient? So do not be harsh with the orphan. And do not chide the one who asks for help; talk about the blessings of your Lord.

## The Disbelievers (109), 1-6

In the name of God, the Lord of Mercy, the Giver of Mercy

Say [Prophet], 'Disbelievers: I do not worship what you worship, you do not worship what I worship, I will never worship what you worship, you will never worship what I worship: you have your religion and I have mine.'

## Purity (112), 1-4

In the name of God, the Lord of Mercy, the Giver of Mercy

Say, 'He is God the One, God the eternal. He begot no one nor was He begotten. No one is comparable to Him.'

*The Prophet Muhammad*
# 5. The *hadith*

The collected reports about the sayings and deeds of the Prophet—known as *hadith* (singular and plural)—are the most important authority for Muslim belief and practice apart from the Qur'an. Extremely numerous and wide-ranging, the *hadith* (text p. 49) reflect not only the setting in which the Prophet lived, but also those of the successive generations of Muslims who collected, edited, and sometimes originated them. The five *hadith* translated here only hint at the topics that these short texts could treat. Note the list of transmitters' names with which each *hadith* begins. This list is called the *isnad*. What does the *isnad*

(*hadith* 1-4) From Juynboll, G.H.A., *The Encyclopedia of Canonical Hadith* (Leiden; Boston: Brill, 2007). (*hadith* 5) From Muslim ibn al-Hajjaj al-Qushayri, *Sahih Muslim bi-sharh al-Nawawi*, vol. 1 (Cairo: al-Matba'a al-Misriyya bil-Azhar). Translated by L. Yarbrough, from the Arabic.

imply about conceptions of religious authority in this society? The first *hadith* would have set a precedent for how Muslims should style their own hair, as they came increasingly to view the Prophet's actions as a model for their own lives. It also reflects the complex attitude of early Islam toward other monotheistic communities (the "People of the Book" are Jews and Christians). The second and third likewise have prescriptive force, and reveal the profound ethical and pious preoccupations of the early Muslims, most of whom at first were Arabs. The fourth *hadith* depicts the Prophet telling a story that reflects the Muslim belief in the resurrection and judgment of the dead, the consequent practice of burial rather than cremation or exposure, and the power of God to save those who fear Him. The fifth, a famous story that is indicative of the supernatural quality of many events that the *hadith* relate, gives a neat synopsis of Muslim faith and practice, with a bit of apocalyptic speculation thrown in for good measure. It may also contain a veiled reference to the Arab-Islamic conquests (text pp. 32-37). If there is such a reference, what is its significance for historians' treatment of the text?

**Zuhri [said, I heard from] 'Ubayd Allah b. 'Abd Allah, [who said, I heard from] Ibn 'Abbas, [who said]:** The People of the Book used to let their hair fall down [upon their foreheads], the polytheists used to part their hair [letting it fall down on either side of their heads], the Prophet used to prefer conforming with the People of the Book in matters for which he had not received a [divine] order, so he let the hair over the forehead fall down; afterwards he resorted to parting his hair.

**Ma'mar—Zuhri—Sa'id b. al-Musayyab—Abu Hurayra—the Prophet:** "There are five obligations incumbent upon a Muslim vis-à-vis his brother: returning his greeting, wishing him well after he sneezes, responding to his invitation, visiting him when he is sick, and following his funeral procession."

**Abu Habiba al-Ta'i—Abu al-Darda'—the Prophet:** "He who only gives a slave his freedom at his death is comparable with someone who only gives away presents when he himself lives in satisfactory circumstances."

**Abu al-Zinad 'Abd Allah b. Dhakwan—al-A'raj 'Abd al-Rahman b. Hurmuz—Abu Hurayra—the Prophet:** "A man who had never done anything meritorious in his life ordered his family at the time of his death to burn his body and to scatter half of the ashes on land and the other half in the sea, adding that if God were to get hold of him, He would punish him as no one was ever punished before. Once the man had died, his people did as they were told. But God ordered the land and the sea to collect his ashes and He asked him: 'Why did you ask your body to be burnt?,' whereupon the man replied: 'Out of fear from You, my Lord, You know best.' Then God forgave him."

**'Umar [b. al-Khattab said,]:** "One day as we were sitting with the Messenger of God, peace and blessings be upon him, there appeared a powerful-looking man, whose hair was as black as his clothes were radiant white. He showed no signs of having traveled, yet none of us recognized him. He sat facing the Prophet, peace and blessings be upon him, knee to knee, and put his palms on the Prophet's thighs. 'O Muhammad,' he said, 'tell me about Islam.' The Messenger of God, peace and blessings be upon him, said, 'Islam is to testify that there is no god but God and that Muhammad is the messenger of God, to pray properly, to give alms, to fast during the month of Ramadan, and to make pilgrimage to Mecca if one is able.' [The visitor] replied, 'You have spoken truly.' We were taken aback that anyone should ask [the Prophet] a question and tell him that he had spoken truly! Then [the visitor] said, 'And tell me about faith.' He replied, 'To believe in God and his angels, books, and messengers, to believe that God decrees all things, good and evil.' He said, 'You have spoken truly.' Then [the visitor] said, 'And tell me about doing good.' He replied, 'To worship God as though you see Him, for although you may not see Him, He sees you.' Then [the visitor] said, 'And tell me about the last hour.' He replied, 'He who is asked knows no more than he who asks.' Then [the visitor] said, 'And tell me about the signs of the last hour.' He replied, 'That the female slave give birth to her mistress, and that the barefoot, naked, and impoverished shepherds vie with one another in building tall structures.' At this [the visitor] left. I waited, then [the Prophet] said, 'Umar, do you know who that questioner was?' I said, 'God and his Messenger know best.' He replied, 'It was Gabriel, come to teach you your religion.'"

*The Prophet Muhammad*

# 6. Muhammad

## Ibn Ishaq

**Ibn Ishaq was born in Medina around 704 and died in Baghdad around 767. While Ibn Ishaq's work, *The Life of God's Messenger* (Ar. *Sirat Rasul Allah*), did not survive in its original form, a later edition of it by Ibn Hisham (died in Egypt around 833) became the most authoritative biography of Muhammad in the Islamic tradition (text p. 48). The reading below is an account**

From Ibn Hisham, 'Abd al-Malik, *The Life of Muhammad*. Trans. A. Guillaume (Karachi: Oxford University Press, 1978).

**from Muhammad's early prophetic career in Mecca. The reading captures the tension between Muhammad's new monotheistic message and the pagan environment of Mecca. What elements in Muhammad's teachings are hardest for the Meccans to swallow? Why is this so? Notice that it is a pagan from Mecca who is interested in reaching compromise and resolution, while it is the monotheist who is exhibits an inclination to quarrel. Is this, in your opinion, a necessary feature of a confrontation between polytheist and monotheist attitudes?**

Yazid b. Ziyad from Muhammad b. Ka'b al-Qurazi told me that he was told that 'Utba b. Rabi'a, who was a chief, said one day while he was sitting in the Quraysh assembly and the apostle was sitting in the mosque by himself, "Why should I not go to Muhammad and make some proposals to him which if he accepts in part, we will give him whatever he wants and he will leave us in peace?" This happened when Hamza had accepted Islam and they saw that the prophet's followers were increasing and multiplying. They thought it was a good idea, and 'Utba went and sat by the prophet and said, "O my nephew, you are one of us as you know, of the noblest of the tribe and hold a worthy position in ancestry. You have come to your people with an important matter, dividing their community thereby and ridiculing their customs, and you have insulted their gods and their religion, and declared that their forefathers were unbelievers, so listen to me and I will make some suggestions, and perhaps you will be able to accept one of them." The apostle agreed, and he went on, "If what you want is money, we will gather for you of our property so that you may be the richest of us; if you want honour, we will make you our chief so that no one can decide anything apart from you; if you want sovereignty, we will make you king, and if this ghost which comes to you, which you see, is such that you cannot get rid of him, we will find a physician for you, and exhaust our means in getting you cured, for often a familiar spirit gets possession of a man until he can be cured of it," or words to that effect.

The apostle listened patiently, and then said: "Now listen to me, 'In the name of God, the compassionate and merciful, H.M. [These are mysterious letters that occasionally begin Qur'anic *suras*. Their meaning is not known], a revelation from the compassionate, the merciful, a book whose verses are expounded as an Arabic Quran for a people who understand, as an announcement and warning, though most of them turn aside not listening and say, 'Our hearts are veiled from that to which you invite us.'" Then the apostle continued to recite it to him. When 'Utba heard it from him, he listened attentively, putting his hands behind his back and leaning on them as he listened. Then the prophet ended at the prostration and prostrated himself, and said, "You have heard what you have heard, Abu al-Walid; the rest remains with you."

When 'Utba returned to his companions they noticed that his expression had completely altered, and they asked him what had happened. He said that he had heard words such as he had never heard before, which were neither poetry, spells, nor witchcraft. "Take my advice and do as I do, leave this man entirely alone for, by God, the words which I have heard will be blazed abroad. If (other) Arabs kill him, others will have rid you of him; if he gets the better of the Arabs, his sovereignty will be your sovereignty, his power your power, and you will be prosperous through him." They said, "He has bewitched you with his tongue." To which he answered, "You have my opinion, you must do what you think fit."

*The Arab-Islamic Conquests*
## 7. A conquest treaty from Spain
### 'Abd al-'Aziz ibn Musa ibn Nusayr

**When the Arab Muslims and their allies took control of a territory for the first time, they were in the habit of making written agreements with the people who lived there (text p. 34). The terms of such agreements set precedents for relations between rulers and ruled. For this reason, they were sometimes tampered with later on, and so the versions contained in the Arabic chronicles are not always reliable. The text below is, however, an example of an authentic-looking conquest treaty; a forger would not have occupied himself with fruit juice and vinegar. Known as the Treaty of Orihuela or of Theodemir, it was contracted in south-east Spain in the year 713—during the last decades of the Arab Muslim expansion—between the Arab general 'Abd al-'Aziz and the Christian, Visigothic noble Theodemir. Its provisions are those that characterized the conquests in most places; the local elites retained their positions, the conquered peoples their religions. Only allegiance and tax payments were demanded in exchange for safety and protection from the new overlords. In time, of course, the state became more involved in the lives of its subjects. At first, however, Arab rule had the loose, ad hoc quality reflected in this document. How would this arrangement need to be changed as the population gradually converted to Islam and mixed with the conquerors?**

From Kennedy, Hugh, *The Great Arab Conquests* (Philadelphia: De Capo Press, 2007).

In the name of God, the Merciful, the Compassionate. This text was written by Abd al-Aziz b. Musa b. Nusayr for Tudmir b. Ghabdush, establishing a treaty of peace and the promise and protection of God and His Prophet (may God bless him and grant him His peace). We [Abd al-Aziz] will not set any special conditions for him or for any among his men, nor harass him, nor remove him from power. His followers will not be killed or taken prisoner, nor will they be separated from their women and children. They will not be coerced in matters of religion, their churches will not be burned, nor will sacred objects be taken from the realm as long as Theodemir remains sincere and fulfils the following conditions we have set for him: He has reached a settlement concerning seven towns: Orihuela, Valentilla, Alicante, Mula, Bigastro, Ello and Lorca. He will not give shelter to fugitives, nor to our enemies, nor encourage any protected person to fear us, nor conceal news of our enemies. He and each of his men shall also pay one dinar every year, together with four measures of wheat, four measures of barley, four liquid measures of concentrated fruit juice, four liquid measures of vinegar, four of honey and four of olive oil. Slaves must each pay half of this.

# 8. A dissident opinion of the Umayyads

## Abu Hamza al-Mukhtar ibn 'Awf

The Kharijis were, along with the groups that would become
known as Sunnis and Shi'is, one of the major factions to emerge
from the quarrels among Muslim Arabs in the first decades after
the Prophet's death. They might be described as meritocratic
purists; they believed that the most righteous Muslim should be
caliph, no matter what his descent. Some of them also believed
that it was their duty to take up arms against any and all who
disagreed with them; they also had a habit of declaring their
opponents to be non-Muslims. It has been suggested that in
these respects they preserved something of the uncompromising
piety that characterized Islam in its earliest decades. In the text
below, a Khariji leader named Abu Hamza looks back on the
Umayyad caliphate, focusing on the ways in which he thinks it
deviated from God's will (the first Umayyad caliph listed is
Mu'awiya; before him are the Rashidun, or "Rightly Guided"
caliphs). Note that he seems to consider it his right and duty to
engage in critique of this sort; this is a very Khariji idea. The
year is 746 or 747. According to what political values does Abu
Hamza judge the Umayyad caliphs? What roles does he assign
to political leaders in the Islamic community? Note that the
*kitab* and *sunna* are the Qur'an and the practice of the early
Muslims, respectively; *fay'* is booty, including land; *amsar* are
new cities established by the Arabs in conquered territories;
*diwan*s are pay-lists of soldiers (the word also came to mean
administrative offices); *sadaqat* are alms taxes that Muslims
had to pay, and which were distributed to eight categories of
people specified in the Qur'an.

O people! The Messenger of God used neither to
advance nor to draw back save with the command of

From Crone, Patricia, and Martin Hinds, *God's Caliph* (Cambridge: Cambridge
University Press, 1986).

God and His revelation. [God] revealed a book to him and made clear to him what he should undertake and what he should guard against, and he was in no way confused about His religion. Then God took him to Himself, after he had taught the Muslims the waymarks of His religion and had placed Abu Bakr in charge of their ritual prayer and [after] the pillar of their religion had become lofty.

When the Muslims put him (Abu Bakr) in charge of their temporal concerns, he fought the apostates and acted by the *kitab* and the *sunna*, striving, until God took him to Himself, may God's mercy be upon him.

'Umar took charge after him. He proceeded according to the mode of conduct (*sira*) of him who had gone before him. He collected the *fay'*, assigned stipends, established *amsar* and *diwans*, gathered the people in night prayer in the month of Ramadan, gave out eighty stripes for wine-drinking, and campaigned in enemy territory. Then he passed on his way, on the path of his companion, having left it (i.e., the matter of the caliphate) to be determined by consultation, may God's mercy be upon him.

Then 'Uthman took charge. For six years he proceeded in a way which fell short of the mode of conduct of his two companions. Then he [acted in a manner which] annulled what he had done earlier, and passed on his way.

Then 'Ali b. Abi Talib took charge. He acted in a proper manner until he established arbitration concerning the book of God and had doubts about His religion. [Thereafter] he did not achieve any goal in respect of what was right, nor did he erect any beacon for that.

Then there took charge Mu'awiya b. Abi Sufyan, who
had been cursed by the Messenger of God and was the
son of one so cursed. He made the servants of God
slaves, the property of God something to be taken by
turns, and His religion a cause of corruption. Then he
passed on his way, deviating from what was right, deceiv-
ing in religion.

Then there took charge his son Yazid, part of [the
object of] the curse of the Messenger of God, a sinner in
respect of his belly and his private parts. He kept to the
path of his father, neither acknowledging what ought to
be acknowledged nor disavowing what ought to be disavowed.

Then Marwan and the Banu Marwan took charge.
They shed forbidden blood and devoured forbidden
property. As for 'Abd al-Malik, he made al-Hajjaj an
*imam* of his, leading to hellfire. As for al-Walid, he was
a stupid fool, at a loss in [his] waywardness, abusing it
(i.e., the caliphate) with benighted senselessness. And
Sulayman, what was Sulayman?! His concern was with
his belly and his private parts. So curse them, may God
curse them! Except that 'Umar b. 'Abd al-'Aziz was from
[among] them: he had [good] intentions and did not act
[upon them]; he fell short of what he intended.

Then there took charge after him Yazid b. 'Abd al-
Malik, a sinner in whom right judgement was not perceived. God has said concerning orphans, 'Then, if you
perceive in them right judgement, deliver their property
to them,' and the affair of Muhammad's nation is of
greater moment than the property of the orphan. [Yazid]
was suspected of wickedness in respect of his belly and
his private parts. Two items of apparel were woven for

him and he wore one as a *rida'* and the other as an *izar*.
Then he sat Hababa on his right and Sallama on his left
and said, "Sing to me, Hababa; give me to drink, Sallama." Then, when he had become drunk and the wine
had taken a hold on him, he rent his two garments,
which had been acquired for one thousand dinars—
[dinars] on account of which skins had been flayed, hair
shaved off, and veils torn away; he took what he spent on
[those two garments] unlawfully and wrongfully. Then
he turned to one of [the girls] and said, "Surely I shall
fly!" Most certainly! Fly to hellfire! Is such supposed to
be the distinguishing characteristic of the caliphs of
God?!

[The last four Umayyad caliphs then come in for similar criticism.]

These Banu Umayya are parties of waywardness.
Their might is self-magnification. They arrest on suspicion, make decrees capriciously, kill in anger, and judge
by passing over crimes without punishment. They take
the alms tax from the incorrect source and make it over
to the wrong people. God has made clear the eight categories [of recipients of *sadaqat*]. Then there came a
ninth category which had no right to them. It set itself in
the midst of [those who did have a right] and said, "The
land is our land, the property is our property, and the
people are our slaves." It took all. That is the party
which decrees other than what God has sent down, and
God has said, "Who so decrees not according to what
God has sent down, they are the unbelievers, the evildo-
ers and the sinners." The[se] people have acted as unbelievers, by God, in the most barefaced manner. So curse
them, may God curse them!

# 9. The dilemma of a Muslim ruler

## Ziya' al-Din al-Barani

Ziya' al-Din ("Light of Religion") Barani (born before 1285 and died after 1357) was a historian and writer on political philosophy serving the rulers of the sultanate of Delhi. The excerpt below is from his *fatawayi Jahandari*, a work meant to instruct the young princes of the sultanate and prepare them for office (a "mirror for princes"). While this text is not from the Abbasid empire or its period, it captures the dilemma that confronted Islamic rulers. The early Abbasid caliphs (text pp. 43–46) found themselves ruling a vast empire of incredible wealth and resources, and took on many of the imperial trappings of the Persian kings who had formerly ruled from their seat of power in Iraq. Could they still maintain the rigorous moral standard attributed to Muhammad and the early caliphs? Is it possible to rule an empire without the trappings of power and the paraphernalia of rulership? Is the Islamic ruler destined to adopt un-Islamic ways? How is Barani's perspective different from that of Abu Hamza (Reading 8 above)?

The governance of men is not feasible and has not been feasible to anyone in the world without the ways of rulers and the majesty and pomp of monarchs. And that one generation when the Rightly Guided Caliphs exercised the authority of the successors of the Prophet in the world with a life of abstinence and poverty, and the world became subject to them, was only possible because the time of the Prophet Muhammad was so near and the effects of his miracles were still being felt. From Adam's

From Barani, Ziya' al-Din, "The Dilemma of the Muslim Ruler," in *Sources of Indian Tradition*, vol. 1. Ed./trans. W.D. de Bary et al. (New York: Columbia University Press, 1958). Translation modified by Michael Cook and used with permission.

day until the extinction of the world, that one generation of theirs has been and will always be considered the wonder of the generations and the rarity of the ages by the first and the last of the generations of the world. The behavior of these caliphs being in all things according to the practice (*sunna*) of the Prophet, if [later] caliphs and kings wish to follow their example they would not be able to maintain their caliphate or royal authority for a single day. Moreover, these four [the Rightly-Guided Caliphs] who did not adopt the habits and customs of sultans for fear of opposing the practice [of the Prophet] gave their lives in imitating the practices of the Prophet. 'Umar, 'Uthman, and 'Ali were martyred by fearless fanatics. Apart from them, it has not been vouchsafed, nor will it ever be, to any caliph or ruler among the caliphs or rulers of Islam to exercise power through such a way of life, and to sacrifice himself through his adherence to the way of life of the practice of the Prophet.

[...]

After them the caliphs and kings of Islam were faced by two opposed alternatives, both necessary for religion and the realm. I mean that if they followed the practices of the Prophet and his mode of life, government and kingship would be impracticable for them; claiming to be kings and yet living the life of mendicants they would not remain alive; and authority, which is the essence of government, would not be enforced among the people at all. [But] if they follow the practices of the Khusraws [the pre-Islamic Persian kings] and adopt their mode of sitting and rising, eating and dressing, and their general manner of life—the destruction of the headstrong, the subduing of the forward, and the taking of any steps necessary for the enforcement of authority among the people—it is necessary to go against the practices of the Prophet, the sum and essence of religion. In the persons and in the environment of kings no practices [of the Prophet] are admissible because prophethood is the perfection of religiosity, and kingship that of earthly bliss; these two perfections are opposed and contradictory to each other and their combination is not within the bounds of possibility. For servitude [to God] is the necessary condition of religiosity, and the necessary conditions of servitude are submission, supplication, poverty, self-abasement, abjectness, need, and humility. [On the other hand] the requisites of kingship, which is the perfection of worldly good fortune, are haughtiness, pride, aloofness from others, luxurious and soft living, lack of civility, grandeur, and might. The qualities enumerated here are among the divine attributes. Kingship is the deputyship and vice-regency of God; there can be no kingship alongside the attributes of servitude. It therefore became necessary for the caliphs and sultans of Islam to adopt the customs of the Khusraws to ensure the exaltation of the the word of truth, the ascendancy of the Muhammadan religion, the superiority of truth, the rooting out and suppression of the opponents and enemies of religion, the carrying on of the affairs of religion, and the maintenance of their own authority [...] Committing the iniquities of the Khusraws is considered among the disapproved and forbidden acts in the Muhammadan religion. [But] just as carrion, though prohibited, becomes permitted in time of dire need, [so also] adopting the customs and traditions of the sultans of the Persians—the crown and the throne, aloofness from others, pride and domination, pomposity in sitting down and getting up, building lofty palaces, keeping court, making people prostrate themselves before one, collecting treasures, misappropriating properties, managing the gifts of kings, wearing gold and jewels and silk cloth and making other people wear them, putting people to death on grounds of policy, keeping large harems [...] and whatever is a necessity of aloof status, pride, and haughtiness, such that a king is not deemed or called a king without it—[ adopting all this] should, from the viewpoint of truth and correct faith, be seen in the same way as carrion becoming permitted in cases of dire need.

[...]

So, O children [of Mahmud, the sultan of Delhi], know well that kingship is not feasible without adopting the customs and practices of the kings of the Persians; and it is known to all the scholars that the customs and practices of the sultans of the Persians are opposed to the practice of the Prophet and to his way of life.

*Al-'Arabiyya: High Arabic Language and Literature*
## 10. Jahiz on singing girls
### 'Amr ibn Bahr al-Jahiz

**Jahiz (776-869) is one of the greatest masters of Arabic literature. Born in Basra, he divided his life between his hometown and Baghdad, then at the pinnacle of its affluence. He wrote works of *belles lettres*, theology and polemics that soon came to epitomize fine Arabic prose style (text pp. 50-51). The excerpt below is from his *Epistle on Singing Girls,* a work claiming to defend the institution of singing girls (i.e., slave girls trained in music and other forms of entertainment), but displaying so much satirical irony that many consider this 'defense' to be a**

From al-Jahiz, 'Amr b. Bahr, *The Epistle on Singing Girls of Jahiz.* Trans./ed. A.F.L. Beeston (Warminster: Aris and Philips, 1980).

**veiled critique. This excerpt offers a glimpse of Abbasid court culture, as well as of Arabic secular literature (*adab*). The excerpt captures Jahiz's deep understanding of human psychology, alongside his comical sarcasm.**

The singing-girl is hardly ever sincere in her passion, or wholehearted in her affection. For both by training and by innate instinct her nature is to set up snares and traps for the victims in order that they may fall into her toils. As soon as the observer notices her, she exchanges provocative glances with him, gives him playful smiles, dallies with him in verses set to music, falls in with his suggestions, is eager to drink when he drinks, expresses her fervent desire for him to stay a long while, her yearning for his prompt return, and her sorrow at his departure. Then when she perceives that her sorcery has worked on him and that he has become entangled in the net, she redoubles the wiles she had used at first, and leads him to suppose that she is more in love than he is. Later she corresponds with him, pouring out complaints to him of infatuation for him, and swearing to him that she has filled the inkwell with tears and wetted the envelope with her kisses; that he is her sole anxiety and care in her thought and mind by night and day; that she desires no other than him, prefers nobody else to her infatuation for him, never intends to abandon him, and does not want him for his money but for himself. Then she puts the letter in a sixth of a sheet of paper, seals it with saffron, ties it up with a piece of lute string, declares it to be concealed from her guardians (in order that the deluded lover may have more confidence in her), and insists on the necessity of his replying. When she gets a reply to it, she asserts that she finds the reply her only consolation, and that she has taken it as a substitute for the sight of him in person, and quotes,

> Many a missive telling the heart's secret, charming in its melodious eloquence, has come when [my] heart has been sore because of the long time I have waited for it; I laughed when I saw it, but wept when I read it; my eyes saw unpleasing news, and the tears started up unbidden to my eye. You tyrant of my soul, my life and death are in your hands.

Then she sings to him,

> My loved one's letter is all night long my bosom companion, at times my confidant and at times my fragrant scent; the start of the missive made me laugh [with joy] , but then he made it too long and caused me to weep.

[...]

Later, she begins to find fault with him, affects to be jealous of his wife, forbids him to glance at her companions, makes him drink out of her half-emptied cup, teases him with bites of her apples or with a salute from her sweet-basil, bestows on him when he departs a lock of her hair, a piece of her robe, or a splinter from her plectrum; presents him at [the Persian holidays of] Nayruz with an embroidered belt and some sugar, at [the Persian holidays of] Mihrjan with a signet ring and an apple; engraves his name on her own signet ring; and if she happens to stumble, lets slip his name. When she sees him, she declaims,

The sight of the lover is sweet to the loved one,
his shunning her is a dread disaster for her.

Then she tells him that she cannot sleep for love of
him, and cannot bear to touch a bite of food by reason
of her yearning for him, and is never weary of weeping
for him when he is away; that she can never think of him
without agitation, or utter his name without trembling,
and has gathered a bowlful of her tears over him. When
she encounters his name, she quotes Majnun's verse,

I love every name that is the same as hers, or like
to it, or in any way resembles it.

[...]
But it sometimes happens that this pretence leads her
on to turning it into reality, and she in fact shares her
lover's torments; so that she will come to his house and
allow him a kiss, or even greater liberties, and give herself to bed, should he think fit [to accept] that from her.
Sometimes she may renounce her craft, in order for her
to be cheaper for him [to buy], and makes a show of ill-
ness and is sullen towards her guardians and asks the
owners to sell her; or she may allege that she is really a
free woman, as a trick to get herself into the lover's possession, and out of anxiety for him lest her high price
should ruin him - specially if she finds him to be sweet-
tempered, clever in expressing himself, pleasant tongued,
with a fine apprehension and delicate sensibility, and
light-hearted; while if he can compose and quote poetry
or warble a tune, that gives him all the more favour in
her eyes.

*The Arab Reception of Antiquity*
# 11. Reconciling the religious and philosophical sciences

## Abu al-Hasan al-'Amiri

**Abu al-Hasan al-'Amiri was a 10th-century philosopher who spent most of his life in Persia. His writings exhibit a blend of Aristotelianism and neo-Platonism alongside a deep investment in defending philosophy vis-à-vis the religious sciences. The excerpt below gives the reader a taste of Islamic philosophy with its penchant for systematic classification (itself part of the classical heritage in Islam). *Hadith* is catalogued with the sciences relying on sense perception since its transmission is based on hearing and speaking. The science of the religious philosophers is theology. After he discusses arithmetic, at the end of the excerpt, he goes on to examine geometry, astronomy, music and mechanics, and then concludes: "From this survey of the utility of the mathematical sciences one can gather that there is no contradiction at all between them and the religious sciences."**

Knowledge means that one grasps something as it is, without mistake and error. There is the knowledge which belongs to the religious community, and there is philosophical knowledge. The masters of the religious sciences are the recognized philosophers. Every prophet is a philosopher but not every philosopher is a prophet.

The religious sciences consist of three branches. One of them relies on sensual perceptions, namely, the science of the *hadith* scholars. The second rests on the intellect, namely the science of the religious philosophers. The third involves both sensual and intellectual percep-

From Rosenthal, Franz, *The Classical Heritage in Islam*. Trans. E. and J. Marmorstein (Berkeley: University of California Press, 1975).

tion, namely, the science of the jurists. Linguistics is an instrument serving all three branches.

The philosophical sciences also consist of three branches. One of them rests on sensual perception, namely, natural science. The second rests on the intellect, namely, metaphysics. The third involves both sensual and intellectual perception, namely, mathematics. Logic is an instrument serving all three branches.

The common people sometimes use the word 'science' for any trade whatsoever. Empiricists sometimes use it for ideas empirically acquired, for example, fortune-telling based on augury through observation of the flight of birds or based on shoulder blades and footprints.

There are sciences which philosophers consider reprehensible, and which, in their opinion, should not be taught to the masses, since they are convinced that their application is more harmful than useful. Such sciences are, for example, magic, conjuring, amulets and alchemy.

[...]

Some scholars of the *hadith* have attacked the philosophical sciences on the assumption that they contradict the religious sciences and that all those interested in the philosophical sciences and occupied with their study forfeit this world and the next. In their view, they contain only impressive words and empty phrases, varnished over with deceptive ideas, so as to deceive poor blockheads and lead astray conceited fools. That is not right. Like the religious sciences, the foundations and branches of the philosophical sciences rest on dogmas in harmony with pure reason and confirmed through fully valid proofs. One knows very well that there should be no contradiction between the demands of the true religion and what proofs confirm and reason demands. Hence, he who masters the philosophical sciences is blessed with three advantages. In the first place, he is extremely close to perfect human virtue in that he is familiar with the true reality of things and has the possibility of controlling them.

Secondly, he has insight into all that reveals the wisdom with which the Creator has created the various things in the world, and he understands their causes and results and the wonderful order and splendid arrangement they have. Thirdly, he is well versed in the arguments against traditional claims and is in no danger of soiling himself with vain dogmas through a blind belief in authority.

As we remarked, the philosophical sciences consist of three branches, namely, mathematics, natural science and metaphysics, while logic serves all of them as an instrument. Now we must mention briefly the good points of each of these four branches and then devote ourselves to the various kinds of religious sciences.

Mathematics has five branches, namely, arithmetic, geometry, astronomy, music and mechanics.

Exercise and skill in arithmetic are a source of the profoundest joy to human reason. An intelligent person who studies the peculiarities of its parts by themselves and in conjunction with one another can never enjoy them enough and is convinced that the value and importance of arithmetic constitute an inexhaustible wonder. Besides, it is free from contradictions and doubts. Furthermore, one appeals to it as an arbitrator in matters of commerce. God has said [Quran 19:94]: "We have counted and calculated them," and [Qur'an 72:28]: "He has counted everything."

# READINGS FOR CHAPTER 3
# THE ARAB WORLD
# FROM 900 TO 1500 CE

*Iraq*
## 12. Whom to hire to run one's affairs

### Nizam al-Mulk

The Seljuq vizier Nizam al-Mulk (text p. 81), who was of
Iranian descent, did much to institutionalize religious learning,
changing the way in which religious knowledge interacted with
political power in the Arabic-speaking lands. He was the first to
establish and support *madrasa*s—colleges of religious law and
theology—west of Iran. It seems that he meant the *madrasa* to
give proper training to religious scholars, who could then staff
the state bureaucracy. In earlier polities of the Arab world, military leaders had not been so involved in the production of a
learned administrative elite. This innovation brought the educated spokesmen of Islam into a closer relationship with political
power than ever before. In this passage, found in a book of
advice for rulers, Nizam al-Mulk urges the ruler to maintain a
religiously "orthodox" retinue. His statements about the good
old days, when only right-thinking men were appointed to office,
represent a pointedly idealized view of the past. Qarmati,
Batini, and Rafidi are words used for Shi'is of different kinds,
Hanafi and Shafi'i are Sunni legal schools, Khurasan is Nizam
al-Mulk's birthplace in eastern Iran, and the Dailamites of the
final paragraph are the predecessors of the Seljuqs (the Buyids
or Buwayhids, text p. 80). Note that Nizam al-Mulk advocates
that civil servants be like the ruler not only in religion, but in
regional origin as well.

From Nizam al-Mulk, *The Book of Government or Rules for Kings*. Trans. H. Darke
(London: Routledge and K. Paul, 1960). Copyright © 1960, Taylor & Francis Books.
Reproduced by permission of Taylor & Francis Books UK.

[I]n all previous ages a public appointment was given to a man who was pure alike in religion and in origin; and if he was averse and refused to accept it, they used compulsion and force to make him take the responsibility. So naturally the revenue was not misappropriated, the peasants were unmolested, assignees enjoyed a good reputation and a safe existence, while the king lived a life of mental and bodily ease and tranquility. But nowadays all distinction has vanished; and if a Jew administers the affairs of Turks or does any other work for Turks, it is permitted; and it is the same for Christians, Zoroastrians and Qarmatis. Everywhere indifference is predominant; there is no zeal for religion, no concern for the revenue, no pity for the peasants. The dynasty has reached its perfection; your humble servant is afraid of the evil eye and knows not where this state of affairs will lead.

In the days of Mahmud, Mas'ud, Tughril and Alp Arslan (may Allah have mercy on them) no Zoroastrian or Jew or Rafidi would have had the audacity to appear in a public place or to present himself before a great man. Those who administered the affairs of the Turks were all professional civil servants and secretaries from Khurasan, who belonged to the orthodox Hanafi or Shafi'i sects. The heretics of Iraq were never admitted as secretaries and tax-collectors; in fact the Turks never used to employ them at all; they said, "These men are of the same religion as the Dailamites and their supporters; if they get a firm footing they will injure the interests of the Turks and cause distress to the Muslims. It is better that enemies should not be in our midst." Consequently they lived free from disaster. Now things have reached such a state that the court and the divan are full of them, and every Turk has ten or twenty of these individuals running after him, and their object is to prevent even a few Khurasanis from entering the service of this court and earning a living here. One day the Turks will realize the iniquity of these people and recall my words, when the divan becomes empty of Khurasani secretaries and officials.

[...]

One day it was reported to the Martyr Sultan Alp Arslan (may Allah sanctify his soul) that Ardam was going to appoint a certain village headman as his secretary. He was enraged to hear it, because the headman was known to be of the Batini sect. He spoke to Ardam in the audience-hall and said, "Are you my enemy and the foe of the state?" When Ardam heard this, he fell on the ground and said, "O Master, what is this you say? I am the least of your slaves; what fault have I committed in service and loyalty to my lord?" The sultan said, "If you are not my enemy why have you taken my enemy into service?" Ardam said, "Who is that?" He said, "The headman of Aba who is your secretary." He said, "What in the world is wrong with him? and even if he turned into a venomous [serpent] what could he do to this empire?" He said, "Go and bring this man here." He was brought in immediately. The sultan said, "Thou wretch, thou sayest that the caliph of Baghdad is not the lawful caliph; thou art a Rafidi." The wretched man said, "O Master, your slave is not a Rafidi; I am a Shi'ite." The sultan said, "O cuckold, what is so good about the Shi'a that you give it precedence over the Batini sect? The one is bad; the other is worse." He commanded the mace-bearers to beat the man, and they threw him half dead out of the palace.

Then the sultan turned to the nobles and said, "It was not this wretched man's fault; it was Ardam's fault for taking an infidel into his service. I have often said that in this country we are foreigners; we conquered this country by force; we are all orthodox Muslims and these Iraqis are heretics, and partisans of the house of Dailam. Today God (be He exalted) has favoured the Turks because they are orthodox Muslims and do not tolerate vanity and heresy.' He then asked for some horse hair; he gave one hair to Ardam and said, "Break it." Ardam broke it. Then he gave him ten hairs and he broke them. But when he twisted many hairs together and said, "Break these," Ardam could not do so. The sultan said, "So it is with enemies; in ones and twos they can be broken but when they become numerous it is impossible. This is the answer to your question, 'What power does this wretched fellow possess and what can he do to the state?' If they infiltrate one by one amongst the Turks, and are allowed to administer their business and get to know about their affairs, then the very moment that revolt breaks out in Iraq, or if the Dailamites attack this country, all these people will secretly and openly make common cause with them and seek to destroy the Turks. You are a Turk, and an officer of the Khurasan army; your administrators, secretaries and officials should all be Khurasanis; and the same should apply to all the Turks, if their interests are not to be damaged. When you make an alliance with your enemy, it is a treason committed against your person and against the king."

*Iraq*
# 13. From the autobiography of 'Abd al-Latif al-Baghdadi

## 'Abd al-Latif al-Baghdadi

**'Abd al-Latif al-Baghdadi (1162-1231) was an important scholar and scientist, who excelled at philosophy and medicine. The excerpt below is taken from his entry in Ibn Abi Usaybi'a's important biographical dictionary of physicians, which quotes an autobiographical text written by 'Abd al-Latif al-Baghdadi himself, alongside Ibn Abi Usaybi'a's comments and additions (after all, 'Abd al-Latif was a friend of Ibn Abi Usaybi'a's grandfather, and a teacher of his father and his uncle). The excerpt provides a glimpse of how medieval Islamic education was conducted, and what people read and studied. Notice how education relied on personal contact between the student and the teacher, and the great role played by memorization. The Nizamiyya law college is the *madrasa* established by Nizam al-Mulk (text p. 81, introduction to Reading 12).**

I was born in 557 [1162 CE] in a house that belonged to my grandfather on Faludhaj Lane, and was raised and instructed under the care of Shaykh Abu al-Najib. I knew neither pleasure nor leisure, and spent most of my time learning *hadith*. Certificates of *hadith* audition were obtained for me from professors in Baghdad, Khurasan, Syria, and Egypt. One day my father [proudly] declared: "I have given you the opportunity to learn *hadith* directly from the top scholars of Baghdad and I have even had you included in the chains of transmission of the older Masters." I was learning calligraphic writing at that time

From Reynolds, Dwight, Kristen Brustad et al., *Interpreting the Self: Autobiography in the Arabic Literary Tradition* (Berkeley: University of California Press, 2001).

and also memorizing the Quran, the *Fasih* [a treatise on Arabic linguistics by Tha'lab, d. 904], the *Maqamat* [picaresque tales by al-Hariri, d. 1122], the collected poems of al-Mutanabbi, an epitome on jurisprudence, another on grammar, and other works of this kind.

When I was old enough, my father took me to Kamal al-Din 'Abd al-Rahman al-Anbari, who was, in those days, the Master of Masters in Baghdad. He was an old classmate of my father's from their days at the Nizamiyya law college, where they had studied law together. It was under his direction that I was to study the introduction to the *Fasih*, but I couldn't understand one bit of his continuous and considerable jabbering, even though his students seem pleased enough with it. So he said, "I avoid teaching younger boys and instead pass them on to my protege al-Wajih al-Wasiti to study under his direction. If and when their situation improves, I then allow them to study with me."

Al-Wajih, a blind man from a wealthy and virtuous family, was employed by some of the children of the Chief Master. He welcomed me with open arms and taught me all day long, showing me kindness in many ways. I attended his study circle at the Zafariyya mosque, and he would teach me the commentaries and discuss them with me. Then he would read my lesson and favor me with his own comments. We would then leave the mosque and he would even help me memorize on the road home. When we reached his house, he would take out the books he himself was studying and I would memorize with him and help him memorize as well. We would then go to Kamal al-Din, to whom he would recite and who would then comment on the lesson, while

I listened. I trained in this way until I surpassed al-Wajih
in both memorization and comprehension, for I used to
spend most of the night memorizing and reviewing. We
continued in this way for a long time, with me affiliated
to both the Master and the Master's Master. My memorizing got better, my recall improved, my understanding
grew, my insights became more acute, and my mind
became keener and more reliable.

[...]

In the year 585AH [1189AD], when there no longer
remained in Baghdad anyone to win my heart or to sat-
isfy my desires, or to help me resolve what was perplex-
ing me, I went on to Mosul. I was disappointed there,
but I did chance upon al-Kamal Ibn Yunus, who was an
expert in mathematics and law, but only partially learned
in the remaining fields of science. His love of alchemy
and its practice had so drowned his intellect and his time
that he dismissed and disdained everything else.

[ ... ]

In Damascus I again came across Professor 'Abd
Allah Ibn Na'ili who had taken up residence at the western minaret. Gathered round him was a group of followers obsessed with him. People were divided into two
camps, one for him and one against. Al-Khatib al-
Dawla'i, a notable of standing and principle, was against
him. It was not long, however, before Ibn Na'ili had himself in quite a mess, at which time his enemies prevailed.
He would lecture defending alchemy and philosophy,
and talk against him soon increased. I used to get
together with him and he would ask me to describe certain procedures so that he could record them, procedures
I thought contemptible and trivial, but to which he

attached great importance and to which he gave himself over completely. I saw through him, though. He was not at all what I had expected. I was thoroughly unimpressed by him and his methods. When I debated science with him, I found that he only had scraps of knowledge. One day I said to him, "If you had devoted the time you have wasted in the pursuit of the Craft [i.e. alchemy] to some of the Islamic or rational sciences, you would today be without equal, waited on hand and foot. This alchemy nonsense simply does not have the answers you seek." I learned from his example and kept my distance from the evils of what befell him: "Contented is he who learns from others." So I pulled myself away, but not entirely. He set off to see Saladin on the outskirts of Acre to complain about al-Dawla'i. He returned sick and was taken to hospital, where he then died. Al-Mu'tamid, [Saladin's] marshal of Damascus, who was himself infatuated with alchemy, confiscated his books.

*Syria/Palestine*
# 14. Those boorish Franks
## Usama ibn Munqidh

The Crusades (text pp. 84-90), despite occasionally shocking violence, did see periods of more-or-less cordial human interaction between northern European Christians and the Muslims of the Levant. The most famous Arab chronicler of these exchanges was undoubtedly Usama b. Munqidh (1095-1188). A poet, warrior, and companion of various local potentates, he

From Usama ibn Munqidh, *The Book of Contemplation*. Trans. P. Cobb (London; New York: Penguin Books, 2008).

made several trips to the Franks as a diplomat, and even made
friends among them, as this short excerpt from his "Book of
instruction by example" (*Kitab al-i'tibar*) reveals. What can you
gather about the scope for interreligious interaction in the
Levant of this time as compared to Western Europe? What
effect do the Crusades seem to have had on the outlooks of the
various parties they embroiled?

Anyone who is recently arrived from the Frankish
lands is rougher in character than those who have
become acclimated and have frequented the company of
Muslims. Here is an instance of their rough character
(may God abominate them!):

Whenever I went to visit the holy sites in Jerusalem, I
would go in and make my way up to the al-Aqsa
Mosque, beside which stood a small mosque that the
Franks had converted into a church. When I went into
the al-Aqsa Mosque—where the Templars, who are my
friends, were—they would clear out that little mosque so
that I could pray in it. One day, I went into the little
mosque, recited the opening formula 'God is great!' and
stood up in prayer. At this, one of the Franks rushed at
me and grabbed me and turned my face towards the east,
saying, "Pray like this!" A group of Templars hurried
towards him, took hold of the Frank and took him away
from me. I then returned to my prayers. The Frank, that
very same one, took advantage of their inattention and
returned, rushing upon me and turning my face to the
east, saying, "Pray like this!"

So the Templars came in again, grabbed him and
threw him out. They apologized to me, saying, "This
man is a stranger, just arrived from the Frankish lands
sometime in the past few days. He has never before seen

anyone who did not pray towards the east."

"I think I've prayed quite enough," I said and left. I used to marvel at that devil, the change of his expression, the way he trembled and what he must have made of seeing someone praying towards Mecca.

*Egypt*
## 15. Hard times on the Nile

### Ahmad ibn 'Ali al-Maqrizi

**Like medieval Europe, the Arab lands of the pre-modern period were subject to occasional outbreaks of plague, as well as economic catastrophe. Egypt stood at particular risk, since a year in which the life-bringing Nile flood failed to reach a certain level would always be followed by a year of scarcity. This natural challenge could be compounded by mismanagement on the part of rulers, who were often inattentive to the populace and its quotidian concerns. In the passage that follows, a famous historian of the Mamluk period, al-Maqrizi (1363-1442) describes the plight of Egyptians of various classes during an economic crisis. This crisis is, according to him, man-made, the result of avaricious currency manipulation and heavy taxation by the Mamluk rulers (text p. 91). The *ajnad al-halqah* are free-born soldiers, as distinct from the *mamluk* slave soldiers. The *dirham* is (in theory) a silver coin, though it is clear from this text that this coin had been devalued in recent years to approximately one fifth of its former value.**

Know—may God guard you with His sleepless eye and His fearsome might—that the population of Egypt is divided on the whole into seven categories. This first

From al-Maqrizi, Ahmad b. 'Ali, *Mamluk Economics*. Trans. A. Allouche (Salt Lake City: University of Utah Press, 1994).

category embraces those who hold the reins of power. The second [is formed of] the rich merchants and the wealthy who lead a life of affluence. The third [encompasses] the retailers, who are merchants of average means, as are the cloth merchants. This also includes the small shopkeepers. The fourth category embraces the peasants, those who cultivate and plow the land. These are the inhabitants of the villages and of the countryside. The fifth category is made up of those who receive a stipend, and includes most legists, students of theology, and most of the *ajnad al-halqah* and the like. The sixth category [corresponds to] the artisans and the salaried persons who possess a skill. The seventh category [consists of] the needy and the paupers; and these are the beggars who live off the [charities of] others. As for [members of the] first category, those who hold the reins of power, their situation during these ordeals is as they wished it to be. To those who lack any sense of observation and have no knowledge of the conditions of existence, [we say] that the members of this category receive more than they did before these ordeals. This is clear when we consider their revenues from land taxes: for instance, a parcel that was taxed 20,000 [silver] *dirham*s before these events is now taxed 100,000 *dirham*s [of account]. It is incorrect to assume that they are wealthier than before, for their wealth has decreased if compared with the wealth of their peers [who lived] before [these ordeals]. This becomes clear when [we realize] that anyone who possessed 20,000 *dirham*s in the past was able to spend whatever he desired or chose, then save whatever amount God permitted, because these were [silver] *dirham*s and were equivalent to 1,000 *mithqal*s of gold or an approximate amount [at the rate of 20 silver *dirham*s per *mithqal*]. As for now, he receives 100,000 *dirham*s [of account], valued at 666 *mithqal*s of gold [at the rate of 5 *dirham*s of account per silver *dirham* and of 150 *dirham*s of account per *mithqal*], that he spends on his daily needs for meat, vegetables, spices, oil, and the like, as well as on the essential clothing for himself and his family, and on his needs for horses, armor, and the like. Before these ordeals, he used to purchase all these items for [only] 10,000 silver *dirham*s or a similar amount. If all people, high and low, were affected— although not in an equal fashion—by the difference between current prices and those that had existed before these ordeals, we would have mentioned it. We must touch briefly upon this matter [later on], God willing. If those holding the reins of power were sincere and inspired with rectitude, they would have realized that they were reaping no benefit at all, neither from the increase of the land [taxes] nor from the increase in the rate of gold that is the origin of this distress and the cause of these ordeals. On the contrary, they are incurring a loss. This situation is the result of deceit on the part of their subordinates who have been seeking to obtain whatever they wish. "But the plotting of evil will hem in only the authors thereof" [Qur'an 35:43].

[...]

The [members of the] third category, i.e., the cloth merchants and the small shopkeepers, are living off whatever profit they can make during these ordeals. They content themselves only with larger profits, even though a few hours later in the same day they will spend the amount they have gained on necessities. Indeed, they will be lucky if they do not have to go into debt for the rest of their needs.

[...]

As for [the members of] the fourth category, those who cultivate and plow the land, most of them have perished as a result of the calamities of the years that we have mentioned and the successive ordeals caused by the lack of irrigation of the lands. However, a number of them have become wealthy, namely, those persons whose lands were irrigated during the years of drought. From cultivating them, they gained large sums of money with which they have been able to support themselves [during] these times. Some of them have accumulated extensive wealth and enjoyed a life of great affluence. They exceeded their goals and surpassed their expectations: "It is God who gave you want or plenty, and to him shall be your return" [Qur'an 2:245].

In the fifth category are the majority of legists and students of theology, legal witnesses, most of *ajnad al-halqah*, and those of similar situation who receive a landed property or a stipend from the sultan or from another source: these are either dead or wishing death because of the calamity that has befallen them.

[...]

The sixth category includes those who possess a skill, salaried persons, porters, servants, stablemen, weavers, masons, unskilled construction workers, and the like. Their wages have increased many-fold. Of this category, only a few have remained, since most have died. Thus, one finds them only after a long search and with great difficulty. "With God rests the end and decision of all affairs" [Qur'an 22:41].

The seventh category comprises the needy and the poor. Most of them have perished of hunger and cold, so that only a minimal fraction of them remains: "He cannot be questioned for His acts, but they will be questioned for theirs" [Qur'an 21:23].

*Egypt*
# 16. Problems of married life
## Ja'far ibn Ahmad

**The medieval Islamic world was a cosmopolitan one, in which people, objects and ideas crossed political and religious boundaries with relative ease. One of the consequences of this cosmopolitanism was the frequent absence of men from their families for long periods of time. Merchants, scholars and people seeking to improve their fortunes travelled away from their families, sometimes staying away for many years at a time or disappearing altogether. These absences brought about a whole range of problems for those who stayed behind. The text below is a 9th century letter written by an Egyptian textile merchant and notary called Ja'far ibn Ahmad to his father. Together with all sorts of business matters, he passes along the complaint of his father's wife Sayyida regarding his prolonged absence. It seems that the husband was staying with one of his other wives and was tarrying in returning. The survival of such a document on the private affairs of a merchant and his wives is very rare and offers a precious glimpse into the everyday life of people who did not make it into the literary historical record. It is especially valuable for preserving the voice of a woman having to deal with the problems brought about by distance and polygamy. The letter**

From Ragib, Yusuf, *Marchands d'étoffes du Fayyoum au IIIe/IXe siècle d'après leurs archives (actes et lettres); II. La correspondance administrative et privée des Banū 'Abd al-Mu'min* (Cairo: Institut français d'archéologie orientale; Paris: Diffusion SEVPO, 1985). Translated by O. Zinger, from the Arabic.

**was written on papyrus and was subsequently torn into two
pieces. Preserved in the dry soil of Egypt for more than a thousand years, parts of the texts are damaged, but the gist is clear
enough. The letter begins with standard pious epistolary formu-
las. Fustat is the capital city built by the Arabs after the Islamic
conquests in Egypt. The reference to "intimacy" refers to the
wife's right to sexual relations with her husband. Notice that the
wife employs a wide range of tactics to pressure her husband to
return; what is the logic behind each of these tactics?**

In the Name of God, the Merciful, the Compassionate.

May God honor you with obedience, strengthen you
with piety, shower you in his mercy with His favor and
gather for you the benefits of this world and the hereafter, for He is all-powerful. [This is] my letter to you,
may God prolong your life. I and those around me [i.e.
the members of his household] are in health and well
being, praise be to God, who has no partner. Your letter
reached me and [the news] of your well being made me
happy. I have praised God greatly for this, and I have
requested His great blessings and abundance of favors
for you, for He is all powerful. I understood what you
mentioned [in your letter], may God prolong your [life],
regarding the matter of Abu al-Asbagh, but he does not
reside in Fustat [In the next few lines he discusses several business matters, unclear due to the preservation of
the papyrus.].

Hamduna informed me that Sayyida has said: "You
left me on the condition that you will be away from me
but a month, and this month it has already been two
months. Were I by myself, without a child, I would not
care about your absence. Had I known that you planned

to spend the Holiday of Sacrifice away from me, I would not have let you leave in peace when you left me in Ramadan. For I allowed you to celebrate Ramadan with them, so that you would celebrate the holiday of sacrifice with me. [Instead,] you have abandoned us like poor people in Ramadan and you also want to leave us on the Holiday of Sacrifice like poor people. And you know that I do not ask you for maintenance or for anything in the world, but I am reprimanding you for my intimacy with you. And regarding your wish to buy [manuscript is unclear], by God, I do not want it! And I do not want to celebrate the Holiday of Sacrifice while you are absent from me. It is enough what I am suffering with my child [....a few unclear sentences follow]. Know that if you do not come to us as you are [unclear] I will also go up to my mother and stay with them for you know that I cannot stand to be by myself [...]

To Abu Ja'far ibn 'Abd al-Mu'min, May God honor him with obedience

From Ja'far ibn Ahmad.

*The Maghreb and al-Andalus*
# 17. Latin and Arabic in al-Andalus
## Alvarus of Cordoba

**Alvarus of Cordoba was one of the prominent leaders of the 9th-century Christian "martyrs movement" that struggled (nonviolently) against Islamic rule in Spain. In this extract, he laments the adoption of Arabic culture by the Christians of his age. Why**

From Menocal, Maria Rosa, *The Ornament of the World* (Boston: Little, Brown, 2002).

**did the Christians adopt Arabic culture with such enthusiasm? According to this text, how would you characterize the relationship between the two religious communities? Can one make a distinction between 'Arabic culture' and 'Islamic culture'? Is such a distinction helpful?**

The Christians love to read the poems and romances of the Arabs; they study the Arab theologians and philosophers, not to refute them but to form a correct and elegant Arabic. Where is the layman who now reads the Latin commentaries on the Holy Scriptures, or who studies the Gospels, prophets or apostles? Alas! All talented young Christians read and study with enthusiasm the Arab books; they gather immense libraries at great expense; they despise the Christian literature as unworthy of attention. They have forgotten their own language. For every one who can write a letter in Latin to a friend, there are a thousand who can express themselves in Arabic with elegance, and write better poems in this language than the Arabs themselves.

*The Maghreb and al-Andalus*

# 18. Andalusi poems on forbidden love and the fall of Granada

**anonymous**

**Arab rule on the the Iberian Peninsula witnessed every imaginable kind of interaction among Muslims, Christians, and Jews. These two poetic excerpts give a sense of the contrasting forms**

From Smith, Colin, ed., *Christians and Moors in Spain*, vol. 3. Ed./trans. C. Melville and A. Ubaydi (London: Aris and Philips, 1992).

that this interaction could take. The first poem, from the later 11th century CE, expresses a Muslim's unrequited erotic longing for a certain Christian girl, and is interwoven with scenes of Christian worship. Similar themes were explored by poets in Iraq at a slightly earlier period. Note that the *qibla* is the direction of Mecca, which Muslims are to face in prayer; 'Amir is the Arab tribe to which belonged the legendary Arab lover Majnun, who endlessly pursued his beloved Layla; an *arta* is a tree that grows in sandy soil, and produces bitter fruit; Nuwaira means "little light," and is the name the speaker has bestowed on the object of his desires. This poem comes from the period of the "party kingdoms" that arose following the fall of the Umayyad Caliphate of Cordoba (text p. 94), and which presided over a flowering of arts and culture. The second poem strikes a note of profound lament at the fall of Granada and other towns during the *reconquista* ("re-conqest") undertaken by Christian kings, and which culminated in 1492, around which time this poem was written (text p. 98). To what does the poet attribute the Muslims' defeat? How does this explanation condition his description of events? Note that "the two noble Iraqs" is a common way of referring to Iraq; the *minbar* is the elevated seat upon which the imam sits while delivering the Friday sermon.

My heart is at the place of the tamarisk trees, a hostage to desires and alarms,

So turn towards them, they are the *qibla* of my desires, even though they treat me badly.

Take a rest from the winding sands in the folds of the mountains covered in blooms,

Stop, you two young men of 'Amir, at the place where the Christian girls are.

I have a girl among the Christians, who bolts like a shy gazelle round the churches.

I am in raptures over her; but passion among the cloisters and the churches is a sin.

In relation to the gazelles of the desert, who would not

prefer the gazelles who live in towns?

I alone celebrate on their Easter Day, among the lofty trees and the *artas*;

They had come from there to a rendezvous, and congregated there at the appointed time,

To stand before a bishop holding a lantern and a staff,

And many priests displaying piety, with signs of ostentatious quietness and humility before God,

His eyes wandering over theirs like a wolf who longs to devour the ewes.

What man could be safe from passion when he had seen these gazelles?

And from moon-like cheeks set above willowy figures?

They recited the scriptures of their Gospels, with beautiful voices and intonations,

Increasing their gazelles' shunning of me, and [raising] the pressure of my passions.

The [only] sun is the sun of beauty, [shining] among them beneath the clouds of [her] veils;

My gaze snatches hers, and her glance kindles my torments.

My insides blaze with the fire of Nuwaira, by whom I have been captivated since my youngest years,

[The fire] has not gone out for a moment, though how often have I wished it; rather, it blazes ever more fiercely.

Wish the gazelle at the bend in the valley a long life, from me, even if it refuses to return my greetings.


[... Halt at] the seat of kingship, Granada, the exalted capital, whose flowers bedeck her;

There is nothing like her in the two noble Iraqs, nothing at all similar in all God's lands.

Sadness contemplates her landmarks, which are cast down; her *minbar* and her throne shed tears.

Both the imam and those who are guided have become deranged; both those who visit her and those who are visited are attending a funeral.

What a situation for one whose souls have been stricken, whose right hand has been cut off and whose destruction has been decreed.

Her spirits are thunderstruck, beyond recovery; like the spirit of Moses when Mount Sinai was flattened.

These buildings [i.e., castles] all around her have been terrified [by bombardments], and her bleary-eyed walls are weeping.

Wadi al-Ash (Guadix) has been shaken and her territories are drunken, though she has not even rinsed her teeth with wine;

She has been plunged in such darkness that, because of her excessive mourning, those with eyes wide open can see no better than the blind [lit: one-eyed].

Baza (Basta) the joyous has not worked out what has befallen her; how could her perceptions be working properly

After the magnitude of her misfortunes and the long duration of the mischief done there, and the disasters that her bosoms have endured?

Whatever I forget, I will not forget Almeria, the victim of terrors it would be despicable to excuse;

If bereavement burnt up those who had suffered, [even] the waves [of her harbour] would have been ignited by the heat of the commotion.

My friends, say farewell to her as a noble place, or else entrust her to whomever her affairs [will] belong to [i.e., God].

We have neglected the rights of the Lord so he has allowed us to perish, all but a few of the bonds of Islam have been broken.

Our [Muslim] community has never distinguished what it is right to do from what is forbidden; see how this disapproval is now [turned on us].

We have obtained what [God] has given us through what we have deserved; such is the evil life for those who lead it.

In our misery, splitting up [disunity] accompanies our unity; we have been brought to circumstances that are blameworthy.

Our enemy has gained power over us because of our sinfulness; the lions and leopards of the enemy have wreaked havoc on us.

Yes, they have pillaged our homelands, our lives and our possessions; its abundance has been allowed [them] as legitimate spoils;

They have seized [ravished] her [Andalusia] without providing a brideprice; no spears have been watered [whetted] for them, nor have her menfolk fought them for her;

The Franks have howled down at us from every hilltop and their vows to the Cross have been completely achieved.

# READINGS FOR CHAPTER 4
# THE ARAB WORLD
# FROM 1500 TO 1800 CE

*The Fertile Crescent under Ottoman Rule*

## 19. A British traveler on Arabs and Turks in the Syrian desert

### William Beawes

A little-known merchant called William Beawes made the journey between Aleppo, Syria and Basra, Iraq in 1745. He was among the first of his countrymen to take this desert short-cut to Britain's newly acquired territories in India. Although Beawes was no expert on the Middle East or its peoples, the unjaundiced freshness of his account makes it a valuable record of travel through this thinly populated region in the 18th century. In this passage, he comments upon the state of intra-Arab and Arab-Turk relations as he saw them, and on his own impression of the Arabs he encountered. How does the political potential of the Arabs compare to their actual condition, according to Beawes? What can you gather about British stereotypes of Arabs in his day? How did his experience square with these? It is worth remembering that Beawes' remarks predate the rise of Arab nationalism by nearly a century.

The greatest unhappiness of the Arabians immediately under the Ottoman tyranny is their disagreement amongst themselves; for were they united, such union would not only secure them from the insults of the Turks (with whom some or other are continually at variance),

From Carruthers, Douglas, ed., *The Desert Route to India* (London: Printed for the Hakluyt Society, 1929).

but render them a powerful people, and having the
desert for a retreat might cultivate the borders, and vend
their camels, cattle, etc., exempt from the extortion and
impositions they are now continually exposed to; for
should any force be then too hard for them, their retreat
might defy the Turks following them, and when safe, to
come back might convince their enemies, by ravaging in
turn, that to be aggressors was neither politick nor prof-
itable; whereas at present the Turks have not only
reduced the wretches within their reach to the utmost
misery, but constantly play the different tribes and petty
bodies one against another to their utter destruction,
who are nevertheless so infatuated as to be at continual
variance amongst themselves, perpetually plundering
and harassing one another, and even value themselves
alternately upon the common enemy to dispose and constitute a sheikh or ruler, whenever the discontented parties have not sufficient strength of their own.

But concerning this matter, I shall not presume to
add. The Arabian politician is burlesque distinction [sic],
I should unwillingly incur, nor am more desirous that the
few particulars I have mentioned of the Arabs should be
deemed an attempt to draw the character of a people
from a month's acquaintance, being sensible that such is
ridiculous, and that men of infinitely superior discern-
ment and experience have long since described the Arabs
at large. But as by some means [sic] those descriptions
where almost every inhumanity is laid to their charge, a
traveller may to his disadvantage be deterred from passing the desert, or executes the journey with unnecessary
suspicions and consequently uneasiness, I have thought
it not amiss to declare the foregoing, and in gratitude to

witness that, however barbarous the real character of these people may be or have been discovered from better occasions of knowing them, a man may travel a great way in their company without one instance to confirm it.

*The Arabian Peninsula*
# 20. Principles of Wahhabism
## Muhammad ibn 'Abd al-Wahhab

**Although Muhammad ibn 'Abd al-Wahhab (text pp. 109-10) espoused a pristine, radical, and militant monotheism that matched his idea of the Prophet's original Islam, his reform program was in fact rather novel in his own context. The passage below gives a sense of his program, in four principles, and of the attitudes and practices he opposed. These practices, which included belief in the intercession of saints and visiting their graves, he likes to call "polytheism" (*shirk*), or "ascribing partners to God." This is a catch-all category whose function is perhaps best compared to that of "heresy" in Christianity. Ibn 'Abd al-Wahhab referred to the "polytheists" (*mushrikun*) of the Prophet's time to show that many of his contemporaries, though they called themselves Muslims, were even further from authentic Islam than non-Muslim contemporaries of the Prophet. For the sake of brevity, the Qur'anic passages that he quotes to support his position have been removed. Although it is not stated explicitly here, can you infer Ibn 'Abd al-Wahhab's view of people who claimed to be Muslims but engaged in *shirk*? Note that "Hanifism" is widely understood is a synonym for Islam.**

You should know, may God guide you to His obedience, that Hanifism, the religion of Abraham, is that you should worship God exclusively. This is what God has

From a translation by Michael Cook, from the Arabic. Used with permission.

enjoined on all people, and for this He created them ...
Once you know that God created you to worship Him,
you should know that worship does not deserve the
name unless conjoined with belief in [God's] unity, just
as prayer does not deserve the name unless conjoined
with ritual purity. When polytheism intrudes into it, it is
voided, just as when a cause of ritual impurity intrudes
into prayer ... Once you know that when polytheism
mixes with worship it voids it, renders the action futile,
and places the agent eternally in hell, then you realise
that your most important duty is to know this. Perhaps
God will save you from [getting caught in] this net of
ascribing partners to God, and this through knowledge
of four principles that God has stated in His Book.

The first is that you should know that the unbelievers
whom the Messenger of God fought affirmed [their
belief] that God is the creator and the sustainer, the giver
of life and death, the one who benefits and harms [peo-
ple], and who controls everything; and [yet] this did not
[suffice to] include them in Islam [...].

The second principle is that they [used to] say: We do
not turn to them [beings other than God] and call upon
them except in seeking closeness [to God] and intercession [with Him]; we want [these things] from Him, not
from them, but through their intercession and getting
close to them [...].

The third principle is that the Prophet came to know
of people who worshipped a variety of things—some
worshipped the sun and moon, some worshipped saints,
some worshipped angels, some worshipped prophets,
some worshipped trees and stones—and [yet] he fought
them [all] and made no distinction between them [...].

The fourth principle is that the polytheists of our own time are further gone in polytheism than the original ones [of the time of the Prophet]. For the original ones used to worship God exclusively when in danger, but worshipped others as well when safe, whereas the polytheism of the polytheists of our own time is continual, in both danger and safety.

*The Arabian Peninsula; Egypt*

# 21. The advent of coffee and coffee-drinkers

### 'Abd al-Qadir al-Jaziri, anonymous

**Coffee first spread in the Middle East around the 15th century, and by the 16th century it was at the center of an interesting controversy. As the two texts below suggest, coffee was first used by Sufis as a stimulant to aid them in their night vigils. Later, its use spread and coffee houses appeared in all the major cities. Coffee was suspect because it was an innovation (after all, Muhammad did not drink coffee) and because as a stimulant it was feared that it could change the drinker's state of mind during prayer (like the effect of alcohol, which is forbidden in Islam). The first text (by 'Abd al-Qadir al-Jaziri on the authority of Shihab al-Din ibn 'Abd al-Ghaffar) shows how important it was to ascertain who were the first to introduce and use coffee, because if coffee was first employed by pious Sufis and well-known scholars, then its use could be permitted. The second text (by a 16th century Turkish traveler in Cairo) shows a very different aspect of the coffee phenomenon: the coffee house. As a welcoming social space, the coffee house could potentially rival the mosque and serve as a place of gathering for suspect social**

From Hattox, Ralph, *Coffee and Coffeehouses: The Origins of a Social Beverage in the Medieval Near East* (Seattle: University of Washington Press, 1988).

**elements. Seen from this angle, one can understand the great coffee controversy in a very different light.**

At the beginning of this [the sixteenth] century, the news reached us in Egypt that a drink, called *qahwa*, had spread in the Yemen and was being used by Sufi shaykhs and others to help them stay awake during their devotional exercises, which they perform according to their well known way. Then it reached us, some time later, that its appearance and spread there had been due to the efforts of the learned shaykh, imam, mufti, and Sufi Jamal al-Din Abu ʿAbd Allah Muhammad ibn Saʿid, known as al-Dhabhani ... We heard that he had been in charge of the critical review of *fatwa*s in Aden, which at that time was a job whose holder decided whether *fatwa*s were sound or in need of revision, which he would indicate at the bottom of the document in his own hand. The reason for his introducing coffee, according to what we heard, was that some affair had forced him to leave Aden and go to Ethiopia, where he stayed for some time. [There] he found the people using *qahwa*, though he knew nothing of its characteristics. After he had returned to Aden he fell ill, and remembering [*qahwa*], he drank it and benefited by it. He found that among its properties was that it drove away fatigue and lethargy, and brought to the body a certain sprightliness and vigor. In consequence, when he became a Sufi, he and other Sufis in Aden began to use the beverage made from it, as we have said. Then the whole people - both the learned and the common - followed [his example] in drinking it, seeking help in study and other vocations and crafts, so that it continued to spread.

[When we heard all this,] I wrote to one of our brothers in God, one of the people of learning and religion in Zabid [a town in the Yemen], the jurist Jamal al-Din Abu 'Abd Allah Muhammad ibn 'Abd al-Ghaffar Ba-'Alawi ... asking that he inform me of which of the people of learning and faith, people whose opinions are respected, drank it, and of its first appearance .... He answered: "I asked a group of elders in our country [about the appearance of coffee], the oldest of whom at present is my uncle, the jurist Wajih al-Din 'Abd al-Rahman ibn Ibrahim al-Alawi—a man over ninety—and he told me ... 'I was at the town of Aden, and there came to us some poor Sufi, who was making and drinking coffee, and who made it as well for the learned jurist Muhammad Ba-Fadl al-Hadrami, the highest jurist at the port of Aden, and for ... Muhammad al-Dhabhani. These two drank it with a company of people, for whom their example was sufficient."

\* \* \*

Also [remarkable] is the multitude of coffee-houses in the city of Cairo, the concentration of coffee-houses at every step, and of perfect places where people can assemble. Early rising worshipers and pious men get up and go [there], drink a cup of coffee adding life to their life. They feel, in a way, that its slight exhilaration strengthens them for their religious observance and worship. From that point of view their coffee-houses are commended and praised. But if one considers the ignorant people that assemble in them it is questionable whether they deserve praise [...] To make it short, the coffee-houses of Egypt are filled mostly with dissolute persons and opium-eaters. Many of them are occupied by veteran soldiers, aged officers (*chaushan* and *mutefer-riqas*). When they arrive in the morning rags and rush mats are spread out, and they stay until evening. Some [of the frequenters of coffeehouses] are drug-users of the slave class; [here follows a section making fun of the Kipchak dialect of these people]. They are a bunch of parasites, *chaushes* and *muteferriqas* by name [only], whose work consists of presiding over the coffee-house, of drinking coffee on credit, talking of frugality, when the matter comes up, and, having told certain matters with all sorts of distortions, of dozing off as soon as the effects of their "grass" subside. In other words, their talk is mostly lies .... But no true word ever comes over their lips.

# 22. A European observer of the Ottoman military

## Ogier Ghiselin de Busbecq

**Ogier Ghiselin de Busbecq (1522-1592) came from Flanders and served as an ambassador of the House of Habsburg (which ruled over the Austrian Empire) to the Ottoman Empire, which at the time ruled the majority of the central Arab lands. When Busbecq arrived in Istanbul in 1552, the Ottoman Empire, ruled by Suleiman the Magnificent, was at the height of its power. Busbecq was a keen observer and gave much thought to the Ottomans' strengths and Austrian weaknesses. It is important**

From Forster, Charles Thornton, and F.H. Blackburne Daniell, eds., *The Life and Letters of Ogier Ghiselin de Busbecq* (London: C.K. Paul, 1881).

**to note that at this point the eventual European domination of the globe did not seem likely and it was an Ottoman example that Busbecq thought European powers should follow.**

The Sultan's hall was crowded with people, among whom were several officers of high rank. Besides these there were all the troopers of the Imperial guard, Spahis, Ghourebas, Ouloufedgis, and a large force of Janissaries; but there was not in all that great assembly a single man who owed his position to aught save his valour and his merit. No distinction is attached to birth among the Turks; the deference to be paid to a man is measured by the position he holds in the public service. There is no fighting for precedence; a man's place is marked out by the duties he discharges. In making his appointments the Sultan pays no regard to any pretensions on the score of wealth or rank, nor does he take into consideration recommendations or popularity; he considers each case on its own merits, and examines carefully into the character, ability, and disposition of the man whose promotion is in question. It is by merit that men rise in the service; a system which ensures that posts should only be assigned to the competent. Each man in Turkey carries in his own hand his ancestry and his position in life, which he may make or mar as he will. Those who receive the highest offices from the Sultan are for the most part the sons of shepherds or herdsmen, and so far from being ashamed of their parentage, they actually glory in it, and consider it a matter of boasting that they owe nothing to the accident of birth; for they do not believe that high qualities are either natural or hereditary, nor do they think that they can be handed down from father to son, but that they are partly the gift of God, and partly the result of good training, great industry, and unwearied zeal.

[...]

From this you will see that it is the patience, self-denial, and thrift of the Turkish soldier that enables him to face the most trying circumstances, and come safely out of the dangers that surround him. What a contrast to our men! Christian soldiers on a campaign refuse to put up with their ordinary food, and call for thrushes, becaficos, and such like dainty dishes! If these are not supplied they grow mutinous and work their own ruin; and if they are supplied, they are ruined all the same. For each man is his own worst enemy, and has no foe more deadly than his own intemperance, which is sure to kill him, if the enemy be not quick. It makes me shudder to think of what the result of a struggle between such different systems must be; one of us must prevail and the other be destroyed, at any rate we cannot both exist in safety. On their side is the vast wealth of their empire, unimpaired resources, experience and practice in arms, a veteran soldiery, an uninterrupted series of victories, readiness to endure hardships, union, order, discipline, thrift, and watchfulness. On ours are found an empty exchequer, luxurious habits, exhausted resources, broken spirits, a raw and insubordinate soldiery, and greedy generals; there is no regard for discipline, license runs riot, the men indulge in drunkenness and debauchery, and, worst of all, the enemy are accustomed to victory, we, to defeat. Can we doubt what the result must be?

*The Maghreb*

# 23. A French observer of the Moroccan military

## Louis Chénier

Louis Chénier was a French diplomat in Morocco several decades after the death of the powerful ruler Moulay Isma'il (text pp. 116-17), whom he describes in the excerpt below. In reading this account, allowance must be made for Chénier's stereotypes of "Oriental despotism," and possibly for a lingering resentment toward Moulay Isma'il, who succeeded for a time in minimizing European influence in his territories. Nevertheless, Chénier's description of Isma'il's crack troops, the *'abid al-Bukhari* (Bukhari slaves) is accurate in its broad contours. The pattern of enlisting foreign troops had been common to many polities of the Arab lands for centuries. However, Isma'il's strategy of affiliating such troops with a revered religious work, the 9th-century *hadith* collection of al-Bukhari (text p. 49), was not so common. Chénier points out that Isma'il probably had an Ottoman precedent in mind. Why would a ruler wish to surround himself with foreign troops? What can you deduce about societies in which this strategy is standard policy? And what might have been the intent behind the association of these soldiers with al-Bukhari?

Here it is proper to observe that the monarchs of Morocco, desirous to imitate the Ottoman court, have sometimes had viziers; but such eminent situations, in this empire, have neither the same splendor nor the same power as those at Constantinople. Authority cannot be delegated, except when it is founded on rational principles, which it is not in a government truly and absolute-

From Chénier, Louis de, *The Present State of the Empire of Morocco*, vol. 2. Trans. P. Motteaux (London: Printed for G.G.J. and J. Robinson, 1788).

ly despotic, where each act depends on the arbitrary will of one man. A vizier, of Morocco, is called by the same title occasionally there as in Turkey; but equal puissance he never can enjoy.

Muley Ishmael arrived at Mequinez at the feast of sacrifices, whither he had convoked all the grandees, who hastened to bring him presents; for, at that court, the visit and the present are not only paid together, but, it is, in some measure, admissible to delay the visit, provided care is taken only to send the present. The ambitious projects of Muley Ishmael, and the various difficulties he had to encounter in the beginning of his reign, made him suppose the necessity of maintaining a body of confidential troops; he therefore conceived the project of forming a corps of negro soldiers, that should immediately be under his command. To accomplish this the more quickly, exclusive of the negroes that Muley Arshid [al-Rashid—text p. 116] already had collected, he purchased himself a great number of blacks, male and female, and accustomed his grandees to send them as presents.

After marrying and setting apart territories for their habitations, he gave a degree of stability to this generation of slaves, educated them in the Mahometan religion, accustomed them to the use of arms, and made soldiers of them, who became formidable to the natives. A monarch so absolute, and so capricious, as as Muley Ishmael, had good reason to fear the fickleness and discontent of his enslaved subjects, whom his violent conduct must continually render liable to revolt, and who could not be kept peaceable but by overawing them with troops, whose interest should also be the interest of the despot.

In this precise situation were the negroes. They were despised by the Moors, as well because of the prejudice entertained concerning their colour, which the white men have every where consigned to slavery, as because of the idolatrous worship they maintained. They also were foreigners. While fighting for the glory of their master, they fulfilled their military duty, and at the same time took vengeance for the hatred in which they were held by the Moors. By this artful policy, and the rivalship which Muley Ishmael knew how to raise between his soldiers and his subjects, this monarch found the means of holding in subjection, during a long reign, all the provinces of an empire accustomed to a change of masters, and which otherwise the barbarity of the prince must soon or late have obliged to rebel.

After having exercised his negroes in military discipline, the Emperor, that he might add to the strength of men the power of superstition, consecrated them, with ceremony, to the prosperity of religion. Following the example of the Sultan Amurath [the Ottoman Sultan al-Murad I, r. 1362-89], who, when he formed the corps of janissaries, sent them to Hadgy Bectasch [a revered Sufi sheikh], that he might bestow his benediction on them, Muley Ishmael appointed his negroes as a patron, and the signal of rallying, Sidi Boccari, one of the commentators of the Koran, on which book he made them take the oath of allegiance. This book, from that time, was, and is still, carried respectfully in the army. It is deposited in a distinguished tent, placed in the centre of the camp, as the image of their worship, and the pledge of their fidelity.

All the troops act under the same auspices, but none,

except the blacks, the Ludaya, or other tribes, destined personally to guard the Emperor, obtain the surname of El-Boccari, which is thus meant to signify those soldiers who are immediately in the service of the prince; that is to say, who constitute the standing army. This negro corps, from that time, became the individual guard of Muley Ishmael, nor did he ever find guards more faithful. His successors, though they have made some reforms, have nearly followed the same plan.

# READINGS FOR CHAPTER 5
# THE NINETEENTH CENTURY

*The Mashriq*
## 24. A Sunni modernist on the conversion of Iraq's Arabs to Shi'ism

### Rashid Rida

In his monthly journal *al-Manar*, the Syrian reformer Rashid Rida (text p. 140, 151) often published letters from readers. The letter with which this passage begins, from 1908, is signed by a "zealous scholar," and entitled "Words concerning Iraq and its people." Its writer is zealous that something be done about the conversion of Iraq's Arab tribes to Shi'ism (text p. 123), which he sees as a threat to both good religion and good governance. Keep in mind that this document predates the end of the Ottoman state, the consequent abolition of the caliphate, and the rise of Arab nationalism to effective hegemony. How does

From [Anon.], *Kalimat 'an al-'Iraq, al-Manar* 11 (1908), p. 41*f.* Translated by L. Yarbrough, from the Arabic.

**Rashid Rida's opinion on this issue in 1900 compare to his new view? What might have brought about the shift? What views do the "zealous scholar" and Rashid Rida take of Shi'ism? Of the Ottoman state? In general, how do these writers envision the relationship of religion to political allegiance? A *sanjaq* is an administrative district; a *mulla* is a Shi'i religious scholar.**

[From a "zealous scholar":] Iraq is, as you well know, an extremely fertile region, richly endowed with fresh air and pure water. Through it run great rivers—the Tigris and the Euphrates, the Diyala and the Karun—snaking throughout the land every which way. Yet most of it lies waste, and the cries of the owl and the raven echo across it. This unfortunate situation has much to do with the difficulty of transport, the loss of security, and the general dearth of education and civilization. The government in that place is, as everywhere else, a kind of organized plunder and corruption, hard at work wrecking the country and wiping out its inhabitants. Most of these folk are distracted by their hardships and blinded to foreign machinations, and so Iraq is fairly bristling with the Martini rifles that England sends at regular intervals, having developed its supply lines in the country.

One of the greatest afflictions is the spread of the Shi'i sect throughout Iraq, such that three quarters of its population are now Shi'i. This is thanks to intensive efforts by Shi'i scholars and their students, and the help they receive from the government, which stays the hand of any Sunni who would resist or gainsay them. In Najaf there is a society of Shi'i scholars, and sixteen thousand students. It is their habit to fan out into the countryside, leading its inhabitants astray. Thus the keenest observers have concluded that the area has been effectively detached from the state, which retains control in name only.

[…]

[Rashid Rida responds]: This letter has reminded us of something that we wrote in the second issue of *al-Manar* (Ramadan 1317[/January 1901]) concerning the spread of the Shiʻi sect in Iraq: "We have read in a certain newspaper that the Ottoman state has made up its mind to send out scholars to the *sanjaq*s of Basra, al-Muntafik, and Karbala' to serve as spiritual guides to the nomadic tribes that reside there. We have read elsewhere that the sultan himself has actually endorsed this initiative. We praise God most high that the Ottoman state has been alerted to this matter before it gets entirely out of hand. For it is the Shiʻa who have seized the initiative, sending preachers and spiritual guides among these and the other Arab tribes that camp along the Tigris and the Euphrates. These preachers have already brought most of the tribes over to the Shiʻi sect.

Typically the Shiʻi *mulla* will go to a tribe, mixing with its sheikh like wine with water. In doing this, he will make use of certain strategies to make the obligations of Islamic law seem easier, taking advantage of the sheikh's predilections. For instance, he will stress the permissibility, among the Shiʻis, of enjoying the company of a great number of women, a matter of considerable importance to these sheikhs. His goal is to become the sheikh's confidant, his bosom friend and political counselor. Thus does the *mulla* find a way to propagate his sect in the tribe very quickly. He usually hardly needs to bother with politics, simply seeing to it that the tribe understands that the rightful head of the Shiʻi sect is the Shah of the Persians, and that the head of the other sect is the [Ottoman] Sultan 'Abd al-Hamid. Obviously, they will throw their support behind the head of their own sect in the event of a disagreement (God forbid) between him and the head of the other sect, even though they live in the territory of the latter. The Ottoman state may find it possible to regain some control over the situation if it selects people of wisdom and sincere zeal for positions in spiritual guidance and education. These will have to be people who care so deeply about reform and religious instruction that they give these things precedence over their own personal benefit. Of course, one who can truly lay claim to wisdom and charisma in preaching should not be deprived of worldly reward; in fact, it might even lead to greater success. After all, all the Shi'i missionaries seem to have done quite well for themselves while propagating their sect. The missionary campaign of the Ottoman state should begin with people along the Euphrates, among whom there remain many who are still Sunnis. It is God who grants success."

This is what we wrote nearly nine years ago. We now say: "Most of those who have responded to the proselytizing of the Shi'i scholars there had scarcely even been Sunni Muslims to begin with. If those missionaries actually succeed in preaching effectively among them, teaching them religious obligations and rulings concerning right and wrong, this will be better for them, religiously speaking, than their former condition. Unlike the writer of the letter above, we do not consider this a religious calamity. Nevertheless, from a political perspective the matter remains important. Politics is still the flashpoint between Sunnis and Shi'a. Without it, there would scarcely be any disagreement. And it is disagreements of this sort that cause us to lose both our religious and our worldly possessions.

Those seeking reform through Islamic unity have been pleased at the rapprochement that has taken place between the two sides in recent years. That was until the recent border disputes. Now, they fear that dreadful old politics will destroy in a single year what the missionaries of reform have built over the course of dozens. We ask God to protect Islam from the evils of politics, and spare Muslims all the discord and harm that it brings."

*The Mashriq*
## 25. The Gulf before oil
### Carsten Niehbuhr

**Carsten Niebuhr (1733-1815), a German mathematician and traveller, was the sole survivor of a Danish scientific expedition. Niebuhr's copies of cuneiform inscriptions in Persepolis were a crucial step in the deciphering of cuneiform and the understanding of ancient Middle Eastern languages like Akkadian, Sumerian and Old Persian. In addition, his travel descriptions are an important source for the history of the Middle East in the 1760s. The excerpt below gives a general description of the Arabs living on the eastern coast of the Persian Gulf (also called the Arabian Gulf). Today, the gulf is home to the ultra-rich gulf states and emirates, like Bahrain, Qatar, Dubai and Abu Dhabi, as well as the oil-producing region of Iran. Comparing Niebuhr's account to present-day conditions gives us a sense of the transformation brought about by the discovery of oil in this area in the 1960s. Ichthyophagi means "fish eaters" – a term given by**

From Niebuhr, Carsten, *Travels through Arabia and Other Countries in the East*, vol. 2. Trans. R. Heron (Edinburgh: R. Morison & Son, 1792).

ancient geographers to various unrelated coast-dwelling people. Niebuhr's last comment makes a comparison between the coastal Arabs and the Greek islands in antiquity. How has the discovery of oil changed the situation that Niebuhr describes?

## Of the Arabs inhabiting around the Persian Gulf

Our geographers are wrong, as I have elsewhere remarked, in representing a part of Arabia as subject to the Monarchs of Persia. So far is it from being so, that, on the contrary, the Arabs possess all the sea-coast of the Persian empire, from the mouths of the Euphrates, nearly to those of the Indus.

These settlements upon the coast of Persia belong not, indeed, to Arabia properly so called. But, since they are independent of Persia, and use the same language, and exhibit the same manners, as the native inhabitants of Arabia, I shall here subjoin a brief account of them.

It is impossible to ascertain the period at which the Arabians formed their settlements upon this coast. Tradition affirms, that they have been established here for many centuries. From a variety of hints in ancient history, it may be presumed, that these Arabian colonies occupied their present situation in the time of the first kings of Persia. There is a striking analogy between the manners ascribed to the ancient Ichthyophagi and those of these Arabs.

They live all nearly in the same manner leading a sea-faring-life, and employing themselves in fishing, and in gathering pearls. They use little other food but fish and dates; and they feed also their cattle upon fish.

They prize liberty as highly as do their brethren in the

desert. Almost every different town has its own sheikh, who receives hardly any revenue from his subjects; but, if he has no private fortune, must, like his subject, support himself by his industry, either in carrying goods, or in fishing. If the principal inhabitants happen to be dissatisfied with the reigning sheikh, they depose him, and choose another out of the same family.

Their arms are a match-firelocks, a sabre, and a buckler. All their fishing-boats serve occasionally as ships of war. But a fleet like this, that must frequently stop to take fish for food, when they should pursue the enemy, can never perform any very great exploits. Their wars are mere skirmishes and inroads, never ending in any decisive action, but producing lasting quarrels, and a state of continual hostility.

Their dwellings are so paltry, that an enemy would not take the pains to demolish them. And as, from this circumstance, these people have nothing to lose upon the continent, they always betake themselves to their boats at the approach of an enemy, and lie concealed in some isle in the Gulf till he have retreated. They are convinced that the Persians will never think of settling on a barren shore, where they would be infested by all the Arabs who frequent the adjacent seas.

[...]

Their government and present political situation seem to me to bear a great resemblance to those of ancient Greece. Hostile engagements are continually a-fighting, and important revolutions happening upon the Persian Gulf; but the Arabs have no historian to spread their fame beyond their own narrow confines.

*The Mashriq*

# 26. A barber of Damascus: Ahmad Budayri al-Hallaq's chronicle of the year 1749

## Ahmad Budayri al-Hallaq

Most historical records tend to preserve only the perspectives of the elites. Therefore, texts written by non-elites (poor people, women, slaves, etc.) are relatively rare and especially precious. The excerpt below is taken from a chronicle written by Ahmad Budayri al-Hallaq, an eighteenth-century barber of Damascus. The chronicle gives a hint of the concerns and worries of the average man of the period. Notice, for example, the repeated mention of the fluctuation of prices of foodstuffs and the constant fear of hunger. Similarly, our barber is critical of the leading personalities in Damascus. He especially enjoys retelling stories that cast these "big-wigs" in negative and often ridiculous light. What are the faults he points out in the actions and manners of the elite? A *ratl* and *wuqiya* are units of weight. A *qirsh* is a silver coin worth forty *masari*. A *mufti* is a scholar authorized to issue *fatwa*s and a *qadi* is a judge.

This year was destined by God to be a blessed one for us and for all our fellow Muslims. As for now, however, the common people continue to suffer under the weight of the high cost of living. However, it must be a positive omen that the year opened with heavy rains.

[...]

High prices continued to mount. A *ratl* of the most inferior kind of bread cost six *masari,* the medium quality eight *masari* and the best quality twelve. A *wuqiya* of

From Tamari, S., trans., "The Barber of Damascus," in Amin, Camron Michael, Benjamin C. Fortna, and Elizabeth Frierson, *The Modern Middle East: A Sourcebook for History* (Oxford; New York: Oxford University Press, 2006).

clarified butter cost seven *masari* and the same measure of oil cost two. The common people were in deep distress.

[...]

I learned recently that Hamid al-Imadi, the *mufti* of Damascus, had been hoarding wheat like all the other bigwigs who don't fear God.

Those responsible for regulating weights and measurements came to the *mufti* and said, "We sell wheat for fifty *qirsh* a sack." He said in return, "Take it easy. Perhaps the price will rise..." If our own Muslim *mufti* has no compassion for his fellow man, how can he possibly be fair?

[...]

The rise in prices in Bilad al-Sham [i.e., the eastern Mediterranean coast] continued unabated. It reached us that the *ratl* of bread in Tripoli cost ten *masari,* and in Gaza and Ramla twenty-five *masari.* Thus, the misfortune and subjugation of the common people continued.

[...]

On Wednesday the 11th of [the month of] Jumada al-Akhira, the new wheat harvest reached market. A sack of wheat sold for forty-five *qirsh.* Earlier, it had been selling for fifty-two. So, the crowds cried foul and rose up attacking bakeries and demanding that the *ratl* of bread sell for three and four *masari.* So, the merchants began to sell at these prices, a fact which was welcomed by the populace who proceeded to celebrate.

Meanwhile, Asad Pasha was in the garden of his father in the area of the al-Aqsab Mosque where he was enjoying a picnic accompanied by the town's bigwigs. When he heard news of the popular unrest, he fell into a furious rage and ordered Mahmud Tafakji Pasha to take his infamous band of ruffians to roam the city and its markets and to warn the bakers that those who dare to sell white bread for anything less than six *masari* and brown for anything less than four will be beaten. So, the situation returned to the way it had been originally.

[...]

On the 3rd of Rajab, the bakers announced that the *ratl* of inferior bread cost four *masari,* the better quality five, and that mixed with barley or corn two. The people of Damascus, particularly the poor, were so overcome with joy that many began to cry with happiness. They began to decorate the market places throughout the city. On that day, the sack of new wheat or barley sold for eight *qirsh*. God graced his worshippers with blessings and generosity.

[...]

Two days before the beginning of Ramadan, the *qadi* of Damascus, Muhammad Efendi Bashmaqji, spent the day in al-Salihiyya with his entire household, including his wife. Late in the day, he was seen heading back to town and the central court carrying a pistol and wearing only one shoe. It appeared he was drunk.

However, I investigated this rumor and found it to be false. In fact, he was not drunk but was caught in a violent rage. Apparently, he was so infatuated with one of his female servants that he was willing to divorce his wife on her behalf. Here's what happened. Realizing her husband was in love with another, his wife decided to make the *qadi's* life unbearable. One day some guests of the servant came to pay her a visit. So, she planned a lavish feast in al-Salihiyya. But the jilted wife conspired to thwart her plans. When the guests arrived and were left without food or drink, the servant started to cry. The *qadi* was so obsessed with this woman that he immediately divorced his wife on her account. He told his entourage to return to the city and he demanded his shoes. One shoe was missing so he descended himself with only one shoe on and rode all the way to the court in this unkempt and agitated manner. His enemies seized the opportunity to accuse him of drunkenness and his wife went as far as lodging a complaint with the central state. An official decree followed which ordered the banishment of the unfortunate *qadi* to Cyprus and the confiscation of his assets which were to be turned over to the wife. She promptly sold these for a sum of almost eight bags of gold coins. By this time, people began to sympathize with the *qadi* except for those who had held a grudge against him for his uprightness and humility.

He was so generous that he regularly opened his pantry during Ramadan and gave away enormous quantities of clarified butter and rice and other staples and even meat. More than thirty people would eat at his place nightly during Ramadan. Because he refused to accept bribes or take sides in legal disputes, there were unscrupulous people in our town who were only too happy to join with his wife against him.

[...]

On the same day, the pasha ordered prostitutes to leave the city. It appears he wanted to banish them to other cities. So, it was announced to neighborhood headmen that they should turn in any suspicious women. Then the town crier announced that all women—save those of the governor's household and that of his chief lieutenant—should not veil. The Pasha's men then began a round of inspections that got progressively intrusive and provoked public outrage. Within only a few days, the "ladies of the night" had returned to their usual haunts in the alleyways and market places. In the end, the governor imposed a tax on them such that each had to pay ten *qirsh* to be collected and regulated by an official of the court.

*The Mashriq*
## 27. Aftermath to a massacre
**anonymous**

The fighting among Christians, Druze, and Sunni Muslims that convulsed the Levant in 1860 (text p. 124) saw some of the Arab world's worst sectarian violence in modern times. In Damascus, Muslims incensed by Christian attacks in Beirut sacked the Christian quarter of the city over the course of three days in July, killing more than 25,000. Among the dead were the American and Dutch consuls. The passage below is the transcript of a speech given in the aftermath by an unnamed Damascene Muslim, and published in the London *Times* on October 6. What are the speaker's reasons for condemning the violence? What can you gather about the debates that were taking place at the time of the speech? A "Zimmi" (often transliterated *dhimmi*) is the name given to a non-Muslim citizen in Islamic law.

Praise be to God, who is free from unrighteousness, and righteousness is one of his attributes! He made His

From [Anon.], "Address of an Influential Moslim to his Co-Religionists in Damascus," in Appendix to Abkariyus, Iskandar, *The Lebanon in Turmoil*. Trans. J.F. Scheltema (New Haven: Yale University Press, 1920).

creatures alike in creating them from the same substance. None can be acceptable before Him but through piety, which is founded upon the observation of the law. Let every one come forward with his works and compare them with the law. If they are in conformity with it, he will be happy, otherwise he will be a great loser. Blessing and peace be upon our Lord Muhammad, who has been sent a mercy to the world, and who spoke in the name of his Lord Most High, saying: "Ye creatures of God, injustice is unlawful for you, having deemed it always unlawful even for me; act not unjustly against each other." And now, ye men, fear God, and know that injustice makes those who commit it hateful and disliked in this life and leads them to torment in the life to come. Is not he who sheds the blood of a Moslem, a Zimmi or a refugee the most unjust man? Yea, is not he that violates a Moslem, Zimmi or refugee woman the most unjust man? Yea, is not he who destroys the house of a Moslem, Zimmi or refugee the most unjust man? The Zimmies and refugees are like unto us, we, Moslems, in all the rights, as it has been related that the lord of men [Muhammad]—may God bless and salute him—has said about the Zimmies: "They have what we have and what is against them is against us." How did the perpetrators of these acts [the massacres at Damascus and elsewhere] feel justified in committing them? How did they think it lawful for them to shed blood, insult women and rob property? Did they find that in a book revealed after the Qoran, or did they rather gather it from the sayings of an apostle sent after the Lord of the sons of Adam? Say to them: "Bring forward your evidence if you are right. Why are you silent? Are you asleep or have you been

deprived of your dreams?" Nay, the devil has possessed
them and led them astray. Indeed, this evil work is no
less than pulling down the foundation of religion and
the doers of it can no longer be included among
Moslems. Whosoever says that it is not right to chastise
and punish these [evil-]doers is one of the deceivers and
offenders. Wake up, ye creatures of God, from your
sleep and slumbers, and submit to the decrees of God
and obey your rulers. Those who despised the law of
God and disobeyed it and offended the Zimmies, shall
be punished in this life and a severe punishment awaits
them in the life to come.

*Strategies against European Intervention*
# 28. Observing the French in Egypt
## Abd al-Rahman al-Jabarti

**When Napoleon's army took possession of Egypt in 1798 (text
p. 126), the French exercised both military and intellectual
power over the population. Their presence also provided local
scholars the chance to observe the habits of Western Europeans
directly. The most famous such observer was 'Abd al-Rahman
al-Jabarti, whose work *Muzhir al-taqdis* gives his fascinating
perspectives on the occupiers. The two passages excerpted below
contain his thoughts about French personal habits and scholarship, respectively. It should be kept in mind that the work was
written for an Ottoman audience, whose favor the author
attempted to curry by comparing the Ottomans favorably to the
French. What of Jabarti's own cultural norms can you detect in
his comments about the French? You should know that he may
be recycling cultural assumptions in his remarks about French**

From al-Jabarti, 'Abd al-Rahman, *Napoleon in Egypt*. Trans. S. Moreh (Princeton:
Markus Wiener Publishers), 1995.

**personal habits; Usama ibn Munqidh (Reading 14 above) had**
**made very similar remarks almost seven centuries earlier. How**
**does Jabarti, himself a scholar, describe the foreign scholarship**
**that has taken up residence in his country? Can any of his**
**assumptions be discerned from the things he chooses to remark?**

They follow this rule: great and small, high and low, male and female are all equal. Sometimes they break this rule according to their whims and inclinations or reasoning. Their women do not veil themselves and have no modesty; they do not care whether they uncover their private parts. Whenever a Frenchman has to perform an act of nature he does so wherever he happens to be, even in full view of people, and he goes away as he is, without washing his private parts after defecation. If he is a man of taste and refinement he wipes himself with whatever he finds, even with a paper with writing on it, otherwise he remains as he is. They have intercourse with any woman who pleases them and vice versa. Sometimes one of their women goes into a barber's shop, and invites him to shave her pubic hair. If he wishes he can take his fee in kind. It is their custom to shave both their moustaches and beard. Some of them leave the hair of their cheeks only. They do not shave their heads nor their pubic hair. They mix their foods. Some might even put together in one dish coffee, sugar, arrack, raw eggs, limes, and so on.

[...]

To the administrators of affairs, the astronomers, scholars, and scientists in mathematics, geometry, astronomy, engraving and drawing, and also to the painters, scribes, and writers [the French] assigned al-Nasiriyya quarter and all the houses in it, such as the house of Qasim Bey, the Amir of the Pilgrimage known as Abu Sayf, and the house of Hasan Kashif Jarkas which he founded and built to perfection, having spent upon it fantastic sums of money amounting to more than a hundred thousand dinars. When he had completed plastering and furnishing it, the French came and he fled with the others and left all that it contained, not having enjoyed it for even a whole month. The administrators, astronomers, and some of the physicians lived in this house in which they placed a great number of their books and with a keeper taking care of them and arranging them. And the students among them would gather two hours before noon every day in an open space opposite the shelves of books, sitting on chairs arranged in parallel rows before a wide long board. Whoever wishes to look up something in a book asks for whatever volumes he wants and the librarian brings them to him. Then he thumbs through the pages, looking through the book, and writes. All the while they are quiet and no one disturbs his neighbour. When some Muslims would come to look around they would not prevent them from entering. Indeed they would bring them all kinds of printed books in which there were all sorts of illustrations and cartes... of the countries and regions, animals, birds, plants, histories of the ancients, campaigns of the nations, tales of the prophets including pictures of them, of their miracles and wondrous deeds, the events of their respective peoples and such things which baffle the mind. I have gone to them many times and they have shown me all these various things and among the things I saw there was a large book containing the Biography of the Prophet, upon whom be mercy and peace. In this volume they draw his noble picture according to the extent of their knowledge and judgement about him. He is depicted standing upon his feet looking toward Heaven as if menacing all creation. In his right hand is the sword and in his left the Book and around him are his Companions, may God be pleased with them, also with swords in their hands. In another page there are pictures of the Rightly Guided Caliphs. On another page a picture of the Midnight Journey of Muhammad and al-Buraq and he, upon whom be mercy and peace, is riding upon al-Buraq from the Rock of Jerusalem. Also there is a picture of Jerusalem and the Holy Places of Mecca and Medina and of the four Imams, Founders of the Schools and the other Caliphs and Sultans and an image of Islambul [i.e., Istanbul] including her Great Mosques like Aya Sofya and the Mosque of Sultan Muhammad. In another picture the manner in which the Prophet's Birthday is celebrated and all the types of people who participate in it [are shown]; also [there are] pictures of the Mosque of Sultan Sulayman and the manner in which the Friday prayers are conducted in it, and the Mosque of Abu Ayyub al-Ansari and the manner in which prayers for the dead are performed in it, and pictures of the countries, the coasts, the seas, the Pyramids, the ancient temples of Upper Egypt including the pictures, figures, and inscriptions which are drawn upon them. Also there are pictures of the species of animals, birds, plants and herbage which are peculiar to each land. The glorious Qur'an is translated into their language! Also many other Islamic books. I saw in their possession the *Kitab al-Shifa'* of Qadi 'Iyad, which they call *al-Shifa' al-Sharif* and *al-Burda* by Abu Siri, many verses of which they know by heart and which they translated into French. I saw some of them who know chapters of the Qur'an by heart. They have a great interest in the sciences, mainly in mathematics and the knowledge of languages, and make great efforts to learn the Arabic language and the colloquial. In this they strive day and night. And they have books especially devoted to all types of languages, their declensions and conjugations as well as their etymologies. They possess extraordinary astronomical instruments of perfect construction and instruments for measuring altitudes, of wondrous, amazing, and precious construction. And they have telescopes for looking at the stars and measuring their scopes, sizes, heights, conjunctions, and oppositions, and the clepsydras and clocks with gradings and minutes and seconds, all of wondrous form and very precious, and the like.

# READINGS FOR CHAPTER 6
# STATE BUILDING AND INDEPENDENCE
# IN THE TWENTIETH CENTURY

*The First World War and the Mandatory Period*

## 29. Behind-the-scenes dealings of the early 20th century

### Various European diplomats

During World War One, European powers made a series of agreements regarding the future of Ottoman territories after the war, both among themselves and with those they considered as representatives of powers in the region. Below, we bring the three most important of such agreements: (1) The 1915 Correspondence between Sharif Hussein (also spelt Husayn) of Mecca and Sir Henry McMahon, the British High Commissioner in Egypt, (2) the 1916 Sykes-Picot Agreement between England and France and (3) The 1917 Balfour Declaration made to the Zionist movement (on all of them, see text pp. 145-6). That the promises made in these agreements overlap is an understatement. What could be the result of such promises? Which of the three agreements would the British be most likely to fulfil?

### (1) The Hussein-McMahon correspondence: Letter no. 4

From Sir Henry McMahon to Sharif Hussein of Mecca, 24 October 1915

I have received your letter of the 29th Shawal, 1333

From http://avalon.law.yale.edu/subject_menus/mideast.asp; and Hurewitz, J.C., ed./trans., *The Middle East and North Africa in World Politics*, vol. 2 (New Haven; London: Yale University Press, 1975-1979), among other sources.

(September 9, 1915), with much pleasure and your expressions of friendliness and sincerity have given me the greatest satisfaction.

I regret that you should have received from my last letter the impression that I regarded the question of the limits and boundaries with coldness and hesitation; such was not the case, but it appeared to me that the time had not yet come when that question could be discussed in a conclusive manner.

I have realised, however, from your last letter that you regard this question as one of vital and urgent importance. I have, therefore, lost no time in informing the Government of Great Britain of the contents of your letter, and it is with great pleasure that I communicate to you on their behalf the following statement, which I am confident you will receive with satisfaction:—

The two districts of Mersina and Alexandretta and portions of Syria lying to the west of the districts of Damascus, Homs, Hama and Aleppo cannot be said to be purely Arab, and should be excluded from the limits demanded.

With the above modification, and without prejudice of our existing treaties with Arab chiefs, we accept those limits.

As for those regions lying within those frontiers wherein Great Britain is free to act without detriment to the interest of her ally, France, I am empowered in the name of the Government of Great Britain to give the following assurances and make the following reply to your letter:

1. Subject to the above modifications, Great Britain is prepared to recognize and support the independence of the Arabs in all the regions within the limits demanded by the Sherif of Mecca.
2. Great Britain will guarantee the Holy Places against all external aggression and will recognise their inviolability.
3. When the situation admits, Great Britain will give to the Arabs her advice and will assist them to establish what may appear to be the most suitable forms of government in those various territories.
4. On the other hand, it is understood that the Arabs have decided to seek the advice and guidance of Great Britain only, and that such European advisers and officials as may be required for the formation of a sound form of administration will be British.
5. With regard to the vilayets [i.e. provinces] of Bagdad and Basra, the Arabs will recognise that the established position and interests of Great Britain necessitate special administrative arrangements in order to secure these territories from foreign aggression, to promote the welfare of the local populations and to safeguard our mutual economic interests.

I am convinced that this declaration will assure you beyond all possible doubt of the sympathy of Great Britain towards the aspirations of her friends the Arabs and will result in a firm and lasting alliance, the immediate results of which will be the expulsion of the Turks from the Arab countries and the freeing of the Arab peoples from the Turkish yoke, which for so many years has pressed heavily upon them.

[...]

It was with very great relief and satisfaction that I heard of the safe arrival of the Holy Carpet [the ornament covering sent annually to the holy Ka'ba in Mecca] and the accompanying offerings which, thanks to the clearness of your directions and the excellence of your arrangements, were landed without trouble or mishap in spite of the dangers and difficulties occasioned by the present sad war. May God soon bring a lasting peace and freedom to all peoples!

[...]

(Signed) A. H. McMAHON.

## (2) The Sykes-Picot Agreement (1916)

[...]

It is accordingly understood between the French and British governments:

That France and Great Britain are prepared to recognize and protect an independent Arab state or a confederation of Arab states (A) and (B) marked on the annexed map, under the suzerainty of an Arab chief. That in area (A) France, and in

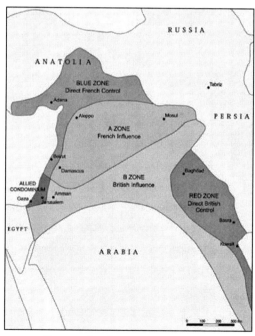

*Zones of influence according to the Sykes-Picot Agreement*

area (B) Great Britain, shall have priority of right of enterprise and local loans. That in area (A) France, and in area (B) Great Britain, shall alone supply advisers or foreign functionaries at the request of the Arab state or confederation of Arab states.

That in the blue area France, and in the red area Great Britain, shall be allowed to establish such direct or indirect administration or control as they desire and as they may think fit to arrange with the Arab state or confederation of Arab states.

That in the brown area there shall be established an international administration, the form of which is to be decided upon after consultation with Russia, and subsequently in consultation with the other allies, and the representatives of the Shereef of Mecca.

That Great Britain be accorded (1) the ports of Haifa and Acre, (2) guarantee of a given supply of water from the Tigris and Euphrates in area (A) for area (B). His Majesty's Government, on their part, undertake that they will at no time enter into negotiations for the cession of Cyprus to any third power without the previous consent of the French government.

That Alexandretta shall be a free port as regards the trade of the British empire, and that there shall be no discrimination in port charges or facilities as regards British shipping and British goods; that there shall be freedom of transit for British goods through Alexandretta and by railway through the blue area, whether those goods are intended for or originate in the red area or (B) area, or area (A); and there shall be no discrimination, direct or indirect, against British goods on any railway or against British goods or ships at any port serving the areas mentioned.

That Haifa shall be a free port as regards the trade of France, her dominions and protectorates, and there shall be no discrimination in port charges or facilities as regards French shipping and French goods. There shall be freedom of transit for French goods through Haifa and by the British railway through the brown area, whether those goods are intended for or originate in the blue area, area (A), or area (B), and there shall be no discrimination, direct or indirect, against French goods on any railway, or against French goods or ships at any port serving the areas mentioned.

[...]

That Great Britain has the right to build, administer, and be sole owner of a railway connecting Haifa with area (B), and shall have a perpetual right to transport troops along such a line at all times. It is to be understood by both governments that this railway is to facilitate the connection of Baghdad with Haifa by rail [...]

There shall be no interior customs barriers between any of the above mentioned areas. The customs duties leviable on goods destined for the interior shall be collected at the port of entry and handed over to the administration of the area of destination.

It shall be agreed that the French Government will at no time enter into any negotiations for the cession of their rights and will not cede such rights in the blue area to any third power, except the Arab state or confederation of Arab states, without the previous agreement of His Majesty's Government, who, on their part, will give a similar undertaking to the French Government regarding the red area.

The British and French Governments, as the protectors of the Arab state, shall agree that they will not themselves acquire and will not consent to a third power acquiring territorial possessions in the Arabian peninsula, nor consent to a third power installing a naval base either on the east coast, or on the islands, of the Red Sea. This, however, shall not prevent such adjustment of the Aden frontier as may be necessary in consequence of recent Turkish aggression.

[...]

## (3) The Balfour Declaration

Foreign Office
November 2nd, 1917
Dear Lord Rothschild,

I have much pleasure in conveying to you, on behalf of His Majesty's Government, the following declaration of sympathy with Jewish Zionist aspirations which has been submitted to, and approved by, the Cabinet:

His Majesty's Government view with favour the establishment in Palestine of a national home for the Jewish people, and will use their best endeavors to facilitate the achievement of this object, it being clearly understood that nothing shall be done which may prejudice the civil and religious rights of existing non-Jewish communities in Palestine or the rights and political status enjoyed by Jews in any other country.

I should be grateful if you would bring this declaration to the knowledge of the Zionist Federation.

Yours,
Arthur James Balfour

*The Salafiyya and the Muslim Brotherhood*
# 30. The founder of the Muslim Brotherhood on politics and religion
## Hasan al-Banna'

The organization founded by Hasan al-Banna' (text p. 150)—the Muslim Brotherhood—is today one of the largest and most influential in the Arab world. Since the time of al-Banna', the Brotherhood has taken many different stances vis-à-vis existing governments, from outright rebellion (as in Hama, Syria, in 1982), to full democratic participation (as in Jordan to the present day), to restrained, strategic involvement (as in Egypt through the end of the Mubarak era). Everywhere it has played an active role in providing social and humanitarian services, and in this capacity has won many adherents. As the following passage from the writings of al-Banna' make clear, accusing the Brotherhood of political maneuvering is a pursuit as old as the organization itself. The writer defends against charges of political opportunism and anti-Westernism, and describes the foundations upon which Islamic reform can (and cannot) be built. Note that this selection is excerpted from several different tracts authored by al-Banna'. What do his means of defending his views reveal about his conception of Islam? In what ways do you think this text might appeal to readers? To what kind of reader will it appeal?

## We and Politics

Other people say that the Muslim Brotherhood are a political group and that their mission is a political one, beyond which they have still other aims. Who knows how far our nation will go in spreading accusations, bandying suspicions, and name-calling, while it aban-

From al-Banna', Hasan, *Five Tracts of Hasan al-Banna'*. Ed./trans. C. Wendell (Berkeley: University of California Press, 1978).

dons a sure way supported by the actual state of affairs, to proceed along a path of mere conjecture inspired by doubts?

O our people, we are calling out to you with the Qur'an in our right hand and the Sunna in our left, and with the deeds of the pious ancestors of the sons of this *umma* as our example. We summon you to Islam, the teachings of Islam, the laws of Islam and the guidance of Islam, and if this smacks of "politics" in your eyes, then it is our "policy"! And if the one summoning you to these principles is a "politician," then we are the most respectable of men, God be praised, in "politics"! And if you wish to call this "politics," say what you like, for names will never harm us when what has been named is made clear and our goals stand revealed.

O our people, let not mere words stand between you and the facts, nor names hide our goals, nor unessentials veil the essential from you. Islam does have a policy embracing the happiness of this world and the godliness of the next: this is our policy, for which we seek no substitute. Therefore govern yourselves according to it, convert others to it, and you will win the glory of the world to come. May you know its glad tidings before long.

[...]

\*   \*   \*

### Islam Is Not a Disturbing Influence on Relations with the West

Similarly, people may imagine that Islamic institutions in our modern life create estrangement between us and the Western nations, and that they will muddy the clarity of our political relations with them just when these were on the point of being settled. This too is a notion rooted in pure fantasy. For those nations which are suspicious of us will like us no better whether we follow Islam or anything else. If they are truly our friends, and mutual trust exists between us, their own spokesmen and leaders have already declared that every nation is free to adopt whatever organization it wishes within its own borders, provided it does not infringe on the rights of others. It is up to all the leaders of these nations to understand that the honor of international Islam is the most sacred honor known to history, and that the principles set down by international Islam to guard this honor and to preserve it are the most firmly fixed and solidly confirmed of principles.

It is Islam which spoke out for the safeguarding of treaties and fulfillment of obligations: "And keep the covenant, for of the covenant question will be made" [Q.17:34]; "Except for those of the polytheists with whom you have a treaty, and who since then have not diminished you in any way and have not helped anyone against you—fulfill your covenant with them up to its stated term. Truly God loves the godfearing" [Q. 9:4]. And He said: "So long as they behave with rectitude toward you, behave with rectitude toward them" [Q.9:7]. And He said, regarding the generous reception of refugees and the good neighborliness of those who receive them: "And if any one of the polytheists seeks refuge with thee, give him refuge so that he may hear God's discourses, then take him to a place of security" [Q. 9:6].

If this is the treatment accorded polytheists, how do

you suppose People of the Book would be treated? The Islam which prescribes these principles and takes its adherents along this path must surely be regarded by Westerners as guaranteeing still another type of security, namely, for themselves. We maintain that it would be to Europe's benefit if these sound concepts governed her own internal relations—this would be better for them and more enduring!

*  *  *

## The Fundamental Sources of the Renaissance in the East Are Not Those of the West

Excellency,

Among the causes which have impelled some of the Eastern nations to deviate from Islam, and to choose to imitate the West, was the study of the Western Renaissance made by their leaders, and their conviction that it was only accomplished by overthrowing religion, destroying churches, freeing themselves from papal authority, controlling the clergy and prelates, putting an end to all manifestations of religious authority in the nation, and definitely separating religion from the general policy of the state. If this is true in the case of the Western nations, it is absolutely untrue for the Islamic nations, since the nature of Islamic doctrines is quite unlike that of any other religion. The jurisdiction of the religious authorities in Islam is circumscribed and limited, powerless to alter its statutes or to subvert its institutions, with the result that the fundamental principles of Islam, across the centuries, have kept pace with the changing eras, and have advocated progress, supported learning, and defended scholars. What happened there is inappropriate for conditions here. There are extensive studies concerning this which take up many volumes: our purpose in this essay is to survey the subject briefly in order to bear it in mind and dispel all ambiguities. We are sure that every fair-minded person will agree with us on this basic principle; accordingly, it is simply not possible that this sentiment should be our guiding precept in our modern renaissance, which must first of all be sustained by the strong pillars of a high morality, a flourishing science, and far-reaching power, which is what Islam enjoins.

*The Founding of Israel and the First Middle East War*
## 31. Israel's declaration of independence

**The text of Israel's Declaration of Independence was worked out in a very short time in the midst of the 1948 War (text p. 155). Its formulation was accompanied by heated debate between secular and religious Jews regarding whether God and divine providence should be mentioned or not. The result is a remarkable document balancing a variety of viewpoints, the wartime circumstances and a vision for the future. The declaration begins by presenting a series of arguments justifying the establishment of Israel. What type of arguments are presented? Next follows the actual declaration and then a series of guiding principles for the nature of the new state and its relations with its neighbours. Has the state of Israel kept true to these principles?**

From http://www.mfa.gov.il/MFA/Peace+Process/Guide+to+the+Peace+Process/ Declaration+of+Establishment+of+State+of+Israel.htm, among other sources.

The land of Israel was the birthplace of the Jewish people. Here their spiritual, religious and political identity was shaped. Here they first attained statehood, created cultural values of national and universal significance and gave to the world the eternal Book of Books.

After being forcibly exiled from their land, the people kept faith with it throughout their dispersion and never ceased to pray and hope for their return to it and for the restoration in it of their political freedom.

Impelled by this historic and traditional attachment, Jews strove in every successive generation to re-establish themselves in their ancient homeland. In recent decades they returned in their masses. Pioneers, *mapilim* [Hebrew for illegal immigrants to Israel] and defenders, they made deserts bloom, revived the Hebrew language, built villages and towns, and created a thriving community controlling its own economy and culture, loving peace but knowing how to defend itself, bringing the blessings of progress to all the country's inhabitants, and aspiring towards independent nationhood.

[Here the declaration recounts the first Zionist Congress of 1897 and the Balfour Declaration of 1917.]

The catastrophe which recently befell the Jewish people—the massacre of millions of Jews in Europe—was another clear demonstration of the urgency of solving the problem of its homelessness by re-establishing in the Land of Israel the Jewish State, which would open the gates of the homeland wide to every Jew and confer upon the Jewish people the status of a fully privileged member of the comity of nations.

[....]

In the Second World War, the Jewish community of

this country contributed its full share to the struggle of the freedom- and peace-loving nations against the forces of Nazi wickedness and, by the blood of its soldiers and its war effort, gained the right to be reckoned among the peoples who founded the United Nations.

On the 29th November, 1947, the United Nations General Assembly passed a resolution calling for the establishment of a Jewish State in the Land of Israel; the General Assembly required the inhabitants of the Land of Israel to take such steps as were necessary on their part for the implementation of that resolution. This recognition by the United Nations of the right of the Jewish people to establish their State is irrevocable.

This right is the natural right of the Jewish people to be masters of their own fate, like all other nations, in their own sovereign State.

Accordingly we, members of the People's Council, representatives of the Jewish community of the Land of Israel and of the Zionist movement, are here assembled on the day of the termination of the British mandate over the land of Israel and, by virtue of our natural and historic right and on the strength of the resolution of the United Nations General Assembly, hereby declare the establishment of a Jewish state in the land of Israel, to be known as the State of Israel.

[...]

THE STATE OF ISRAEL will be open for Jewish immigration and for the Ingathering of the Exiles; it will foster the development of the country for the benefit of all its inhabitants; it will be based on freedom, justice and peace as envisaged by the prophets of Israel; it will ensure complete equality of social and political rights to all its inhabitants irrespective of religion, race or sex; it will guarantee freedom of religion, conscience, language, education and culture; it will safeguard the Holy Places of all religions; and it will be faithful to the principles of the Charter of the United Nations.

THE STATE OF ISRAEL is prepared to cooperate with the agencies and representatives of the United Nations in implementing the resolution of the General Assembly of the 29th November, 1947, and will take steps to bring about the economic union of the whole of the Land of Israel.

WE APPEAL to the United Nations to assist the Jewish people in the building-up of its State and to receive the State of Israel into the comity of nations.

WE APPEAL—in the very midst of the onslaught launched against us now for months—to the Arab inhabitants of the State of Israel to preserve peace and participate in the building of the State on the basis of full and equal citizenship and due representation in all its provisional and permanent institutions.

WE EXTEND our hand to all neighbouring states and their peoples in an offer of peace and good neighbourliness, and appeal to them to establish bonds of cooperation and mutual help with the sovereign Jewish people settled in its own land. The State of Israel is prepared to do its share in a common effort for the advancement of the entire Middle East.

WE APPEAL to the Jewish people throughout the Diaspora to rally round the Jews of the Land of Israel in the tasks of immigration and building and to stand by them in the great struggle for the realization of the age-old dream—the redemption of Israel.

Placing our trust in the "Rock of Israel," we affix our signatures to this proclamation at this session of the Provisional Council of State, on the soil of the homeland, in the city of Tel Aviv, on this Sabbath eve, the 5th day of Iyar, 5708 AM (14th May 1948).

## 32. The Palestinian National Covenant

The PLO (Palestine Liberation Organization) was founded in 1964. After the defeat in the Six Day War (text p. 160), its founding charter was substantially amended in 1968. There is a complex controversy as to whether this covenant was or was not amended following the 1990s peace process with Israel (text p. 168). Like Israel's Declaration of Independence above, the Palestinian National Covenant presents an argument for Palestinian independence. What are the similarities and differences between the two arguments? Notice the great importance laid in this document on the definition of who is a Palestinian and on defining the relationship between the Palestinian struggle for independence and the concerns of Arab nationalism. On the basis of these two documents, what are the prospects for the resolution of the conflict?

1. Palestine is the homeland of the Arab Palestinian people; it is an indivisible part of the Arab homeland, and the Palestinian people are an integral part of the Arab nation.
2. Palestine, with the boundaries it had during the British Mandate, is an indivisible territorial unit.
3. The Palestinian Arab people possess the legal right

From http://avalon.law.yale.edu/20th_century/plocov.asp; and http://www.mfa.gov.il/MFA/Peace+Process/Guide+to+the+Peace+Process/The+Palestinian+National+Charter.htm, among other sources.

to their homeland and have the right to determine their destiny after achieving the liberation of their country in accordance with their wishes and entirely of their own accord and will.

4.  The Palestinian identity is a genuine, essential, and inherent characteristic; it is transmitted from parents to children. The Zionist occupation and the dispersal of the Palestinian Arab people, through the disasters which befell them, do not make them lose their Palestinian identity and their membership in the Palestinian community, nor do they negate them.

5.  The Palestinians are those Arab nationals who, until 1947, normally resided in Palestine regardless of whether they were evicted from it or have stayed there. Anyone born, after that date, of a Palestinian father—whether inside Palestine or outside it—is also a Palestinian.

6.  The Jews who had normally resided in Palestine until the beginning of the Zionist invasion will be considered Palestinians.

7.  That there is a Palestinian community and that it has material, spiritual, and historical connection with Palestine are indisputable facts. It is a national duty to bring up individual Palestinians in an Arab revolutionary manner. All means of information and education must be adopted in order to acquaint the Palestinian with his country in the most profound manner, both spiritual and material, that is possible. He must be prepared for the armed struggle and ready to sacrifice his wealth and his life in order to win back his homeland and bring about its liberation.

8.  The phase in their history through which the

Palestinian people are now living is that of national struggle for the liberation of Palestine. Thus the conflicts among the Palestinian national forces are secondary, and should be ended for the sake of the basic conflict that exists between the forces of Zionism and of imperialism on the one hand, and the Palestinian Arab people on the other [...]

9. Armed struggle is the only way to liberate Palestine. This is the overall strategy, not merely a tactical phase. The Palestinian Arab people assert their absolute determination and firm resolution to continue their armed struggle and to work for an armed popular revolution for the liberation of their country and their return to it. They also assert their right to normal life in Palestine and to exercise their right to self-determination and sovereignty over it.

[...]

12. The Palestinian people believe in Arab unity. In order to contribute their share toward the attainment of that objective, however, they must, at the present stage of their struggle, safeguard their Palestinian identity and develop their consciousness of that identity, and oppose any plan that may dissolve or impair it.

[...]

15. The liberation of Palestine, from an Arab viewpoint, is a national duty and it attempts to repel the Zionist and imperialist aggression against the Arab homeland, and aims at the elimination of Zionism in Palestine. Absolute responsibility for this falls upon the Arab nation - peoples and governments - with the Arab people of Palestine in the vanguard. Accord-

ingly, the Arab nation must mobilize all its military, human, moral, and spiritual capabilities to participate actively with the Palestinian people in the liberation of Palestine. [...]

16. The liberation of Palestine, from a spiritual point of view, will provide the Holy Land with an atmosphere of safety and tranquility, which in turn will safeguard the country's religious sanctuaries and guarantee freedom of worship and of visit to all, without discrimination of race, color, language, or religion. Accordingly, the people of Palestine look to all spiritual forces in the world for support.

17. The liberation of Palestine, from a human point of view, will restore to the Palestinian individual his dignity, pride, and freedom. Accordingly the Palestinian Arab people look forward to the support of all those who believe in the dignity of man and his freedom in the world.

18. The liberation of Palestine, from an international point of view, is a defensive action necessitated by the demands of self-defense. Accordingly the Palestinian people, desirous as they are of the friendship of all people, look to freedom-loving, and peace-loving states for support in order to restore their legitimate rights in Palestine, to re-establish peace and security in the country, and to enable its people to exercise national sovereignty and freedom.

19. The partition of Palestine in 1947 and the establishment of the state of Israel are entirely illegal, regardless of the passage of time, because they were contrary to the will of the Palestinian people and to their natural right in their homeland, and inconsistent

with the principles embodied in the Charter of the United Nations; particularly the right to self-determination.

20. The Balfour Declaration, the Mandate for Palestine, and everything that has been based upon them, are deemed null and void. Claims of historical or religious ties of Jews with Palestine are incompatible with the facts of history and the true conception of what constitutes statehood. Judaism, being a religion, is not an independent nationality. Nor do Jews constitute a single nation with an identity of its own; they are citizens of the states to which they belong.

21. The Arab Palestinian people, expressing themselves by the armed Palestinian revolution, reject all solutions which are substitutes for the total liberation of Palestine and reject all proposals aiming at the liquidation of the Palestinian problem, or its internationalization.

22. Zionism is a political movement organically associated with international imperialism and antagonistic to all action for liberation and to progressive movements in the world. It is racist and fanatic in its nature, aggressive, expansionist, and colonial in its aims, and fascist in its methods. Israel is the instrument of the Zionist movement, and geographical base for world imperialism placed strategically in the midst of the Arab homeland to combat the hopes of the Arab nation for liberation, unity, and progress. Israel is a constant source of threat vis-à-vis peace in the Middle East and the whole world. [...]

24. The Palestinian people believe in the principles of justice, freedom, sovereignty, self-determination,

human dignity, and in the right of all peoples to exercise them.

# 33. The Hamas charter

**Hamas (in Arabic, "enthusiasm" and acronym for "the Islamic Resistance Movement") was established in 1988, in the midst of the Intifada (text p. 168) as a chapter of the Egyptian Muslim Brotherhood (text pp. 150-151). Today it rules the Gaza Strip and challenges the Fatah for the leadership of the Palestinian National Authority. How does this charter compare with the Palestinian National Covenant? On the basis of these two documents, what are some of the obstacles to Palestinian unity?**

## The Charter of the Islamic Resistance Movement (Hamas)

### Ideological Origins

Article 1

The basis of the Islamic Resistance Movement is Islam. From Islam it derives its ideas and its fundamental precepts and view of life, the universe, and humanity; and it judges all its actions according to Islam and is inspired by Islam to correct its errors.

### The Islamic Resistance Movement's Connection to the Society of the Muslim Brotherhood

From Mishal, Shaul, and Avraham Sela, *The Palestinian Hamas* (New York: Columbia University Press, 2000). Copyright © 2000, Columbia University Press. Reprinted by permission.

Article 2

The Islamic Resistance Movement is one of the wings [chapters] of the Muslim Brotherhood in Palestine. The Muslim Brotherhood Movement is a world organization, one of the largest Islamic movements in the modern era. [...]

**Palestine Is an Islamic Endowment (waqf)**

Article 11

The Islamic Resistance Movement believes that the land of Palestine is an Islamic *waqf* [an inalienable religious endowment] [endowed] to all Muslim generations until the day of resurrection. It is not right to give up it or any part of it. Neither a single Arab state nor all the Arab states, neither a king nor a president, not all the kings or presidents, not any organization or all of them—be they Palestinian or Arab—have such authority, because the land of Palestine is an Islamic *waqf* [endowed] to all Muslim generations until the day of resurrection. [So] who has the legitimate right to represent all Islamic generations until the day of resurrection?

**The Islamic Resistance Movement's View of Homeland (watan) and Nationalism (wataniyya)**

Article 12

According to the Islamic Resistance Movement, nationalism is part and parcel of its religious creed. Nothing is loftier or deeper in nationalism than [waging] a holy war (*jihad*) against the enemy and confronting him when he sets foot on the land of the Muslims. This becomes an individual obligation (*fard 'ayn*) of every Muslim man and woman: the woman is allowed to fight the enemy [even] without her husband's permission, and the slave without his master's permission.

[....]

**The Role of the Muslim Woman**

Article 17

The Muslim woman has a no lesser role than that of the Muslim man in the war of liberation; she is the manufacturer of men and plays a major role in guiding and educating the [new] generations. The enemies have realized her role; hence they think that if they can guide her and educate her in the way they wish, away from Islam, they will have won the war. Therefore, you can see them attempting to do this through the mass media and movies, education and culture and using as their intermediaries their craftsmen, who are part of Zionist organizations that assume various names and shapes, such as the [Free] Masons, Rotary Clubs, and espionage gangs, all of which are nests of saboteurs and sabotage [...]

Article 18

The woman in the fighting (*mujahid*) house and family, whether she is a mother or a sister, has the most important role in taking care of the home and raising the children according to Islamic concepts and values and educating her sons to observe the religious precepts in preparation for the duty of jihad awaiting them. Therefore, it is necessary to pay attention to the schools and curricula for Muslim girls so that they will become righteous mothers, [who are] aware of their role in the war of liberation.

[...]

## The Palestine Liberation Organization

Article 27

The Palestine Liberation Organization [PLO] is the movement closest to the Islamic Resistance Movement in that it consists of fathers, brothers, relatives, and friends. Can a Muslim turn away from his father, his brother, his relative, or his friend? Our homeland is one, our plight is one, our destiny is one, and our enemy is common to all of us.

Due to the circumstances that surrounded the formation of the organization [the PLO] and the ideological confusion that prevails in the Arab world as a result of the ideological invasion which has befallen the Arab world since the defeat of the Crusades and that has been intensified by Orientalism, the [Christian] mission and imperialism, the organization has adopted the idea of a secular state, and this is how we view it. [But] secular thought is entirely contradictory to religious thought.

[...]

When the Palestine Liberation Organization has adopted Islam as its system of life, we will become its soldiers and the fuel of its fires that will burn the enemies. Until this happens—and we pray to Allah that it will be soon—the position of the Islamic Resistance Movement toward the Palestine Liberation Organization is that of a son toward his father, a brother toward his brother and a relative toward his relative who suffers the other's pain when a thorn hits him, who supports the other in his confrontation with the enemy and wishes him guidance and righteous conduct. [...]

### The Members of Other Religions: The Islamic Resistance Movement is a Humanistic Movement

Article 31

The Islamic Resistance Movement is a humanistic movement. It cares about human rights and is committed to Islam's tolerance of the followers of other religions. It is hostile only to those who are hostile toward it or stand in its way so as to impede its moves or frustrate its efforts. In the shadow of Islam, it is possible for the followers of the three religions—Islam, Christianity, and Judaism—to coexist in safety and security. Safety and security are possible only in the shadow of Islam and recent and ancient history is the best witness to that effect.

*Ba'th Party and Nasserism*
# 34. The heady years of Arab nationalism
## Gamal 'Abd al-Nasir

**It would be difficult to overstate the extent to which Arab nationalist ideology dominated mid-20th-century politics. The widespread ebullience that it encouraged among the citizens of**

From A.Y. Ahmad, ed., *al-Majmu'a al-kamila li-khutab wa-ahadith wa-tasrihat Jamal 'Abd al-Nasir*, vol. 2 (Beirut: Markaz Dirasat al-Wahda al-'Arabiyya, 1995). Translated by L. Yarbrough, from the Arabic.

Arab countries contributed to its own undoing in the aftermath
of the catastrophic 1967 war with Israel. At the time of the
excerpt below, however, the future of the movement still looked
bright. Here we encounter the leading light of Arab nationalism,
Gamal 'Abd al-Nasir (text pp. 157-60), on August 4, 1959,
addressing a group of women teachers in Alexandria. Notice the
confidence and rhetorical flourish with which he speaks. To
what challenges does Nasser allude? What seem to be the solutions he envisions? And what roles does he imagine women playing in effecting these solutions? How does his outlook contrast
to that of Hassan al-Banna' (Reading 30 above), who was writing only a few decades earlier, and whose ideas would flourish
anew in the rubble of Arab nationalism a decade later?

What I have seen today has made me very happy. I'll
begin by thanking those responsible for organizing this
camp, and for the training. I also want to thank them for
something I saw today for the first time: I saw Arab
women carrying out training in military science. This is
a thing that inspires confidence, and inspires pride, and
inspires assurance.

I want to celebrate the steadiness in instruction and
seriousness in training that I have witnessed today. And
I want to express to you my great happiness at what I
sensed, and what I saw. To be honest, it was a surprise to
me. It filled me with pride and affection. Arab women
today are fully half of society. They carry a great responsibility: to join with men in building this nation.

After the proclamation of a revolution of equality in
rights and duties, and after we have seen Arab women
walking side by side with Arab men for the sake of building the nation in labor, and in building factories, and in
technical instruction, and in military training, after all
this, Arab women must feel and believe that they have a

great role to play in building this nation, and in building its future. I see before me the instructors responsible for the entire next generation. You bear a heavy responsibility, for you will produce the next generation. We need the next generation to be a generation free of the traces of colonialism, coming forth in freedom, and discovering freedom, and discovering revolution and progress.

But this society still bears the traces of colonialism. It is you who must free us of these traces. You must instruct the new generation, enabling them to build this nation and continue building until all that we aspire to has been attained. Arab women represent half of Arab society. They are in a position to influence this society, whether they wish to or not, and their influence is great indeed. They influence the household, they influence the family, they influence the schools, and they influence this society at each and every stage.

If we are to build the society we hope for, then it falls to you to work to create that society. It will consist of both the individual and the people [as a whole], as well as those who work to raise them and instruct them so that they are able to bear the responsibility cast upon our shoulders, and even heavier burdens. For the responsibility of the future will be far greater than that which we now bear.

The Arab women of today, as I see before me, provide the highest example. They are shining examples with respect to their work: their work to raise the condition of the nation. This work will have great results: spiritual results, material results and abstract results.

All of us in this nation are working for a single goal, a single objective: the building up of this nation, creating a society pervaded by material comfort, in which every person experiences justice, freedom, and equality. A socialist, democratic, cooperative society, liberated from all exploitation, whether political, economic, or social.

Each one of you can participate in this work, in creating this society by the faith that I see before me today. Faith in the nation, faith in the future, faith that it will be a future that grows continually brighter. Each year will be better than the one before, that our children might have opportunity in the future that was not available to us, in our time, or to our ancestors in the past.

All of us are working, standing in solidarity, to become a society pervaded by material comfort, in which each and every person can taste happiness. A society in which production increases, in all sectors. And along with this increase in production, there will be justice in the distribution of that production, such that no minority will dominate a majority. This will be a society in which every person feels that he has the same opportunities available to his fellows, and in which all citizens feel that there is no discrimination among them, and no distinctions save according to their efforts, and according to their work.

You are not only capable of building such a society; in fact, you carry great responsibility for building up this society. For you are teachers, entrusted with the responsibility of raising the next generation. It must rest upon a firm foundation, so that it is able to complete this task.

I thank you once again, and express my admiration for what I have seen today. I wish for you continual progress and good fortune.

*The Sadat Era*

# 35. Sadat in Jerusalem

## Anwar al-Sadat

**Egyptian President Muhammad Anwar al-Sadat and Israeli Prime Minister Menachem Begin shared the 1978 Nobel Peace Prize for their roles in bringing about the Camp David accords (text p. 161). These accords were preceded by Sadat's surprise trip to Jerusalem, which cost Egypt much support in the wider Arab world, and probably precipitated his assassination (text p. 163). During the Jerusalem trip, Sadat made a famous speech before the Knesset, Israel's national legislative body, in West Jerusalem. The excerpt below contains relatively little of the pro-peace rhetoric that formed the core of the speech. Rather, it gives some of the speech's firmer, more confrontational moments: the important "facts" as Sadat presented them, his admonitions to Israel's leadership, and the bases on which he envisioned the conclusion of a peace agreement. Many of the points he makes are calculated to discourage his listeners from drawing certain conclusions from the content of his Knesset speech, or from the fact that he was giving it at all. Can you infer what some of these common interpretations of Sadat's actions might have been? Based on your readings elsewhere, how many of the five bases for peace that Sadat sets forth in the last section excerpted have now been achieved?**

Let us be frank with one another as we answer the big question: How can we achieve a durable and just peace?

[...]

Before I make public my answer, allow me to assure you that my clear and frank answer rests on several facts, that every one cannot help but recognise.

First fact:

From http://sadat.umd.edu/archives/speeches/AADI%20Sadat%20Speech%20to%20Knesset%2011.20.77.pdf; and http://www.ibiblio.org/sullivan/docs/Knesset-speech.html, among other sources.

Nobody can have happiness at the expense of the wretchedness of others.

Second fact:

I have never spoken, and I will never speak in two different ways. I have not and will never adopt a two-faced policy. I have never conferred with anybody except through one language, one policy and one face.

Third fact:

Direct confrontation and the straight line are the shortest and most successful road to clear-cut objectives.

Fourth fact:

The call for a durable and just peace based on respect of the U.N. resolutions has been adopted today by the entire world and has become a cogent expression of the international community's will, either in the official capitals where policy and decisions are made, or on the level of world public opinion which influences the processes of policy and decision-making.

Fifth fact:

Which may be the most salient and clear-cut of all facts, is that the Arab nation is not seeking a durable and just peace from a position of weakness or instability. On the contrary, it possesses all the potentialities of power and stability. Hence its word emanates from a genuine will to achieve peace, a word that proceeds from a civilised awareness that in order to avert a definite catastrophe for us and for you and for the entire world, we have no other alternative but to establish a durable and just peace; a peace that cannot be shaken by storms, or tampered with through doubts or shaken by ill and distorted intentions.

Proceeding from these facts, I would like, while wishing to bring you to see the image as I conceive it, to sincerely warn you against thoughts that might occur to you.

The commitment to be frank compels me to say the following:

First:

I did not come to you to conclude a separate agreement between Egypt and Israel, for this has no place in Egyptian policy. The problem does not concern Egypt and Israel alone. Hence, any separate peace between Egypt and Israel or between any of the front-line states and Israel is bound to fall short of establishing a durable and just peace in the entire area. Furthermore, it would not be possible to achieve the just and durable peace so pressingly advocated by the entire world in the absence of a just solution to the Palestinian problem even though peace may have [been] achieved between all the front-line states and Israel.

Second:

I did not come to you seeking a partial peace in the sense that we put an end to the state of belligerency at this stage, shelving the whole problem to be tackled at a later stage. This will not be the radical solution leading us to durable peace. In addition to this, I did not come to you to agree upon a third disengagement in Sinai, or the Golan and the West Bank, for this would only mean that we are postponing the lighting of the fuse to a future date. It would also mean that we lack the courage to face up to peace and we are too weak to shoulder the burden and responsibilities of a durable and just peace. I came here to you to build together a durable and just peace and to prevent any Arab or Israeli bloodshed. For this reason I declared that I was ready to go to the end of the world.

[...]

I tell you today, and declare to the whole world, that we accept to live with you in durable and just peace. We do not want to encircle each other with rockets ready to destroy or with missiles of feuds and hatred. I have declared more than once that Israel has become an established fact recognised by the entire world. The two super-powers have committed themselves to security and the safe-guarding of its existence. And since we really and sincerely want peace, we welcome you to live among us in real peace and security.

[...]

To tell you the truth, peace cannot be real unless it rests on justice and not on the occupation of the land of others. It is not right that you should demand for yourselves what you deny to others. In all frankness, and in the spirit that impelled me to come to you today, I say to you: You should give up once and for all the dreams of conquest, and the belief that force is the best way to deal with the Arabs. You should assimilate the lessons of confrontation between us. Expansion will gain you nothing. So that we may speak clearly, our land is not subject to bargaining nor is it a topic of debate. Our national and regional soil is to us like the sacred valley in which God spoke to Moses. None of us can, nor would, give up one inch of that soil, nor would we accept the principle of discussing, or bargaining about it.

Let me tell you truthfully: Today we have a good chance for peace, an opportunity that cannot be repeated, if we are really serious in the quest for peace. If we throw or fritter away this chance, the curse of mankind and the curse of history will befall the one who plots against it.

[...]

Conceive -- with me -- a peace agreement in Geneva, which we herald to a world thirsty for peace.

A peace agreement based on the following:

First: Termination of the Israeli occupation of the Arab territories occupied in 1967.

Second: Achievement of the basic rights of the Palestinian people and their right to self-determination, including the right to establish their own state.

Third: The right of each state in the area to live in peace within secure borders guaranteed by agreed-upon procedures that would ensure the proper security of international borders, in addition to appropriate international guarantees.

Fourth: All the states of the area should be committed to conduct their relations with one another, according to the aims and principles of the United Nations Charter, particularly, not to resort to the use of force, and to resolve any differences among them through peaceful means.

Fifth: Termination of the present state of belligerency in the area.

# 36. Political jokes from Egypt and Syria

**A culture of dark humor often proliferates under authoritarian regimes. Circulating jokes can be a way of expressing critique and frustration within a medium that is often more tolerated**

(*Egypt*) From Samer Shehata, "Nasser, Sadat, and Mubarak in Egyptian Political Jokes," *Folklore* 103 (1991). (*Syria*) From Wedeen, Lisa. *Ambiguities of Domination* (Chicago; London: University of Chicago Press, 1999).

than formal political or social protest. The reading below contains a selection of such political jokes from Egypt and Syria.
What do these jokes reveal about the ways in which Egyptians
and Syrians view their countries? Is there a difference between
the Egyptian jokes and the Syrian ones?

## Egypt

A fox in the Western Desert escaped to Libya and the
Libyans asked, "Why do you come here?" The fox said,
"Because in Egypt they arrest camels." The Libyans
said, "But you are not a camel." The fox then said, "Of
course not, but try telling that to the police!"

\*   \*   \*

A little ancient Egyptian statue was found, but no one
could find out anything about it. They summoned
experts from abroad, and still they couldn't find out a
single thing about it. The secret police heard about the
statue, and they said, "Give it to us for twenty-four
hours."

"Twenty-four hours! What can you do in twenty four
hours?"

"None of your business. Just give it to us."

They took it, and before the day was over, they came
back with it and said, "This is King So-and so, son of
So-and-so; he ruled at such and such a time and place,
and ... , and ... , and!" They told them everything.

"How did you find all that out? Did you locate his
tomb?"

"No sir! He confessed!"

\* \* \*

Anwar al-Sadat was in a very important meeting with all of his ministers when he got an urgent phone call from [his wife] Jihan. He got up and took the phone call and asked Jihan what the emergency was. Jihan said, "Oh Anwar, Anwar, our house has been robbed!" Sadat said, "Impossible, I've been sitting here with all the crooks in Egypt!"

\* \* \*

There was an international conference on surgical operations and representatives of many of the countries of the world attended. The French surgeon told about a man who was in a serious accident and was hurt badly and had to have his heart and kidneys replaced. "Today," the French surgeon said, "he is a professional wrestler." The English surgeon spoke about a man who was a marathon runner and was hurt badly and had both of his legs replaced and today was still a champion marathon runner. All the representatives, in turn, told about the best operations performed in their countries. Finally, the Egyptian surgeon got up and told of a man who had a brain that didn't work and had it replaced with the brain of a monkey and was now president of Egypt.

\* \* \*

When Nasser became president he wanted a vice-president who was dumber than he was, so as not to cause him trouble or pose a threat to his power, so he chose Sadat. When Sadat became president he too wanted a vice-president dumber than he was and picked Mubarak. Mubarak has not yet found anyone in Egypt dumber than himself.

## Syria

Bush, Gorbachev, and Asad are in a race. Bush's bodyguard carries him until they reach a river. The river has crocodiles in it, and the bodyguard refuses to cross it: "I have children, family responsibilities ... " They return. Gorbachev's bodyguard carries him to the river, and he too refuses to cross it: "I have children, family responsibilities ... " They also return. Asad's bodyguard carries Asad to the river and dives in, dodging the crocodiles. The other bodyguards are amazed and ask: "How could you do it?" Asad's bodyguard replies: "I have children, family responsibilities ... "

*     *     *

An Israeli and a Syrian are standing at the border. The Israeli says to the Syrian, "In Israel we've got running water, we've got electricity, and we've got working telephones." The Syrian, puzzled about how to reply, says, "Well in Syria, we've got Asad." [The word *asad* in Arabic means lion...] The Israeli is perplexed. He scratches his head and goes away. The next day the scenario is repeated. On the third day the Israeli comes back and says, "Now we have an 'asad' too." The Syrian, thinking that the Israelis have managed to get a hold of another Asad, responds, "Now you won't have running water, electricity, or working telephones either."

\* \* \*

A man had to go to the bathroom. So he entered the public restrooms at the Suq al-Hamadiyya [Damascus' large market]. He knocked on the door. The man inside said "Yes." He knocked on the door a second time. The man inside said "Yes." The man outside said, "Where do you think we are, at the polls?"

\* \* \*

An officer wants to pray. He asks his guards: "Is there an 'Alawi mosque here?" The guards go and search and come back without finding one. They tell him that there is only a Sunni mosque in the area. The officer says, "It's O.K. Let's enter it and pray." They enter to pray. He sees an imam delivering a speech, and shouts at him, "Stop that blathering." He orders one of his guards to complete the speech. The guard ascends and begins the speech. When he finishes, he asks the officer, "How was my speech, was it good?" The officer replies, "You are a donkey. You said Muhammad is the cousin of Asad and we believed you. You said God is his uncle and we believed you. But how can we believe that the Ka'ba [a shrine in Mecca dating from pre-Islamic times and holy to Muslims] is among the achievements of the Corrective Movement [the 1970 revolution that brought Asad to power]?"

\*   \*   \*

Asad is passing by the American consulate. He notices a long line outside the door. He asks his bodyguards, "Why is there such a long line outside the American consulate?" The bodyguards only shrug their shoulders. Asad goes into the consulate and demands to see the consul. He asks the consul, "What are all these people doing waiting in line outside the consulate?" The consul replies, "They all want visas to go to America." Asad thinks for a moment, and then says, "Give me a visa too; I want to go to America." So the consul obliges and gives him the visa. He steps outside only to find that no one is waiting in line. The place is empty. "What happened?" Asad asks his bodyguard. The guard replies, "When they found out you were going, they decided to stay."

*The Lebanese Civil War and the Iran-Iraq War*
# 37. Impressions of the Lebanese civil war

### Mishka Moujabbar Mourani

**Mishka Moujabbar Mourani is a Lebanese-Greek writer who lived through Lebanon's devastating civil war (text pp. 165-67). In the following short story, she gives a fictionalized, retrospective view of life in Beirut during the war. What can you gather about the social and economic mobility of the characters? How did the experience of war affect them, and their attitudes toward the religious divisions within Lebanese society? Note that the**

From Mourani, Mishka Moujabbar, "The Fragrant Garden," in Khalaf, Roseanne Saad, ed., *Hikayat: Short Stories by Lebanese Women* (London: Telegram, 2006).

"demarcation line," or "green line," was a hazardous strip of no man's land that divided the city between warring militias in East and West Beirut; a Maronite is a member of the largest Christian group in Lebanon, which is in communion with the Roman Catholic Church.

## The Fragrant Garden

The neighbourhood of Gemmayzeh, just beyond Beirut city centre, was too close to the demarcation line during the war. As a result, for twenty years the area had been left pretty much to its own devices. While the war raged on, its ancient alleyways and traditional houses were abandoned or occupied by cowering people who had nowhere else to go.

For various reasons, the reconstruction that followed the war did not quite reach this quaint quarter either. Some of the old houses were renovated and transformed into expensive villas by an enterprising woman who was keen on both charging rent and preserving what little heritage remained in Gemmayzeh. Apart from that, the area remained untouched. One evening we were invited to the home of some friends who lived in the area overlooking Gemmayzeh. When we arrived we found them sitting in the garden with their guests. It was a lovely October evening, and the air was heavy with the scent of jasmine.

As is often the case when Beirutis get together, the conversation somehow managed to turn to the war years, even though the war ended some fifteen years ago.

"The other day my daughter asked me if the war had left any scars," said a lawyer who had shuffled back and forth between Tripoli and Paris. "It seems her teacher had been discussing post-traumatic stress disorders and the problems faced by the lost generation."

"What did you tell your daughter?" asked an attractive artist in her forties.

"I was taken aback by the question, actually. I didn't think that I was scarred. But then my daughter asked me a curious question. 'What about Teta (grandmother)? Did the war affect her?' Suddenly, I started to weep because when my mother had died during the war I was unable to attend her funeral."

"I feel like I wasted my youth," said the artist. "I still can't account for those fifteen years of war, or even the years that followed. Many of my friends never married, and in our culture women marry young." Then she turned to me. "Where were you during the war?"

"I stayed in Beirut."

"Here in Gemmayzeh?"

"No, I lived in West Beirut. I moved after I got married, but by then the war had ended."

"I went to Paris soon after the war started," said our hostess. "I couldn't risk staying. My son had just been born and my husband was able to relocate his work. I know it must have been a horrible time to be in Lebanon."

I thought for a moment. "There was much that was terrible, yes, and yet, in an odd way, it was a unique experience. I have never lived as intensely as I did during the war."

"Intensely?"

"Perceptions were heightened, experiences were more vivid. I can't explain it. I felt I was really alive. I wrote poems mostly, that were compact and intense reactions to what was happening. I looked forward to going to school, to spending time with the kids I taught. There was heightened meaning to our everyday lives. In fact, I haven't felt that way since the war ended."

"I remember the summer of 1989," my husband said. "I was one of the few people remaining in Beirut. My wife's family had gone to the US and left me the key to their apartment, on the sixth floor of a building in Zarif. I had offered to feed the cat and water the plants while they were away. My sister and her family had gone to the mountains in the north, and she too had a cat; so she left me the key to her place on the seventh floor of a building about a ten-minute walk from the Zarif apartment. I lived on the eleventh floor of a building in Kraytem, about a half-hour away from both houses. By then the war had been raging for fourteen years, and, although I'm a Maronite, living in West Beirut was the only choice available to me."

My husband was keen to share his war experience. "The shelling that summer ravaged the city. Fuel was scarce, and basic amenities were unavailable, but I soon developed a ritual. Because the electricity was cut most of the time, I had to walk down the eleven flights of stairs before heading to the Sporting Club where I would swim for an hour. The beach was the only place I could have a shower, albeit with brackish water, since there was no running water in any of the flats. Occasionally I played chess with some of the regulars there, but mostly I donned my mask and flippers to go skin-diving, relishing the cool serenity of the Mediterranean," he explained to the interested guests.

"Every afternoon I walked to my sister's house as

there was very little fuel and taxis were a luxury. Once there, I climbed the seven flights of stairs to her apartment, fed the cat, walked down again and headed to Zarif to do the same thing. It was a thirty-minute walk back to my building and, once again, I had to climb up eleven flights of stairs to my apartment. I developed different ways of making the trek up the stairs easier. Sometimes maintaining a steady, slow pace helped preserve energy. Or counting backwards and focusing on how many floors were left rather than how many I had climbed," my husband continued.

"In the evening, I would often meet my neighbour, a gnarled and gruff Sunni, on the landing between our two apartments; it was the safest place to be during heavy bouts of shelling. Like underground garages, these spaces became the community centres of wartime Beirut. People who barely acknowledged each other before the war began to spending long, intimate evenings together, united by their need for preservation and survival; he said with a distant look in his eyes.

"My neighbour and I found we had a lot in common. We had long discussions over bottles of whisky in the dim light of a battery-powered lamp. Confidentially he would tell his friends that he really liked his Maronite neighbour. "An excellent young man, were it nor for his name!" The guests in the garden chuckled. My husband's name literally means "the Maronite."

"Funny thing about all this is that when the horror of the shelling stopped, and a ceasefire was agreed upon, eventually leading to the end of the war some months later, I was miserable," my husband admitted. "Many of the people who stayed behind had the same reaction.

Instead of feeling relieved or overjoyed, I was upset, lost. People returned from wherever they had taken refuge. Normal life resumed, but I couldn't take it. My space was suddenly invaded by all the people returning from cities where normal life is taken for granted. They had no idea what every shell hole in the wall or every pothole in the street meant. The pace of life quickened and became banal. People were busy again. It actually made me nauseous."

Our host shook his head: "And here we are fifteen years later still coming to terms with this devastating war."

The delicate jasmine blossoms shivered in the breeze, wrapping us in their fragrant perfume. The white flowers fell gently in our laps as we sat silently in the fragrant garden, an anachronism in this city of unruly concrete.

# READINGS FOR CHAPTER 7
# THE BEGINNING OF THE
# TWENTY-FIRST CENTURY

*The Iraq War*
## 38. The dark days of Iraqi discord
### Ayatollah Sistani

Grand Ayatollah 'Ali al-Sistani (b. 1930) is one of the most respected religious authorities in Shi'i Islam (text p. 177). He has studiously avoided direct political involvement throughout his career, but in the years following the 2003 U.S.-led regime change he issued a number of influential statements from his office in Najaf, Iraq, regarding the conduct of his followers in the public sphere. In general, these statements discouraged involvement in sectarian violence, and strongly urged participation in democratic elections. In the passage below, from 2005, some followers of Muqtada al-Sadr (text p. 177) ask Sistani for a ruling about how to deal with a specific threat made against Iraqi Shi'is by the notorious Jordanian militant Abu Mus'ab al-Zarqawi. What are the means by which Sistani advocates accomplishing the goals he has in view? Would you describe this statement as indicative of a political or an apolitical stance on the part of a religious leader?

**The Sadrist faction seeks a pronouncement from His Eminence al-Sayyid al-Sistani concerning the threats of al-Zarqawi.**

In His exalted name:

[To] His Eminence the Grand Ayatollah al-Sayyid 'Ali

From Sistani, 'Ali, *al-Nusus al-sadira 'an Samahat al-Sayyid al-Sistani fi al-mas'a-la al-iraqiyya*. Ed. H. al-Khaffaf (Beirut: Dar al-Mu'arrikh al-'Arabi, 2007). Translated by L. Yarbrough, from the Arabic.

al-Sistani (may his shadow long endure)

Peace be upon you, and God's mercy and blessings.

Your Eminence is well aware of the threats that have recently been made by the agents of the "sinister triad" [Ba'thists, Wahhabis, and Iraqi Sunni fighters] against the followers of Ahl al-Bayt [i.e., Shi'is], God's peace be upon them [i.e., upon Ahl al-Bayt, the family of the Prophet]. These threats have been proclaimed by a certain al-Zarqawi, as a declaration of war against the Shi'is in Iraq. What is your view concerning this grave matter? What can be done to prevent harm to the followers of Ahl al-Bayt? What is your counsel to the Shi'a in particular, and to Iraqis in general? May God reward you with the best of rewards He bestows upon those who do good.

The Sons of the Martyr al-Sadr II, God bless his soul
Kufa


In the name of God, Compassionate and Merciful

The essential goal of such threats, and of the heinous crimes that preceded and followed them, which have targeted tens of thousand of innocent Iraqis, is to sow discord among this noble people. It is to ignite the fire of civil war in this great land, to prevent the recovery of its sovereignty and its security, and to prevent its people, weakened by the wounds of occupation and the totalitarian subjugation that went before it, from working for the return of its vitality, and from progressing upwards and onwards.

Most Iraqis, however—praise God—are fully aware of these vicious goals, and will not allow the enemy to carry out its heinous plans, regardless of the oppression and harm they endure, and how much of the guiltless blood of their families and loved ones is spilled upon the pure soil of their land.

We express our great sorrow at every drop of Iraqi blood that is shed from oppression and animosity, and we feel pain at the cries of the bereaved, the weeping of orphans, and the groans of the wounded. At the same time, we call on the faithful from among the followers of the Imams of Ahl al-Bayt (i.e., Shi'is) to continue in self-control, and for them to take even greater prudence and caution. We urge them to cooperate with the Iraqi forces who have been tasked with their oversight and protection. They are working to prevent the infiltration of criminals and their supporters into our cities and residential areas. We also call upon all Iraqis to work in strengthening the unity of this people, and strengthening the bonds of familiarity and affection among us. This will be accomplished by making it impossible—by what we say and by what we do—for anyone to belong to this deviant sect, or to offer to it any support whatsoever. Likewise, it is of the greatest importance to raise awareness among those who foolishly think well of such people, and to alert them to the deviance of their ideas, the evil of their objectives, and the terrible consequences of their actions.

We call upon the Iraqi government to work earnestly and tirelessly to provide security and stability to all Iraqis, to protect all their rights, and to prevent harm to them, without regard to their ethnic, religious, or intellectual affiliations. We call upon the Iraqi judiciary to do its part by trying in a timely manner those accused in cases of murder and injury, assigning appropriate sentences to those proved guilty. None shall hold them blameworthy in this matter [an allusion to Qur'an 5:54].

We ask God most high, all-powerful, to lead all involved by the hand toward the greater good of Iraq, and her strengthening, stability, and independence, and to turn all Iraqis from all evil and hateful acts. For He is all-hearing, and answers supplications. Peace be upon you, and the mercy and blessings of God.

21 Sha'ban 1426 [25 September 2005]

The Office of al-Sayyid al-Sistani (may his shadow long endure)

Najaf

## 39. Israel's mid-life crisis?

### David Grossman

**David Grossman is a well known Israeli writer and peace activist. In summer 2006, during the fighting between Israel and Hezbollah (text p.175), his son Uri, a soldier in the Israeli army, was killed. The following excerpt is taken from a speech delivered by Grossman at the annual memorial ceremony for Yitzhak Rabin, the Israeli Prime Minster behind the Oslo Agreements who was assassinated in 1995 (text pp.168-169). In this speech, Grossman criticizes severely Israel's political leaders for not exhausting every effort to attain peace. While many Israelis disagree with Grossman's political views, he captured in this speech the deep frustration and anger that many Israelis are feeling today at the current state of their country. How might a Palestinian or a Lebanese respond to Grossman's speech? What**

From "David Grossman's Speech at the Rabin Memorial," trans. O. Scharf, *Haaretz* English online edition, 6 November 2006. Copyright © *Ha'aretz* Daily Newspaper Ltd. Used with permission of author.

**are the similarities and differences between Grossman's critique
and frustrations and the anger against Arab governments in the
Arab street?**

[...]

It is not easy to take a look at ourselves this year.
There was a war, and Israel flexed its massive military
muscle, but also exposed Israel's fragility. We discovered
that our military might ultimately cannot be the only
guarantee of our existence. Primarily, we have found
that the crisis Israel is experiencing is far deeper than we
had feared, in almost every way.

I am speaking here tonight as a person whose love for
the land [of Israel] is overwhelming and complex, and
yet it is unequivocal, and as one whose continuous
covenant with the land has turned his personal calamity
into a covenant of blood.

I am totally secular, and yet in my eyes the establishment and the very existence of the State of Israel is a
miracle of sorts that happened to us as a nation – a political, national, human miracle.

I do not forget this for a single moment. Even when
many things in the reality of our lives enrage and depress
me, even when the miracle is broken down to routine and
wretchedness, to corruption and cynicism, even when
reality seems like nothing but a poor parody of this miracle, I always remember. And with these feelings, I
address you tonight.

"Behold, land, for we have been so very wasteful,"
wrote the poet Saul Tchernikovsky in Tel Aviv in 1938.
He lamented the burial of our young again and again in
the soil of the Land of Israel. The death of young people is a horrible, ghastly waste.

But no less dreadful is the sense that for many years, the State of Israel has been squandering, not only the lives of its sons, but also its miracle; that grand and rare opportunity that history bestowed upon it, the opportunity to establish here a state that is efficient, democratic, which abides by Jewish and universal values; a state that would be a national home and haven, but not only a haven, also a place that would offer a new meaning to Jewish existence; a state that holds as an integral and essential part of its Jewish identity and its Jewish ethos, the observance of full equality and respect for its non-Jewish citizens.

Look at what befell us. Look what befell the young, bold, passionate country we had here, and how, as if it had undergone a quickened aging process, Israel lurched from infancy and youth to a perpetual state of gripe, weakness and sourness.

How did this happen? When did we lose even the hope that we would eventually be able to live a different, better life? Moreover, how do we continue to watch from the side as though hypnotized by the insanity, rudeness, violence and racism that has overtaken our home?

[....]

One of the most difficult outcomes of the recent war is the heightened realization that at this time there is no king in Israel [Judges 17:6], that our leadership is hollow. Our military and political leadership is hollow. I am not even talking about the obvious blunders in running the war, of the collapse of the home front, nor of the large-scale and small-time corruption. I am talking about the fact that the people leading Israel today are unable to connect Israelis to their identity. Certainly not with the healthy, vitalizing and productive areas of this identity, with those areas of identity and memory and fundamental values that would give us hope and strength, that would be the antidote to the waning of mutual trust, of the bonds to the land, that would give some meaning to the exhausting and despairing struggle for existence

[...]

Rabin decided to act, because he discerned very wisely that Israeli society would not be able to sustain itself endlessly in a state of an unresolved conflict. He realized long before many others that life in a climate of violence, occupation, terror, anxiety and hopelessness, extracts a price Israel cannot afford [....]

We have been living in this struggle for more than 100 years. We, the citizens of this conflict, have been born into war and raised in it, and in a certain sense indoctrinated by it. Maybe this is why we sometimes think that this madness in which we live for over 100 years is the only real thing, the only life for us, and that we do not have the option or even the right to aspire for a different life.

[...]

Any reasonable person in Israel, and I will say in Palestine too, knows exactly the outline of a possible solution to the conflict between the two peoples. Any reasonable person here and over there knows deep in their heart the difference between dreams and the heart's desire, between what is possible and what is not possible by the conclusion of negotiations. Anyone who does not know, who refuses to acknowledge this, is already not a partner, be he Jew or Arab, is entrapped in his hermetic fanaticism, and is therefore not a partner.

[…]

Turn to the Palestinians, Mr. Olmert, address them over the heads of Hamas, appeal to their moderates, those who like you and I oppose Hamas and its ways, turn to the Palestinian people, speak to their deep grief and wounds, acknowledge their ongoing suffering.

[…]

Go to the Palestinians, Mr. Olmert, do not search all the time for reasons for not to talk to them [….] You owe it to those whom you would ask to sacrifice their lives should another war break out. Therefore, if President Assad says that Syria wants peace, even if you don't believe him, and we are all suspicious of him, you must offer to meet him that same day.

[…]

From where I stand right now, I beseech, I call on all those who listen, the young who came back from the war, who know they are the ones to be called upon to pay the price of the next war, on citizens, Jew and Arab, people on the right and the left, the secular, the religious, stop for a moment, take a look into the abyss. Think of how close we are to losing all that we have created here. Ask yourselves if this is not the time to get a grip, to break free of this paralysis, to finally claim the lives we deserve to live.

# 40. A manifesto of the Arab Spring
## The April 6 Youth Movement

The April 6 Youth Movement traces its origins to 2008, when it was formed to support a workers' strike in the Nile Delta town of al-Mahalla al-Kubra. It maintained an online presence after the strike, and served as a means of connecting and organizing young, educated, politically aware Egyptians. This structure was instrumental in organizing the protests of January 25, 2011, that led eventually to a "revolution" that overthrew President Hosni Mubarak. In the following passage, posted on the group's blog, the April 6 Youth Movement introduces itself and expresses its aspirations for Egypt. The revolution was brought about by the confluent concerns of a variety of constituencies in Egypt, and this document certainly does not represent all of them. However, it does give a hint of the prevailing mood during the months of the revolution, and of the hopes that animated young, internet-savvy political organizers. Compare the "solution" urged in this document to those championed by al-Banna' (Reading 30) and Nasser (Reading 34). Despite the differences, can you trace any threads from earlier readings to the events of the 2011 revolution? Given the continued power of the Muslim Brotherhood in contemporary Egyptian politics, what scope do you foresee for the integration of ideas like those of al-Banna' with those expressed here? What adjustments will both need to make in order to get along? What room, if any, remains for Arab nationalism?

**[Who we are]**

We are a group of Egyptian youth, of varying ages and political inclinations. We have had a dream that has led us to establish a youth political movement. It is inde-

From http://shabab6april.wordpress.com /أبريل-6-حركة-الحرية-عصر/ (last accessed 30 July 2011). Translated by L. Yarbrough from the Arabic.

pendent of any party organization or preexisting political current, and seeks to establish a critical mass, which will do its part to maintain steady pressure and work cumulatively toward change.

We launched the movement on 6 April 2008, after calling for the well-known 6 April strike throughout Egypt. This call was made by various means, among which was Facebook. We were among the first groups in the world to use this social site for political mobilization.

We had confidence in our ability to resist and remain steadfast against this totalitarian regime. We believed also in the possibility that a collective effort, in which the youth would play their part alongside all the other factions and classes of society, could move Egypt beyond the catastrophic Mubarak regime by pushing for a democratic transformation.

From the beginning, it became something of a motto for us that our generation had the right to try. Either we would succeed, or we would become an instructive precedent for generations to come. We consider ourselves, and indeed are broadly considered by outside observers, to be the origin [literally: the "mother movement"] of the popular movement that has depended, since its very inception, upon the concerted use of modern technology and all available mass media to mobilize and organize.

**The vision**

Our vision is for the 6 April youth organization to become a mass entity that participates in the oversight of the democratic transition. It will assist in evaluating governments, authorities, and laws, and the performance of the various apparatuses in the state. It will also do its part to produce a healthy political climate, by supporting measures that contribute to the formation of a healthy, well informed political regime. Conversely, it will resist any measures that harm the democratic system or political life in Egypt, and stand in the way of the advancement of civilization.

**What we want**

We want to see Egypt a country blessed with civilian democracy and a healthy political climate that affords freedom of opinion and expression, freedom to establish political parties, syndicates, and associations simply by notifying the authorities, and freedom of assembly.

We want to see Egypt a country in which predominate the principles of freedom, diversity, tolerance, acceptance of others, and citizenship, as well as principles of social justice, principles of human dignity and equality among citizens.

We want the people truly to participate in decision making in Egypt, by sound electoral practices that result in the selection of deserving candidates, in all places and at all levels of responsibility.

We want Egypt to be a democratic country, with a separation of powers, transparency, and oversight of the executive authority and the mechanisms for the devolution of power.

We want the president to have fewer powers, and for there to be mechanisms for investigating and holding accountable office holders at all levels.

We want priority in legislation given to the benefit of the people, and not to the benefit of a particular class that is linked to the authorities.

We want Egypt to be an advanced country, with a proper educational organization, such that it can avail itself of its entire human and material potential in order to realize its advancement in all spheres, gaining control over the means of science and advancement.

# References for Primary Source Readings

## Chapter 1

1. Ibn Khaldun, 'Abd al-Rahman. *The Muqaddimah: An Introduction to History.* Trans. F. Rosenthal. Princeton: Princeton University Press, 1981, pp. 249-66, 305-8.
2. Hoyland, Robert. *Arabia and the Arabs: From the Bronze Age to the Coming of Islam.* London; New York: Routledge, 2001, pp. 70-71, 244.
3. Arberry, A.J. *Arabic Poetry: A Primer for Students.* Cambridge: Cambridge University Press, 1965, pp. 34, 36.

## Chapter 2

4. Abdel Haleem, M.A.S., trans. *The Qur'an: A New Translation.* Oxford; New York: Oxford University Press, 2004, pp. 14-16, 50-51, 425, 441, 444.
5. (*hadith* 1-4) Juynboll, G.H.A. *The Encyclopedia of Canonical Hadith.* Leiden; Boston: Brill, 2007, pp. 28, 50, 231, 364. (*hadith* 5) Trans. L. Yarbrough, from the Arabic; see Muslim ibn al-Hajjaj al-Qushayri, *Sahih Muslim bi-sharh al-Nawawi,* vol. 1. Cairo: al-Matba'a al- Misriyya bil-Azhar, 1929-30, p. 157*f.*
6. Ibn Hisham, 'Abd al-Malik. *The Life of Muhammad.* Trans. A. Guillaume. Karachi: Oxford University Press, 1978, pp. 132-33.
7. Kennedy, Hugh. *The Great Arab Conquests.* Philadelphia: De Capo Press, 2007, p. 315.
8. Crone, Patricia, and Martin Hinds. *God's Caliph.* Cambridge: Cambridge University Press, 1986, pp. 129-30, 132.
9. Barani, Ziya' al-Din. "The Dilemma of the Muslim Ruler," in *Sources of Indian Tradition,* vol. 1. Ed./trans. W.D. de Bary et al. New York: Columbia University Press, 1958, pp. 471-74. Translation modified by Michael Cook.

10. al-Jahiz, 'Amr b. Bahr. *The Epistle on Singing Girls of Jahiz*. Trans./ ed. A.F.L. Beeston. Warminster: Aris and Philips, 1980, pp. 31-33.
11. Rosenthal, Franz. *The Classical Heritage in Islam*. Trans. E. and J. Marmorstein. Berkeley: University of California Press, 1975, pp. 63-65.

**Chapter 3**

12. Nizam al-Mulk. *The Book of Government or Rules for Kings*. Trans. H. Darke. London: Routledge and Paul, 1960, pp. 164-67.
13. Reynolds, Dwight, Kristen Brustad et al. *Interpreting the Self: Autobiography in the Arabic Literary Tradition*. Berkeley: University of California Press, 2001, pp. 158-60.
14. Usama ibn Munqidh. *The Book of Contemplation*. Trans. P. Cobb. London; New York: Penguin Books, 2008, p. 147.
15. al-Maqrizi, Ahmad b. 'Ali. *Mamluk Economics*. Trans. A. Allouche. Salt Lake City: University of Utah Press, 1994, pp. 73-76.
16. Trans. O. Zinger, from the Arabic; see Ragib, Yusuf. *Marchands d'étoffes du Fayyoum au IIIe/IXe siècle d'après leurs archives (actes et lettres); II. La correspondance administrative et privée des Banū 'Abd al-Mu'min*. Cairo: Institut français d'archéologie orientale; Paris: Diffusion SEVPO, 1985, pp. 5-6.
17. Menocal, Maria Rosa. *The Ornament of the World*. Boston: Little, Brown, 2002, p. 66.
18. Smith, Colin, ed. *Christians and Moors in Spain*, vol. 3. Ed./trans. C. Melville and A. Ubaydi. London: Aris and Philips, 1992, pp. 75, 77, 183, 184.

**Chapter 4**

19. Carruthers, Douglas, ed. *The Desert Route to India*. London: Printed for the Hakluyt Society, 1929, pp. 39-40.
20. Trans. Michael Cook, from the Arabic. Used with permission.
21. Hattox, Ralph. *Coffee and Coffeehouses: The Origins of a Social Beverage in the Medieval Near East*. Seattle: University of Washington Press, 1988, pp. 14-15, 113-14.
22. Forster, Charles Thornton, and F.H. Blackburne Daniell, eds. *The Life and Letters of Ogier Ghiselin de Busbecq*. London: C.K. Paul, 1881, pp. 153-55, 221.
23. Chénier, Louis de. *The Present State of the Empire of Morocco*, vol.

2. Trans. P. Motteaux. London: Printed for G.G.J. and J. Robinson, 1788, pp. 187-91.

## Chapter 5

24. Trans. L. Yarbrough, from the Arabic; see [Anon.], *Kalimat 'an al-'Iraq, al-Manar* 11 (1908), p. 41*f.*
25. Niebuhr, Carsten. *Travels through Arabia and Other Countries in the East*, vol. 2. Trans. R. Heron. Edinburgh: R. Morison & Son, 1792, pp. 137-40.
26. Tamari, S., trans. "The Barber of Damascus," in Amin, Camron Michael, Benjamin C. Fortna, and Elizabeth Frierson, *The Modern Middle East: A Sourcebook for History*. Oxford; New York: Oxford University Press, 2006, pp. 563-68.
27. [Anon.]. "Address of an Influential Moslim to his Co-Religionists in Damascus," in Appendix to Abkariyus, Iskandar, *The Lebanon in Turmoil.* Trans. J.F. Scheltema. New Haven: Yale University Press, 1920, pp. 200-201.
28. al-Jabarti, 'Abd al-Rahman. *Napoleon in Egypt.* Trans. S. Moreh. Princeton: Markus Wiener Publishers, 1995, pp. 28-29, 108-10.

## Chapter 6

29. Widely available government documents; see, among other sources, http://avalon.law.yale.edu/subject_menus/mideast.asp; Hurewitz, J.C., ed./trans. *The Middle East and North Africa in World Politics*, vol. 2. New Haven; London: Yale University Press, 1975-1979, pp. 17-18, 50-51, 62-63.
30. al-Banna', Hasan. *Five Tracts of Hasan al-Banna'.* Ed./trans. C. Wendell. Berkeley: University of California Press, 1978, pp. 74-75, 121-23.
31. Widely available; see http://www.mfa.gov.il/MFA/Peace+Process/Guide+to+the+Peace+Process/Declaration+of+Establishment+of+State+of+Israel.htm
32. Widely available; see http://avalon.law.yale.edu/20th_century/plo-cov.asp; http://www.mfa.gov.il/MFA/Peace+Process/Guide+to+the+Peace+Process/The+Palestinian+National+Charter.htm
33. Mishal, Shaul, and Avraham Sela. *The Palestinian Hamas.* New York: Columbia University Press, 2000, pp. 181-87.
34. Trans. L. Yarbrough, from the Arabic; see A.Y. Ahmad, ed. *al-*

*Majmu'a al-kamila li-khutab wa-ahadith wa-tasrihat Jamal 'Abd al-Nasir*, vol. 2. Beirut: Markaz Dirasat al-Wahda al-'Arabiyya, 1995, pp. 741-43.

35. Widely available government document; see http://sadat.umd.edu/archives/speeches/AADI%20Sadat%20Speech%20to%20Knesset%2011.20.77.pdf; http://www.ibiblio.org/sullivan/docs/Knesset-speech.html

36. (Egypt) Samer Shehata. "Nasser, Sadat, and Mubarak in Egyptian Political Jokes." *Folklore* 103 (1991), pp. 80-87. (Syria) Wedeen, Lisa. *Ambiguities of Domination*. Chicago; London: University of Chicago Press, 1999, pp. 120-29.

37. Mourani, Mishka Moujabbar. "The Fragrant Garden," in Khalaf, Roseanne Saad, ed., *Hikayat: Short Stories by Lebanese Women*. London: Telegram, 2006, pp. 95-99.

**Chapter 7**

38. Trans. L. Yarbrough, from the Arabic; see Sistani, 'Ali. *al-Nusus al-sadira 'an Samahat al-Sayyid al-Sistani fi al-mas'ala al-iraqiyya*. Ed. H. al-Khaffaf. Beirut: Dar al-Mu'arrikh al-'Arabi, 2007, pp. 142-43.

39. "David Grossman's Speech at the Rabin Memorial." Trans. O. Scharf, *Haaretz* online edition, 6 November 2006. Used with permission of the author.

40. Trans. L. Yarbrough, from the Arabic; see http://shabab6april.word-press.com /عصر-الحرية-حركة-6-ابريل/(last accessed 30 July 2011).

# Bibliography

## General Works

Jonathan P. Berkey, *The Formation of Islam: Religion and Society in the Near East, 600-1800* (Cambridge: Cambridge Univ. Press, 2003).
Michael Cook, general ed., *The New Cambridge History of Islam*, 6 vols. (Cambridge: Cambridge Univ. Press, 2010).
Ulrich Haarman and Heinz Halm, eds., *Geschichte der arabischen Welt*, 4th revised and expanded edition (Munich: C. H. Beck, 2001).
Albert Hourani, *A History of the Arab Peoples* (New York: Warner Books, 1992).
Bernard Lewis, *The Arabs in History*, 6th ed. (Oxford and New York: Oxford Univ. Press, 1993 [first ed.: London and New York: Hutchinson's University Library, 1950]).

## Pre-Islamic Arabia

G. W. Bowersock, *Roman Arabia* (Cambridge, Mass.: Harvard Univ. Press, 1983).
Robert G. Hoyland, *Arabia and the Arabs from the Bronze Age to the Coming of Islam* (London and New York: Routledge, 2001).
Jan Retsō, *The Arabs in Antiquity: Their History from the Assyrians to the Umayyads* (London and New York: Routledge Curzon, 2003).

## The Beginnings of Islam

Hartmut Bobzin, *Mohammed*, 3rd ed. (Munich: C. H. Beck, 2006 [2000]).
_____. *Der Koran* (Munich: C. H. Beck, 1999).
Michael Cook, *Muhammad* (Oxford: Oxford Univ. Press, 1983).
_____. The Koran: *A Very Short Introduction* (Oxford: Oxford Univ. Press, 2000).
Patricia Crone. *Slaves on Horses: The Evolution of the Islamic Polity* (Cambridge: Cambridge Univ. Press, 1980).
_____. *The Meccan Trade and the Rise of Islam* (Princeton: Princeton Univ. Press, 1987).

Fred McGraw Donner, *The Early Islamic Conquests* (Princeton: Princeton Univ. Press, 1981).

G. R. Hawting, *The First Dynasty of Islam*, 2nd ed. (London; New York: Routledge, 2000).

Hugh Kennedy, *The Early 'Abbāsid Caliphate: A Political History* (Totowa, NJ: Barnes and Noble, 1981).

_____. *The Prophet and the Age of the Caliphates: The Islamic Near East from the Sixth to the Eleventh Century* (Harlow: Longman, 2004 [1986]).

Rudi Paret, *Mohammed und der Koran* (Stuttgart: W. Kohlhammer, 1957) (reprinted numerous times).

_____. *Der Koran* (Stuttgart: W. Kohlhammer Verlag, 1999).

Montgomery Watt, *Muhammad at Mecca* (Oxford: Clarendon Press, 1953).

_____. *Muhammad at Medina* (Oxford: Clarendon Press, 1956).

Julius Wellhausen, *The Arab Kingdom and Its Fall*, trans. Margaret Graham Weir (Beirut: Khayats, 1963 [first English ed.: Calcutta: Univ. of Calcutta, 1927]).

## 'Arabiyya

Johann Fück, *Arabiya: Untersuchungen zur arabisch Sprach- und Stilgeschichte* (Berlin: Akademischer Verlag, 1950).

Hamilton A. R. Gibb, *Arabic Literature: An Introduction* (Oxford and New York: Oxford Univ. Press, 1962).

Wolfhart Heinrichs, *Neues Handbuch der Literaturwissenschaft,* vol. 5: *Orientalisches Mittelalter* (Wiebelsheim: Aula Verlag, 1990).

Charles Pellat, *The Life and Works of Jāḥiẓ*, translation of selected texts, trans. D. M. Hawke (London: Routledge & K. Paul, 1969).

## Arab Reception of Antiquity

Ahmad Dallal, *Islam, Science, and the Challenge of History* (New Haven: Yale Univ. Press, 2010).

Dimitri Gutas, *Greek Thought, Arabic Culture: The Graeco-Arabic Translation Movement in Baghdad and Early 'Abbāsid Society (2nd-4th, 8th-10th centuries)* (London and New York: Routledge, 1981).

Franz Rosenthal, *The Classical Heritage in Islam*, trans. E. and J. Marmorstein (Berkeley: Univ. of California Press, 1975).

George Saliba, *Islamic Science and the Making of the European*

*Renaissance* (Cambridge, Mass.: MIT Press, 2007).

Gotthard Strohmaier, *Von Demokrit bis Dante. Die Bewahrung antiken Erbes in der arabischen Kultur* (Hildesheim, Zurich, and New York: Georg Olms, 1996) (Olms Studien 43).

Juan Vernet, *La cultura hispanoárabe en Oriente y Occidente* (Barcelona: Ariel Historia, 1978).

## The Mamluks

David Ayalon, *The Mamluk Military Society* (London: Variorum Reprints, 1979).

Daniel Pipes, *Slaves Soldiers and Islam: The Genesis of a Military System* (New Haven: Yale Univ. Press, 1981).

## Tenth to Fifteenth Centuries

Mark R. Cohen, *Under Crescent and Cross: The Jews in the Middle Ages*, 2nd ed. (Princeton: Princeton Univ. Press, 2008 [1994]).

Francesco Gabrieli, *Arab Historians of the Crusades*, selected and trans. from Arabic sources by Francesco Gabrieli; trans. from Italian by E. J. Costello (Berkeley: Univ. of Calif. Press, 1969). [Original title: *Storici Arabi delle Crociate*]

Sidney H. Griffith, *The Church in the Shadow of the Mosque: Christians and Muslims in the World of Islam* (Princeton: Princeton Univ. Press, 2008).

S. D. Goitein, *Jews and Arabs: Their Contacts through the Ages*, 3rd ed. (New York: Schocken Books, 1974 [1955]).

Gustav E. von Grunebaum, *Medieval Islam: A Study in Cultural Orientation*, 2nd ed. (Chicago: Univ. of Chicago Press, 1966 [1946]).

Heinz Halm, *The Empire of the Mahdi: The Rise of the Fāṭimids*, trans. Michael Bonner (Leiden and New York: E.J. Brill, 1996).

_____. *Die Kalifen von Kairo: Die Fatimiden in Ägypten 973-1074* (Munich: C. H. Beck, 2003).

Joel Kraemer, *Humanism in the Renaissance of Islam: The Cultural Revival during the Buyid Age*, 2nd ed. (Leiden and New York: Brill, 1996).

Maurice Lombard, *The Golden Age of Islam*, trans. Joan Spencer, new preface by Jane Hathaway (Princeton: Markus Wiener Publishers, 2004).

Macolm C. Lyons and D.E.P. Jackson, *Saladin – The Politics of Holy War* (Cambridge and New York: Cambridge Univ. Press, 1982).

Hans Eberhard Mayer, *The Crusades*, trans. John Gillingham (Oxford and New York: Oxford Univ. Press, 1972 [1965]).
Adam Mez, *The Renaissance of Islam*, trans. Salahuddin Khuda Bukhsh and D. S. Margoliouth (New York: AMS Press, 1975 [1st English ed., London: Luzac & Co., 1937]).

## From 1500 to 1800

Jane Hathaway (with contributions by Karl K. Barbir), *The Arab Lands under Ottoman Rule, 1516-1800* (New York: Pearson Longman, 2008).
Abraham Marcus, *The Middle East on the Eve of Modernity* (New York: Columbia Univ. Press, 1989).

## The Nineteenth Century

Khaled Fahmy, *All the Pasha's Men* (Cambridge: Cambridge Univ. Press, 1997).
Albert Hourani, *Arabic Thought in the Liberal Age 1798-1939* (Cambridge and New York: Cambridge Univ. Press, 1962 [reprinted numerous times]).
Josef Matuz, *Das Osmanische Reich. Grundlinien seiner Geschichte* (Darmstadt: Wissenschaftliche Buchgesellschaft, 1985).
P. J. Vatikiotis, *The History of Egypt from Muhammad Ali to Sadat* (Baltimore: John Hopkins Univ. Press, 1969).
M. E. Yapp, *The Making of the Modern Near East, 1792-1923* (New York: Longman, 1996).

## The Twentieth Century

Henner Fürtig, *Kleine Geschichte des Irak* (Munich: C. H. Beck, 2003).
Toby Craig Jones, *Desert Kingdom: How Oil and Water Forged Modern Saudi Arabia* (Cambridge, Mass.: Harvard Univ. Press, 2010).
Gudrun Krämer, *A History of Palestine: From the Ottoman Conquest to the Founding of the State of Israel*, trans. Graham Harman (Princeton: Princeton Univ. Press, 2008).
Reinhard Schulze, *Geschichte der islamischen Welt im 20. Jahrhundert* (Munich: C. H. Beck, 1994).
M. E. Yapp, *The Near East since the First World War: A History to 1995* (New York: Longman, 1996).

# Index of Names

# About the Author, Editors, and Translators

**Heinz Halm,** University of Tübingen, is one of the world's leading scholars on the Middle East and especially on Shi'ism. His books, which have been translated into numerous languages, include: *The Shi'ites: A Short History* and *The Empire of the Mahdi: The Rise of the Fatimids*. Professor Halm is the editor of *Die Welt des Orients*, and his shorter studies have appeared in the *Encyclopaedia of Islam*, *Encyclopaedia Iranica*, and numerous learned journals.

**Luke Yarbrough** (coeditor), Princeton University, researches the intersection of religious affiliation and political inclusion in the early centuries of Islam. His writing has appeared in *Islamic Law and Society* and the *Journal of Religion*, among other places. His teaching interests include Middle East and comparative history, Islamic thought, and the history and theory of inter-communal relations in the Middle East and the Mediterranean basin.

**Oded Zinger** (coeditor), Princeton University, researches the dynamics and realities of married life in medieval Egypt. His teaching interests include the history of non-Muslims in the Islamic world, everyday life through documentary material, and gender and the history of the family in the Middle East.

**Allison Brown** (translator) has translated German scholarly books and essays since 1988. Her main fields of interest include history, art, and the social and political sciences, especially women's and cultural studies. She has an MA in translation science and is certified by the state of Berlin to translate official documents into English.

**Tom Lampert** (translator) studied political science at Stanford University and completed his doctorate on Max Weber at Cornell University. Since 1998, Lampert has been a freelance translator and author of scholarly books and articles, including *One Life* (Houghton Mifflin Harcourt, 2004), comprising eight biographies based on archival material from Nazi Germany. He lives in Bad Kreuznach.

CPSIA information can be obtained at www.ICGtesting.com
Printed in the USA
BVOW050051021111

274977BV00003B/1/P